Evaluating
Social Science
Research

Evaluating Social Science Research

Paul C. Stern

Institution for Social and Policy Studies
Yale University

New York   Oxford
OXFORD UNIVERSITY PRESS
1979

Library of Congress Cataloging in Publication Data

Stern, Paul C   1944–
    Evaluating social science research.

    Bibliography: p.
    Includes index.
    1. Social science research.   2. Social sciences—
Methodology.   I. Title.
H62.S7545   300′.7′2   78-16235   ISBN 0-19-502480-X

Printed in the United States of America

Preface

THIS BOOK is the result of a concern shared by several people who have been on the psychology faculty at Elmira College. We felt that our students were insufficiently prepared to devise research or even, in many cases, to read critically in the professional journals. We decided to design a course explicitly for training students in the skills of critically evaluating empirical research. First entitled "Advanced General Psychology," the course was used as a prerequisite for Experimental Psychology and other upper level courses. As interest in the course spread to faculty and students outside psychology, the course broadened into "Evaluating Social Science Research."

This course has been useful to students in several disciplines because its primary focus is on the development of cognitive skills that are appropriate for analyzing any empirical research. These skills, combined with some knowledge of the relevant content areas, give students a good background for critical reading of empirical research in a number of fields.

In the course and in this book, the emphasis is on evaluation of research instead of acquisition of a new methodological vocabulary. Although terms common in methodology textbooks are used, the main interest is in getting students to apply the concepts; I am less concerned about whether they learn to define the terms. This emphasis is reflected in heavy reliance on exercises and problems—students develop critical capacities by practicing them and by getting feedback on their progress.

This book was developed for a particular twelve-week course, yet the rationale behind it is equally valid in other educational contexts. Most likely, it will be used by instructors who, like myself, find themselves teaching research methods to students who do not yet know how to review a body of empirical literature. For such instructors, it will supplement books that emphasize conducting research, handling statistics, and writing research reports, but do not deal with the first step in the research process: the evaluation of existing knowledge about a possible research question.

My hope is that the book will also be used outside of curricula aimed at training people to do competent empirical research. Most undergraduate students will never conduct empirical research, yet the skills taught here are valuable for them too. In fact, the most gratifying outcomes of teaching "Evaluating Social Science Research" are the changes in students who have seen the value of their critical skills in their nonacademic lives. These students report that they now question the poorly supported claims of "experts" whose word they once would have taken on faith. Some put it more strongly: They feel an increased sense of personal control and power because they are able to make important judgments for themselves and need not be dependent on what they hear or read in the popular media. Such reports point to the greatest value of explicit training in critical thinking skills, and they confirm that—at least sometimes—material that has a place in a curriculum can also help people to gain an education.

This work is the result of my interaction with students over a period of five years, and it has benefited greatly from constant revision. But the book owes its very existence to a person I have never met. Dr. James E. Bell preceded me at Elmira College and left behind the idea of teaching a course such as the one eventually created. He also left behind some of his teaching materials. I owe to him the concept of teaching critical thinking through examples and problems, and also some of the terminology used, especially in the first chapter. Dr. Bell continues to teach critical thinking in a more accepting educational atmosphere at Howard Community College in Maryland.

Jim Bell's ideas came to me through Dr. Richard Ek, my colleague at Elmira until 1976, who has provided continual moral and intellectual support for the preparation of these materials. His support and encouragement have been invaluable. Rick continues his educational work at Corning Community College in New York.

I also wish to thank all the students who served as Teaching Fellows over the last five years and who helped teach this material. Special thanks are due to Kathy Parsons, Jan Guild, Eileen Kirkpatrick, Jerry Bortz, Bob Dietrich, Gary Millspaugh, George Greger, Marsha Kokinda, Beth Dalton, Laurel Tormey, Linda Maceda, and Penny Chick, each of whom, in one way or another, is responsible for some of what is in this book. Comments and criticism from other Teaching Fellows and students have also been of great value.

In the typing and preparation of this volume, I have been greatly assisted by the work of Sue Stern, Kim Sykes, Phyllis Peters, Melissa Williams, Linda Maceda, and especially Chris Hummer, who has always managed to find the time to help when it was needed most. Finally, I want to thank Sue and Sarah Stern, who somehow put up with endless hours of my writing and typing in attic, basement, and elsewhere over the years, postponing other things we could have done.

New Haven   P.C.S.
September 1978

Contents

Introduction   3

1   Scientific and Nonscientific Statements of Fact   7
EXERCISES 17, ANSWERS TO EXERCISES 19, PROBLEMS 21

2   Methods of Gathering Scientific Evidence   24
Naturalistic Observation   25
Retrospective Case Study   27
Sample Study   32
Correlational Study   33
Experiments: Within-subjects and Between-subjects   38
EXERCISES 44, ANSWERS TO EXERCISES 51, PROBLEMS 56

3   Evaluating Scientific Evidence: I   61
Naturalistic Observation: Problems Caused by the Presence of an Observer   64
Retrospective Case Study: Problems of Selection, Distortion, and Memory   72
Sample Study: Problems of Operational Definitions and Generalizing about Populations   76
Correlational Research: The Problem of Subject Variables   82

Within-subjects Experiment: The Problem of "Time-tied" Extraneous Variables 91

Between-subjects Experiment: The Importance of Randomization 94

EXERCISES 97, BRIEFER EXERCISES 97, ANSWERS TO BRIEFER EXERCISES 101
BRIEFER PROBLEMS 106, COMPLETE EXERCISE 109, ANSWERS TO COMPLETE EXERCISE 111
COMPLETE PROBLEMS 114

4 Evaluating Scientific Evidence: II 117

Landauer, T. K. & Whiting, J. W. M.
"Infantile Stimulation and Adult Stature of Human Males" 118

Rosenhan, D. L. "On Being Sane in Insane Places" 147

QUESTIONS ABOUT "ON BEING SANE IN INSANE PLACES" 162, ANSWERS 163

5 Reviewing a Body of Literature 167

Darley, J. M. & Latane, B. "Bystander Intervention
in Emergencies: Diffusion of Responsibility" 172

Latane, B. & Darley, J. M. "Group Inhibition of Bystander Intervention
in Emergencies" 180

Piliavin, I. M., Rodin, J., & Piliavin, J. A. "Good Samaritanism:
An Underground Phenomenon?" 188

Dietrich, R. "The Effect of Group Size
on Bystander Intervention in Emergencies" 211

Appendix: Asking Answerable Questions and Finding Scientific Evidence 219

References 233

Index 237

Evaluating
Social Science
Research

Introduction

This book is designed to help you answer two important questions:

1. How can I find out about something I want to know more about?
2. When I do find out, how will I know what to believe?

These two questions cover a huge area of education, and you may wonder how this book can claim to do so much. My goals are actually narrower than this. The material here will be most useful if the things you want to know about have certain characteristics.

1. The focus is on questions of *fact*, rather than questions of *value*. Values are relevant to this book only when they raise questions of fact. If you want to know, for example, whether racial integration is good for children, this book will not be of any direct help. Such a value question cannot be decided until you are clear about what you mean by "good." But if you value integration, you may believe in it because it increases understanding between people. This belief raises a question of fact: Do people raised in integrated environments understand others better than comparable people raised in segregated surroundings? Whether or not they do is a factual question, and this book deals with such questions.

A question of fact is one that we try to answer by making observations with our senses and checking the accuracy of these observations against the observations of others. A fact is an observation that can be verified by others—it is a step beyond our individual feelings and impressions.

2. The focus is on questions of fact, not questions of *theory*. The process of making inferences from theory is relevant to this book because inferences from

theory raise questions of fact. For example, Marx's theory produced predictions about the transition from capitalism to socialism. To ask whether these transitions have occurred as Marx predicted is to raise a factual question, and an affirmative answer to this question would provide some evidence for Marx's theory. Similarly, Freud's theory can be made to yield predictions about what happens to people who are deprived of the opportunity to dream. For example, a person would be expected to dream more than usual after dream deprivation. Whether or not this occurs is a factual question and, again, the answer to the question is evidence for or against Freud's theory. Theories are tested by making them produce factual statements and by appealing to the evidence that would confirm or disconfirm these statements.

This book does not attempt to show you how to make predictions from theories, but it does teach you how to pass judgment on the factual accuracy of predictions. You will not learn how to derive such predictions as "Dream time increases after dream deprivation," but you will learn the skills you need to judge the truth of this statement.

3. The focus is on factual questions about people, their institutions, their interactions, and their behavior. We will also look at some questions concerning the behavior of lower animals. These questions fall within the traditional disciplines of psychology, sociology, anthropology, economics, education, political science, psychotherapy, and so on. I am focusing on these questions because the research methods used to study them are fairly similar, as are the difficulties of getting acceptable answers. Thus, what you learn about evaluating research on a problem related to education will be useful in evaluating research on a sociological problem.

4. The focus is on *evaluating* research someone else has already done. If there are no facts pertaining to your question, this book won't help much; it is not a guide for gathering actual evidence. However, if you become good at evaluating other people's research, you will have acquired a skill necessary for doing good research of your own.

With all these restrictions, many different kinds of questions still "qualify." Here are some examples:

Are women more conforming than men?
Is there really a "Catholic vote" in presidential elections?
Can a teacher's expectation influence a pupil's IQ?
Do anti-abortion laws increase the birth rate?
Does marijuana use impair memory?
What is the effect of a ½% increase in the prime interest rate on the money supply?
Is it true that schools inculcate "middle-class values?"
Is schizophrenia an inherited disease?

Are sex role differentiations related to the means of subsistence of a culture?

Do people learn better when they are a little anxious?

Of course, it's impossible to "cover" all these topics in one place, and this is not my purpose. This book aims to provide the tools you need to arrive at the best possible answer to your own question of fact, whatever it is. I am assuming that you already have two things when you begin. First: *a subject area you want to find out about.* You are in good shape if you have an interest you can phrase as a question, such as, "What causes juvenile delinquency?" or "Is marijuana psychologically harmful?" If your interest cannot yet be put in question form, consult the Appendix, which is devoted to showing how to turn a general interest into a question answerable by scientific evidence. Second: *at least an elementary knowledge of the language people use in talking about your kind of question.* If you have in mind a sociological question, you should have the equivalent of a sociology course's worth of knowledge of sociological language (or else a stong determination to learn). I am not assuming prior knowledge of statistics, although such knowledge will certainly help you to understand scientific articles. The most essential statistical concepts are explained as they become necessary.

As you start to pursue your question, you will learn new and more specialized language that is meaningful to researchers working on your question. You will also gain exposure to the current theories and methods used in research about your subject. The less you know about the question you are asking, the more you should expect to learn.

In working through this book, you will be learning:

To ask questions so that they are answerable
To use library resources to find facts about your question
To use standards of evidence employed by social scientists in judging statements of fact

Although it is possible to learn each of these skills separately, it makes more sense to present them together. If you have a genuine interest in a topic or question, it will be beneficial to learn how to use library resources so that you can frame an answerable question and find the facts you need to try to answer that question.

Because this book cannot be written exclusively for your own personal interest area, you should be doing two things as you progress through it: improving the skills you need, using examples in the book for practice, and practicing your skills in your own area of interest, by reading scientific material on that subject.

The book is divided into five chapters and an Appendix:

Chapter 1: *Scientific and nonscientific statements of fact*
Chapter 2: *Methods of gathering scientific evidence*

Chapter 3: *Evaluating scientific evidence: I*
Chapter 4: *Evaluating scientific evidence: II*
Chapter 5: *Reviewing a body of literature*
Appendix: *Asking answerable questions*

The chapters are presented in a logical order, with the material in each building on what was presented earlier. The Appendix is intended as a reference whenever you begin to search for bibliography and can, therefore, be used at various points in the chapter sequence. The language in the Appendix assumes mastery of the first two chapters.

Each chapter is devoted to a limited number of related skills. The student's goal is not to memorize terms and definitions, but to learn to *use concepts* when evaluating scientific writing. Exercises and problems are included to allow the student to practice until the skills are well established, and additional problems may be used for further practice. When you finish the book, you should be able to define a question and find and critically evaluate the available scientific evidence relevant to that question. Thus, you will be better able to know what to believe.

CHAPTER **I**

Scientific and Nonscientific Statements of Fact

Any statement that you can try to confirm or disconfirm by looking at the evidence of the senses (or sensing technology) is a statement of fact. This includes statements that are true, those that are false, and statements about which truth or falsity is undetermined. Thus, both the statement "Smoking causes cancer" and the statement "Smoking is unrelated to cancer" are statements of fact by this definition. Whatever one believes about the truth or falsity of these statements, we can agree that the way to confirm or disconfirm them is by appeal to the senses of doctors (who can, with the help of technology, diagnose cancer), and to the senses of anyone at all, who can determine whether someone is a smoker. Although there may be some disagreement about the relationship between smoking and cancer, and while at least one of the statements must be false, both statements are factual in the present sense.

Some statements are not factual in this sense. Consider the statement "Socialism is the best form of government." This is a value statement because of the judgment given by the use of "best." You wouldn't try to confirm or disconfirm it until you knew what its author meant by "best." Thus, before trying to confirm or disconfirm, you would appeal to the author for a definition. Note that definitions are *not* statements of fact. Suppose the author of the statement about socialism said, "By 'best,' I mean 'provides the highest possible standard of living'." This is the author's definition, and you wouldn't try to confirm or disconfirm it at all. (You could, of course, agree or disagree with it.) If you combine the value statement about socialism and the definition that is given to the value word "best," you now have a factual statement: "Socialism gives its people a higher standard of living than any other form of government." This statement is factual in that you would look for evidence to confirm or disconfirm it. It may not be possible to find the evidence that would lead to a clear-cut confirmation or disconfirmation, but this does not change the way you would go about confirming or disconfirming.

Some statements in theoretical discussions are also not factual statements. These include statements that relate parts of a theory to each other, such as "A neurotic symptom both conceals and expresses a repressed wish." While such a statement seems to refer to something in the world, we do not know where or how to look for confirmation until we know more about what the author means by "neurotic symptom," "conceals," "expresses," and "repressed wish." If the abstractions contained in the statement are related to actual people and events so that we know what exactly the author is referring to, the statement can be turned into a statement of fact.

In short, the distinction between statements of fact and other statements is in the way you go about confirming them (and whether you even try to confirm them; you don't, with definitions). If you want to make observations to answer a question, it is probably factual. If it seems that no amount of evidence would matter, it is nonfactual.

The main point of this chapter is to make clear the minimum requirements for scientific statements. A discussion of statements of fact will make these requirements stand out. Here are some interesting statements of fact:

> "Properly spaced children from small families are brighter."
> "In a normal two-person conversation more than 65 percent of the social meaning is carried by nonverbal messages."
> "Today the war of national liberation . . . has become a favorable breeding-ground for mental disorders."
> "A child learns its native language by patient and persistent experiment."
> "In large cities, crime rates are higher in disadvantaged Negro areas than anywhere else."

These statements are taken from books and periodicals that attempt to give authoritative information. But are these statements believable? As they stand, none is supported by any evidence. That is, the authors have not, as far as we know now, presented any firsthand knowledge of what they are talking about. They are making assertions of fact, but they have not (yet) reported any personal experience, observations, or data to support their assertions. Such bare statements of fact, with no supporting evidence, are called *unsupported assertions.*[1]

1. The term "unsupported assertion," and many ideas throughout this book, are owed either directly or indirectly to Dr. James F. Bell (Bell, no date). Citations of references in this book use the style of the American Psychological Association: articles are cited by author and date, and the references will

Unsupported assertions are commonly found in such popular sources as television ads: "Bufferin enters the bloodstream twice as fast as aspirin," political speeches: "American military strength is second to none," and magazines, especially of the sensational type: "New sex therapy saves thousands of marriages." My reaction to such statements is always: sounds interesting, but is there any evidence? In the case of TV ads, enough people share my reaction that many ads have been compelled to cite their evidence: "According to EPA tests, Chevette delivers 40 miles per gallon on the highway, 24 in the city," or whatever. We expect any reputable source to cite the evidence for its statements of fact.

All the statements of fact quoted at the beginning of this section are supported by something more than just words. We are right to call them all unsupported assertions as they stand, but let us also see what kind of support the authors offer for their statements.

The statement about small families being brighter comes from the publication *Intercom* (Small Families are Smarter, 1976), which says it is based on "an intriguingly simple theory posed by Psychologist Robert Zajonc of the University of Michigan." So, small families have brighter children because Zajonc's theory says so. If you can trust Zajonc, or if you believe in the reputations of psychologists at the University of Michigan, you can believe that small families have brighter children. *Intercom* seems to be *appealing to authority*. A statement is supported by appeal to authority if the best evidence offered is that someone else (besides the author) says it is so. The problem with appeals to authority is that there is no factual support for the authority's statement of fact. In a sense, the author has appealed to someone's unsupported assertion. You may say that a psychologist at the University of Michigan wouldn't make an unsupported assertion, but it is not safe to take anyone's statements on faith. Certainly another psychologist would not accept Zajonc's statement without supporting evidence, even though he is respected in the field.

The statement about nonverbal communication also turns out to be an appeal to authority. The statement comes from a book by David W. Johnson (1973), and is supported by a reference to another source (McCroskey, Larson, & Knapp, 1971). Because we have no idea whether McCroskey et al. have factual evidence to support their statement, we have to conclude that Johnson is making his statement merely on the other writers' authority. If we are unsatisfied with this as evidence, as we should be, we must go to the McCroskey book to see if their statement is supported by evidence.

We can distinguish *appeal to authority* from mere *unsupported assertion* by the fact that in an appeal to authority someone besides the author believes the statement.

---

be found, alphabetically by author, at the end of the book. My style of citing sources may serve as a model for students in disciplines commonly using this style (e.g., psychology, education, speech and hearing). Students in other disciplines may consult their respective professional journals for stylistic models.

This is the essential difference. Although it sometimes matters to us who is cited as an authority, and while it is reassuring to have a recognized authority on one's side, with scientific questions it is the evidence, not its source, that matters. You may suspect that some authorities are better than others, but the best way to get believable facts is by looking for the evidence on which the authorities based their conclusion. It is safer to err by being too skeptical.

Both appeals to authority and unsupported assertions are distinguished by the fact that they offer no *observable evidence*. The only support offered for the statement is verbal. To be believed, statements of fact must be based on observations. When we encounter an assertion, even by a psychologist at the University of Michigan, it is best to consider it unsupported until we find the observations that support it. Once we know what was observed, we can make our own judgments.

This last statement is central to understanding what constitutes acceptable scientific evidence: *Once we know what was observed, we can make our own judgments.* Not all observations are scientifically useful. The most basic criterion for scientifically acceptable evidence is that everyone knows what was observed. Some examples will make this clearer.

Consider the statement "Today the war of national liberation . . . has become a favorable breeding-ground for mental disorders." The author of this statement was Frantz Fanon (1966), a black Algerian psychiatrist writing about the war for Algerian independence. The statement is followed by forty pages of evidence in the form of Fanon's observations of patients he interviewed while working in Algeria during this protracted guerilla war. Fanon presents brief case descriptions of people with "mental disorders," including cases of impotence, psychosis, homicidal impulses, and the murder by 13- and 14-year-old Algerian boys of their European playmate. If we are to decide whether we agree with Fanon that the war of national liberation breeds mental disorders, we must know what he observed, then decide whether these observations justify the conclusion.

Fanon says he has observed "the war of national liberation" and the "mental disorders" he says were "bred" by the war. Wars of national liberation and mental disorders are not things you can observe in the same way you can observe trees, trucks, 14-year-old boys, and other concrete objects. It is usually easy to get observers to agree about which things are trees (in spite of a few disagreements about large bushes) or trucks, or 14-year-old boys (again, in spite of disagreements in some questionable cases), but it is not merely as easy to get observers to agree about which events are "wars of national liberation" and which people are suffering from "mental disorders." The key terms in Fanon's statement are *abstractions*, and to know what was observed, we must have a concrete understanding of the abstractions. We must know exactly what events Fanon refers to by the terms "the war of national liberation" and "mental disorders." *For observations to be scientifically useful, their abstractions must be concretized.*[2] This is the only way we can know exactly what the author is talking about.

There are two ways to concretize an abstraction. The first is by pointing to every instance. This is practical when there are few instances. For example, when Fanon talks of "the war of national liberation," he makes it clear that he is referring only to the war that was going on in Algeria from 1954 until his book was written in 1961. He does not intend to make a statement about all "wars of national liberation," although what he has observed may also occur outside Algeria. For Fanon's purposes, "war of national liberation" has been concretized. However, we may be more interested in the *kinds* of conditions that breed mental disorders than the fact that one particular war may have had this effect. We may also be more interested in the effects of wars of national liberation in general than in the effects of the Algerian war. We may want to know what to expect in the future. Scientists like to draw general conclusions and, where possible, to make predictions. If we are interested in the effect of wars of national liberation, in general, on mental health, we must concretize "war of national liberation" in some way that allows us to know one when we see one. The same is true if we want to make a statement about 14-year-old boys in general, or about such abstractions as prejudice, anxiety, competition, power, intelligence, alienation, or learning.

If we cannot enumerate all instances of an abstraction, or if we want the abstraction to be useful when new instances occur, we must have rules for using the abstraction. Consider Fanon's abstraction "mental disorders." If we want to know how to identify a mental disorder, we need some rules for proceeding. Here are some possible rules:

1. When dealing with hospitalized patients, we can classify people by the most current diagnosis in the medical record. We can specify those diagnoses we consider to be "mental disorders."

2. We can empanel three psychiatrists to examine people in the way they see fit, ask them to decide whether the person has a "mental disorder" or not, and classify people as having mental disorders only when all three psychiatrists agree they do.

3. We could employ a standard psychological test, such as the MMPI (Minnesota Multiphasic Personality Inventory), and state that all people scoring above X value on certain specified scales of the test will be classified as having mental disorders.

4. We could interview people, asking them about their thoughts, feelings, physical complaints, and so on, and decide to classify anyone with more than X number out of a specified list of symptoms as having a "mental disorder."

2. The terms "concretized abstraction" and "unconcretized abstraction" are drawn from *Clear Thinking for Composition,* by Ray Kytle (Kytle, 1969).

It should be obvious that many other rules for proceeding can be devised. All the above rules have certain things in common. First, the abstractions in the rules are much more concrete than the original abstraction. It is easier to agree on who is a psychiatrist, what a patients's current recorded diagnosis is, or what the score on a personality test or symptom checklist is than it is to agree on whether a person has a "mental disorder." Second, the rules are stated so that you must, to find out who has a mental disorder, perform a series of *operations* either on the person or the person's records. Because the term "mental disorder" is defined by a series of operations, the four sets of rules stated above are called *operational definitions*. Operational definition is the predominant method of concretizing abstractions in science; it is unusual for an abstraction to be concretized by enumerating instances.

The first requirement for observations to have scientific value is that *abstractions be concretized*. This is generally done by using *operational definitions* for each abstraction. It is necessary to concretize abstractions so that we know just what was observed. Unless we can agree on what Fanon means by "mental disorders," it makes no sense to debate whether the war of national liberation bred them. The test of whether an abstraction is adequately concretized is whether independent observers use it in the same way. Operational definitions are used to make it easier for observers to agree, but we should not accept an operational definition as adequate on faith. Consider, for example, rule 4. The symptoms a person complains of might depend on who is doing the interviewing. Thus, the same person may be classified as having mental disorders if the interviewer is female, or a medical doctor, or a fellow Algerian, but not if the interviewer is male, or a nonmedical person, or a European. The fact that operations have been defined for using an abstraction does not guarantee that different observers would use the abstraction in the same way. The same problem exists with the panel of psychiatrists: Unanimous agreement will depend on which psychiatrists are included in the panel. The use of a test such as the MMPI would eliminate much of this problem, because there is no room for interpreting the answers; however, other psychological tests, such as the Rorschach, are evaluated differently by different observers. In short, for observations to have scientific value, there must be assurance that different observers of the same people or events would use the abstractions in the same way. The technical term for this is *reliability*.

Reliability is the second requirement for observations to have scientific value. Independent observers must use the same abstractions in the same way. If psychiatrists are almost always in agreement about who has a "mental disorder," there is high *interjudge reliability*. If a person reports the same history of symptoms from one week to the next, there is high *test retest reliability* (the same questions get the same responses). If someone's score on the odd numbered items on the MMPI is very close to his/her score on even numbered items, the test has high *split-half reliability*. Regardless of the technical terms referring to types of reliability, the notion of reliability is that to the extent something looks the same every time it is measured, the measurement technique is reliable. Reliable measurement is a requirement for scientifically acceptable observations.

One might quarrel with some of the operational definitions suggested for "mental disorders." Even if they successfully concretize the abstraction, and even if they can be made to give reliable observations, they may not measure what Fanon was talking about. Can you really evaluate the mental status of an Algerian peasant in wartime with a test developed using peacetime Americans (the MMPI)? Is there a symptom checklist that adequately reflects the types of mental disorders suffered by people who have witnessed their families being tortured, or who have survived a mass murder? Fanon is talking about bizarre and frightening circumstances, and it is hard to believe that any standard set of operations can accurately measure or describe the effects of such events on people's mental state.

The question being raised here is one of the *validity* of the operational definitions. Do they in fact measure what they set out to measure? Obviously, this question is crucial to the evaluation of scientific evidence, and it is the first question to ask about an operational definition after determining that it is reliable. I will postpone discussion of validity for two reasons: It is too complex to discuss adequately without further background and, more importantly, observations can be scientifically useful even though their validity is questioned. If we have reliably measured *something* about Algerians in the war of national liberation, we have usable information, even if what we have measured is not "mental disorder." We may have a measure of psychiatrists' prejudice, or cultural differences in response to standard test materials, or something yet undefined. If an invalid measure of mental disorder is used, it will be useless for the study of mental disorder but, if the measure is reliable, it may become scientifically useful for some other purpose. Thus, for observations to have scientific value, they must *reliably concretize abstractions*. Whether the operational definitions are *valid* is an important question that is discussed in Chapter 3, when we deal with the problem of evaluating scientific evidence.

In summary, for observations to have scientific value, they must satisfy two conditions: All abstractions must be concretized (this is usually done by providing operational definitions), and the observations must be reliable. If we have assurance that independent observers use the abstractions in the same way, we know that given the same events or people, we could reproduce what the author did. Given the same Algerians, and a reliable operational definition of mental disorder, anyone would agree pretty well about which Algerians suffered from mental disorders. These are the basic requirements for scientifically acceptable observations.

When observable evidence does not meet these criteria, we call it *casual observation*. The term "casual" suggests the absence of the care and precision required to ensure that one's observations could be repeated by another observer. If the criteria of concretized abstractions and reliability are met, we will call the observations *scientific evidence*.

Let us look briefly at some of the examples of factual statements to see which qualify as scientific evidence.

Fanon said, "the war of national liberation . . . has become a favorable breeding-ground for mental disorders." This statement, in itself, is an unsupported assertion until Fanon provides some evidence to support it. His evidence is in the form of case descriptions of people he met in his work as a psychiatrist. In short, Fanon has made observations. Our problem is to decide whether the evidence is or is not scientific. First, are the abstractions concretized? As I have already said, Fanon makes clear that by "the war of national liberation" he refers to a particular war in Algeria. This is concrete, and does not need an operational definition. What about "favorable breeding-ground" and "mental disorders?"

Nowhere does Fanon define "favorable breeding-ground," yet it seems fairly clear what he means. He must mean that mental disorders begin more easily, or more frequently, in a war of national liberation than in other situations. "Favorable breeding-ground" implies a comparison between a war of national liberation and something else, some "normal" situation. Fanon's statement can be translated into a statement about the relative frequency of "mental disorders," such as, "The proportion of people suffering mental disorders in a nation increases during a war of national liberation." Thus, we know exactly what is meant by "favorable breeding-ground" once we are clear about what constitutes a "mental disorder."

But "mental disorders" remains unconcretized. Fanon presents cases, but do we know how he decided that the people had mental disorders? Here is what Fanon says: "We shall mention here some Algerian cases which have been attended by us and who seem to us to be particularly eloquent. We need hardly say that we are not concerned with producing a scientific work. We avoid all arguments over semiology, nosology, or therapeutics. The few technical terms serve merely as references" (Fanon, 1966, p. 204). Fanon gives it away by disclaiming interest in producing a scientific work—he knows his observations do not qualify as scientific evidence. The reason why they are nonscientific should be clear. He has selected cases "who seem to us to be particularly eloquent." In other words, the criterion for selection was the subjective judgment of Fanon and, possibly, his co-workers. Further, he avoids "all arguments over . . . nosology." That is, he does not wish to discuss diagnosis. But we cannot agree on who has a mental disorder without setting up a procedure for reliable diagnosis. In other words, Fanon has selected cases that potently promote his point, and has avoided all the essential steps toward producing scientifically acceptable evidence. The advantage of Fanon's work over what sometimes appears in print is that he knows what he has done and admits it. His justification for this procedure seems to be that some of the cases he reports are so bizarre and unusual that these particular mental states could only have been bred in total war. The examples are intended to speak for themselves. Still, the evidence is weak; it does not meet acceptable scientific criteria; it is *casual observation*.

Earlier in the chapter, I quoted the statement "Properly spaced children from small families are smarter," which was published in *Intercom* and attributed to psychologist Robert Zajonc. The quoted statement is unsupported; when attributed to Zajonc, it is an appeal to authority. But does Zajonc have observations to support his assertion? The article in *Intercom* says that Zajonc's theory is supported by "earlier large-scale studies in Scotland, France, and The Netherlands." If there was a study, one can assume that observations were made. But is the evidence scientifically acceptable? We must look at the original assertion to see if the abstractions are concretized. Abstractions: "properly spaced children," "small families," "smarter." *Intercom* describes the studies as having found that "first-born children from small families did better on intelligence tests than later-borns and children from large families, regardless of race, class, or income level." This is all the information *Intercom* gives on these studies. It is hard to be sure whether the evidence is scientific. What is a "small family?" If the studies define "small family" and "large family" by the number of children present, and show that the more children, the lower the average intelligence test score of each, we know what is meant: It is usually easy to agree on how many children are in a family. We can hope this is what the studies did, but we are not certain. The term "smarter" seems to be operationally defined as intelligence test scores. If the same intelligence test was used for all the children in a study, and "smarter" is operationally defined as the score on the test (higher scores being "smarter"), again we know what was done. Given the name of the test, we could repeat the study. But what about "properly spaced?" While these studies *may* give scientific evidence about the assertion "children from small families are smarter," they seem to say nothing about the companion assertion "properly spaced children are smarter." The latter assertion at this point is based on no more than Zajonc's authority. To be certain whether the assertion about children from small families is supported by scientific evidence or mere casual observation, one must look at the studies themselves. However, since "small families" is so easily concretized and since "smarter" seems to refer to doing "better on intelligence tests," we can at least expect that the evidence will prove to be scientific. Still, it is best to be skeptical, and say the statement is based on *at least* casual observation.

More examples will follow shortly, for you to work on individually. When you begin reading about subjects of interest, you will have to constantly evaluate whether or not statements of fact are based on evidence, and whether the evidence is or is not scientifically acceptable. The best way to improve this skill is to practice.

In this and the other chapters of this book, there are exercises, followed by suggested answers to the questions. These are followed by more problems, for which I have not provided discussion. Constant practice and discussion of the points on which you are unclear are the best ways of gaining the confidence necessary for evaluating scientific writing.

The exercises for this chapter test your ability to use the following key terms:

> unsupported assertion (defined on p. 8)
> appeal to authority (p. 9)
> casual observation (pp. 13–14)
> scientific evidence (pp. 13–14)
> concretized abstraction (pp. 10–11)
> unconcretized abstraction (pp. 10–11)
> operational definition (pp. 11–12)
> reliability (p. 12)

A diagram summarizing the distinctions among the four types of statements of fact appears in Figure 1. You may find it helpful in making the distinctions and in mastering the exercises.

Figure 1. Decision-making procedure for distinguishing among four types of statements of fact.

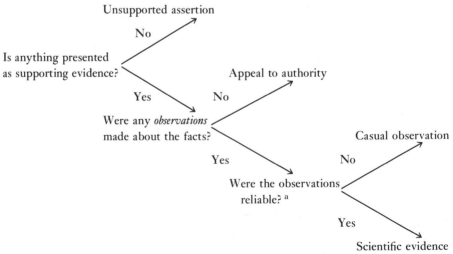

ªObservations can't be reliable unless the relevant abstractions are concretized.

Exercises

These exercises are designed to give you practice in using the key terms on new material.

For each statement of fact, classify it as either an unsupported assertion, an appeal to authority, a casual observation, or scientific evidence. For casual observations, identify an unconcretized abstraction. For scientific evidence, identify a concretized abstraction, and the operational definition stated or implied for this abstraction.

Sometimes the statement you are given is divided into parts. When working these exercises, evaluate the first part on the basis of what is present in that statement. When working subsequent parts, you may refer back to the previous statements to judge what is said in context. Thus, if an abstraction is unconcretized at first, but is concretized in a later part of the statement, only the later part can be judged as scientific evidence.

Write your answers in the spaces provided. If you have any doubts about the answer, write them down too. You can use your notes to clarify the points you are uncertain about.

(1) Everyone knows that alcohol in moderation has therapeutic effects.

(2) I've never met a man I didn't like.

(3a) Cigarette smoking *is* dangerous to health. (3b) The Surgeon General's Committee *unanimously* decided to apply the word "cause" to the smoking–mortality relationship.

(3a)

(3b)

(4a) Tryon (1940) selectively bred strains of maze-dull and maze-bright rats. (4b) By the eighth generation, the maze-bright rats made an average of 25 errors in their first 19 trials in a standard maze, while the maze-dull rats made an average of 120 errors in their first 19 trials in the same maze.

(4a)

(4b)

(5) According to Rogers (1971) leaderless groups can be as effective as other encounter groups with trained leaders.

(6a) Dr. Stanley Schachter reports that the effects of a drug depend on the subject's expectations of what the drug will do. (6b) Subjects injected with epinephrine and given no information about its effects were more strongly influenced in their reports of their mood by the experimenter's confederates (stooges) than were subjects who had been accurately informed that the drug was a stimulant.

(6a)

(6b)

(7a) According to research by Dr. J. P. Jones, women who tolerate stress well have less difficulty from menstrual cramping than women who have difficulty tolerating stress. (7b) Jones conducted detailed interviews with 100 consecutive female patients admitted to Sanford Memorial Hospital, and found that those women she classified as high in tolerance to stress were less likely to report a history of painful menstrual cramping than the women classified as low in stress tolerance.

(7a)

(7b)

(8a) Early experience with weaning has profound effects on personality. (8b) A study of children weaned at six months found them to be more possessive than a comparable group of children in the same study who were weaned at one year. (8c) The two groups did not differ, however, in their scores on the MMPI (a personality test) given when they reached age 20.

(8a)

(8b)

(8c)

Answers to Exercises

(1) Unsupported assertion. No evidence is given.

(2) Casual observation. The generalization is based on personal experiences. "Liking" is not concretized.

(3a) Unsupported assertion.

(3b) Appeal to authority. We do not know the basis for the committee's decision. Although we'd like to believe that such a committee would only act on evidence, we can only take their conclusion on authority, given what we know. (Note that the statement is an unsupported assertion about the Surgeon General's Committee, but in the context, read it as a statement about the effects of smoking.)

(4a) Unsupported assertion about Tryon. Taken as a statement about the rats, it is an appeal to Tryon's authority. If you had the reference, you could decide whether Tryon has scientific evidence that he created these two different strains.

(4b) This statement is the evidence for the assertion that the rats were, in fact, maze-dull and maze-bright. The abstractions "bright" and "dull" are concretized in terms of *number of errors in 19 trials of running a maze* (the operational definition of dullness or brightness). Call this scientific evidence.

(5) The statement about leaderless groups is an appeal to authority. It is not clear whether Rogers' statement is based on any observations of groups. (If you

read Rogers, you will find that it is, and you will be able to evaluate the quality of the observations.)

(6a) Appeal to authority. This is essentially the same as 5.

(6b) This is Schachter's evidence. It can be called scientific if all abstractions are concretized. "Epinephrine" is fairly concrete; it is operationalized as administration by injection (since the dosage and time of injection are unspecified, epinephrine is incompletely concretized; the operational definition is incomplete). "Given information" is also concretized; it is operationally defined as being "informed that the drug was a stimulant," as opposed to being told nothing about the drug's effects. "Mood" is made somewhat concrete; it is operationalized as the people's *reports* of their mood. Since we don't know if they merely described their mood, or used a more reliable form of reporting, such as a questionnaire or checklist, the operational definition is incomplete. "Influenced" seems to refer merely to the fact that the mood reports differed for the two groups; this is concrete. In spite of reservations, especially about the abstraction "mood," this statement can be said to be based on scientific evidence.

(7a) There is no scientific evidence in this statement, although it does make reference to "research." If we can assume that "research" always involves some kind of observation, this must be casual observation, because "tolerating stress well" and "difficulty from menstrual cramping" are unconcretized. However, if Jones' "research" was done in the library, Jones made no relevant observations, and the statement is an appeal to authority.

(7b) Here is Jones' evidence, and she *did* make observations. Her evidence is scientific if the abstractions are concretized so that reliable observations can be made. "Women" is concretized. "Menstrual cramping" is also concretized: women either report a history of painful cramps or they don't. "Tolerance for stress," however, isn't clearly concretized. The doctor classified the women on her own, providing no set of rules that another observer could use to measure stress tolerance. We have no way of knowing whether another doctor would have classified the women the same way Jones did. Call this a casual observation.

(8a) Unsupported assertion.

(8b) "A study" presumes that there were observations made. "Weaning" is now concretized as "weaned at six months" versus "weaned at one year." While we might ask if these are the ages when weaning began or when it ended, this is still fairly concrete. "Personality" (the term in statement 8a) is here narrowed to "possessiveness" (presumably a part of personality), but there is no attempt made to concretize "possessiveness." Casual observation.

(8c) "Weaning" is used the same way as in 8b—fairly concrete. "Personality" is here operationally defined as scores on a particular test, given at a particular time. Though the MMPI may not cover all of personality, the language is concrete and the observations here are reliable. Scientific evidence.

Problems

Try your skills on these problems. Answers are not provided. For each statement of fact, classify it as an unsupported assertion, an appeal to authority, a casual observation, or scientific evidence. For casual observations, identify an unconcretized abstraction. For scientific evidence, identify a concretized abstraction and give the operational definition that is stated or implied for the abstraction. If you have any doubts, explain your answer.

(1) Reward is most effective when given immediately after a response.

(2) Dr. X found that when patients with senile psychoses are given a chance to play a normal role, their symptoms of senility and psychosis diminish.

(3a) Dr. Y has produced evidence that exposure to televised violence increases children's aggressive behavior. (3b) Children in this study watched either a violent TV film (a gunfight from an old Western) or a nonviolent film that also involved physical activity (a cowboy chasing a runaway stagecoach, from the same Western). After the film, each child was observed individually through a one-way mirror during a ten-minute free play period in a room with toys. The number of aggressive acts performed by children who watched the violent film was more than double the number of aggressive acts of children who watched the nonviolent film.

(3a)

(3b)

(4a) The available evidence on privacy indicates that people confined together in pairs are less anxious and perform better when privacy is not provided. (4b) Taylor, Wheeler, and Altman (1968) found that subjects confined in pairs for eight days in a single room reported themselves less anxious than similar subjects confined in two adjoining rooms (where they could have complete privacy) for the same length of time. (4c) In another study, Altman, Taylor, and Wheeler

(1971) reported that groups allowed privacy performed less well on group tasks than nonprivacy groups. (Studies cited above are taken from Freedman (1973).)

(4a)

(4b)

(4c)

(5) Research by Kornhauser (1962, cited by Watson & Johnson, 1972) concluded that 57% of skilled factory workers had good mental health, as compared to 37% of semi-skilled workers and 12% of those doing repetitive work.

(6a) Oakes (1970) reports significant effects of the steroids in birth control pills on users' feelings of aggression, hostility, nurturance, and affiliation. (6b) Women whose pills were high in estrogen concentration scored higher on self-reported aggression and hostility than women taking pills high in progestin. (6c) Women taking high-progestin pills scored higher in their reports of nurturance and affiliation. (Cited by Bardwick, 1973.)

(6a)

(6b)

(6c)

(7a) Social maturity depends partly on intelligence. (7b) The most socially mature kids in my second-grade class are also the most intelligent.

(7a)

(7b)

CHAPTER **2**

Methods
of Gathering
Scientific
Evidence

Chapter 1 set forth the basic requirements for scientifically useful observations. The purpose of this chapter is to introduce you to the major methods social scientists use to gather evidence. You will see that the method a scientist uses is dictated by the kinds of questions he/she can ask, by the amount of knowledge or theory at the scientist's disposal, and by the amount of control the scientist has over events. Although there are many useful distinctions among the methods of gathering scientific evidence, it is convenient to divide these methods into six categories:

> naturalistic observation
> retrospective case study
> sample study
> correlational study
> within-subjects experiment
> between-subjects experiment

In the course of learning to distinguish these six methods, you will learn some other language useful for evaluating evidence. You will also begin to see how each method has its particular advantages and disadvantages. This knowledge will become increasingly useful when you begin to judge scientific reports.

Let me introduce the six methods in the context of an interest you may share with me. We have all heard of the "population explosion" and many of us are concerned about the effects that a vastly increased population might have on individuals and on society. Let us suppose that we are following up our concern by looking for scientific evidence on the effects of crowding, or dense populations, on individuals, their behavior, and their feelings. We are starting out with a general question something like this: "What effects does crowding have on people?" Our goal is to find a scientifically acceptable answer.

Our question contains a key abstraction: "crowding." For evidence to be scientifically acceptable, this abstraction must be concretized in some way. We might choose to make up an operational definition, but most scientists, when they know as little as we do now, would choose the other method of concretizing—they would enumerate a situation (one that intuitively involves "crowding") and observe what happens in that situation. The observations could still be scientifically acceptable, since the situation has been concretely specified. For example, a scientist could observe behavior on a New York subway in rush hour. If the number and location of the people were recorded, we would know concretely what was observed, even though crowding has not been operationally defined. For observations of this type to be useful, they must be carefully *recorded in concrete language*. This method of gathering evidence is called naturalistic observation, and it has some definite rules.

Naturalistic Observation

Naturalistic observation is a method of gathering evidence based on complete and accurate recording of events, as they occur, with minimal interference with the events. (Naturalistic observation is usually used when a scientist begins with a general question, such as "What effects does crowding have on people," or other questions of the type "What is the nature of X situation?")

> *Complete and accurate recording:* This is necessary for the data to be scientifically useful. Completeness helps eliminate biases that show up when a scientist records only what seems important. Once any arbitrary selection is made by the observer, we are not seeing the whole event, but rather the event as the observer sees it. Accuracy is necessary for reliability: The events must be recorded in *concrete language* because this is the only language that independent observers would be likely to agree on.
>
> *Events as they occur:* The most complete records are those made on the spot. Memories are faulty and tend to be selective. When events are filtered through an observer's memory, the observer's report is bound to emphasize one person's idea of what is important and to deemphasize everything else.
>
> *Minimal interference:* It is impossible to make a complete record of events without being noticed (barring hidden cameras), and it is therefore next to

impossible to make a record without interfering with events. But, to be "naturalistic," it is important to make an attempt to be relatively unobtrusive, and to avoid any deliberate tampering with naturally occurring events.

Naturalistic observations can sometimes be found in a secretary's notes for the minutes of a meeting. Scientific examples include Jane van Lawick-Goodall's observations of chimpanzee society (1971), and some of Jean Piaget's early work on cognitive development in children. These works tend to be filled with highly detailed accounts of behavior (without inferring motives or thoughts), with any conclusions clearly separate from the evidence on which they are based. Thus, another scientist could agree with the observations of the author but disagree about conclusions.

An example of naturalistic observation of the effects of crowding can be found in Konrad Lorenz's work, *On Aggression* (Lorenz, 1966).[1] Lorenz noted in his observations of the Beau Gregory, a tropical fish, that the fish would attack other members of its species when they intruded into the area occupied by the original fish. Beau Gregories do not similarly attack members of other species, and the "intruding" fish, even though larger, generally retreats from such attacks. It seems as if Beau Gregories have a territory, possibly a "hunting ground," that they defend from encroachment. In the Beau Gregory, one response to being crowded seems to be aggressive attack.

Lorenz's observations of the Beau Gregory can clearly be separated from his conclusions (which appear in the last two sentences of the preceding paragraph). It is possible to agree with the observations but reject the conclusions. But the observations are at least consistent with the conclusions, and they were valuable to Lorenz in that they suggested a general theory that goes beyond the observations. From such observations, with several species of animals, Lorenz theorized that there is a territorial instinct: Animals in general need territory, and respond to invasions of their territory with aggression. It is often true of naturalistic observations that they help suggest theory. They also raise questions that lead to further research. We now know, for example, that crowding is, in at least some species and situations, related to *aggression*. To ask the question "How are crowding and aggression related?" is to suggest a direction for research on crowding.

Before looking at other types of research, some limitations of naturalistic observation can be mentioned briefly. Although the behavior of the Beau Gregory suggested the theory of a territorial instinct, the same observations may be consistent with other theories. For example, the aggressive behavior may reflect a competi-

1. This and other examples of research on crowding used in this chapter were suggested by the discussion in Jonathan Freedman's book, *Crowding and Behavior* (Freedman, 1975).

tion for food, rather than for territory. Aggression may result from scarcity of life-sustaining resources, and territory thus is not the central issue. Naturalistic observations may yield information that is consistent with a theory, yet it is not always possible to rule out other explanations. To find out whether Beau Gregories are instinctively territorial or merely compete for food, we would have to observe them in a setting where there was unlimited food. Since this does not occur in the natural environment, other methods are needed.

Naturalistic observation has suggested that crowding may cause aggression. One way to test this possibility would be to look at situations in which aggression has taken place, and try to determine whether crowding was a contributing factor. We would then look for a naturally occurring instance of aggression and go *back in time* to see if crowding was an antecedent condition. We might, for example, talk to people right after a fight and ask them to recall the causes. We would then try to evaluate whether feelings of being crowded or being intruded upon were among the causes mentioned. In this method of gathering evidence, it is again unnecessary to operationally define such terms as "aggression" and "crowding," so long as we faithfully record a description of the fight and the statements of the participants. From this concrete information, we can draw tentative conclusions. This method is very much like naturalistic observation, except that: (1) events are not observed as they occur, and (2) because of this, records cannot be complete. The account of events depends on the recollections of the participants, after the fact. We call this method *retrospective case study*.

Retrospective Case Study

Retrospective case study attempts to answer a fairly general question (of the type "Why did X happen?") by gathering evidence after the fact. This evidence might come from talking to people involved, or from looking at records of the events, in newspapers, medical records, artifacts, and so forth. A question such as "What factors led to the demise of the U.S.–Soviet alliance after World War II?" lends itself to this method. A retrospective case study may study an individual ("Why did he commit suicide?"), or a social system ("Why did the babysitting cooperative collapse?"). The hope is usually that a detailed knowledge of what happened in a particular case will lead to principles by which to understand other, similar cases.

Let's look at an example of a retrospective case study that is relevant to the question of whether crowding causes aggression. During the 1960's, a number of riots occurred in crowded black neighborhoods in many American cities. It would be interesting to us to find out whether the crowded conditions contributed to the violence. We can look for data in the report of the National Advisory

Commission on Civil Disorders (1968). This Commission, chaired by Otto Kerner, then Governor of Illinois, gathered retrospective data on riots and near-riots that occurred in the United States during 1967, in an attempt to find out why the riots happened.

The Kerner Commission researchers used a variety of methods characteristic of the retrospective case study. They interviewed city officials to obtain their accounts of events, and they interviewed rioters, police, nonparticipant members of the community, and others who had firsthand information about events. They conducted surveys of attitudes of blacks and whites in the affected cities. They consulted census data to create profiles of the socioeconomic conditions of blacks and whites in each of the cities studied, both in the neighborhood of the riot and elsewhere in the city. Information was gathered on income, unemployment, age distribution of the population, and many other factors. Weather conditions preceding and during the riot were also recorded. In short, a vast amount of information was gathered in an attempt to find a pattern to the riots: What did cities with riots have in common?

Regarding the effects of crowding, the Commission found that "the final incident before the outbreak of disorder, and the initial violence itself, generally took place in the evening or at night at a place in which it was normal for many people to be on the streets" (National Advisory Commission, 1968, p. 6). The Commission concluded that "crowded ghetto living conditions" were one of the factors that recurred in the 1967 disturbances. However, crowding was not considered one of the basic causes. The basic causes of the rioting, according to the Commission, were white racism, discrimination, frustrated hopes of blacks, a social climate encouraging violence as a form of protest, increased racial pride among blacks, and the actions of the police, who symbolize white power. Crowding was seen as a less important factor, and one that in turn depended on segregation in housing and on patterns of migration of blacks into, and whites out of, the cities. Crowding seems to contribute to violence, but not because of an innate territoriality. The Commission's conclusions suggest that crowding served only to make an unpleasant situation more intolerable.

The report of the Kerner Commission is a good example of a retrospective case study. It asks the question "Why did the riots happen?" and attempts to answer it by gathering information about the past. An advantage of this approach is that there is no other practical way to study mass violence except retrospectively. We cannot make naturalistic observations because we cannot accurately predict when riots will occur. Even if we could, we might feel ethically bound to try to stop the violence; nor can we ethically incite a riot in order to study it. Thus, retrospective study is sometimes the only possible method. At other times, the retrospective method is much more practical than the alternatives. To find a relationship between childhood experiences and later delinquency, or neurosis, or personality development, it is easier to begin with the recollections of the people being studied than it is to observe children and await their development.

The retrospective method also has its limitations. People tend to remember what makes sense to them. Memories of what preceded a riot are colored by a person's ideas about the causes of riots, and memories of childhood are influenced by a person's present feelings about parents and siblings. Thus, memories are distorted by prejudice and preconceptions, and it is often difficult to find other witnesses who can either confirm or question someone's recollections. Furthermore, the results of a study depend on the questions that are (or aren't) asked. The cause of the 1967 riots may have been something that was completely neglected by the Kerner Commission's investigators. Problems like these are discussed in more detail in Chapter 3.

Both naturalistic observations and retrospective case studies are valuable because they provide concrete observations, relatively uncluttered by anyone's theories and conclusions. From such observations, it is possible to produce theories to try to explain the events. We can then look to new events to test the theories. Lorenz's observations suggested the theory of an innate territorial instinct, and this theory implies that crowding will always produce aggression. The Kerner Commission report led to a theory of the causes of urban riots, which in turn suggested that when certain specified social conditions exist, crowding can contribute to riots. In short, both naturalistic observation and retrospective case study help to turn a relatively vague question into a theoretical analysis. The theory, in turn, suggests *hypotheses* for future research.

Hypotheses and Variables

A *hypothesis* is a statement of possible fact, usually focusing on one or more abstractions. Here are some examples:

"Animals *respond aggressively* to *crowding*."
"Most Americans *think they are not making enough money*."
"People with *premarital sexual experience* have more *stable marriages*."
"*Intelligence* does not depend on *race*."
"*Education* makes people more *tolerant of other beliefs*."
"The effect of a *deterrent strategy* on the *opponent's response* increases as the *risk of war* increases."

The phrases in italics are the abstractions central to each hypothesis. The prominence of abstractions in these statements suggests the possibility of operationalizing the abstractions and making observations to test the truth of these hypotheses. This is the strategy that is used in the remaining methods of gathering scientific evidence.

It will make sense at this point to look more closely at the process of operationalizing. An operational definition is a *procedure* for classifying, ordering, or measuring something. In the case of "crowding," an operational definition would give us rules for either

> *classifying* situations (as crowded or not crowded)
> *ordering* situations (as uncrowded, mildly crowded, moderately crowded, and severely crowded, for example)
> *quantifying* crowdedness (in a city, we could measure it in terms of the average number of residents per square mile).

When we operationalize "crowding," we are seeing it as a property ("crowdedness") that is measurable by its presence or absence, or else by the amount of it that is present. The concept "crowding" has become the measurable *variable* "crowdedness."

A *variable* is any property of a person, thing, event, setting, and so on that is not fixed. Variables may be properities that are different in different places (crowding in Manhattan vs. central Wyoming) or different times (crowding in Saigon before vs. after the war) or different people (some people feel crowded while others in the same place do not). Variables may be relatively concrete concepts such as height, number of people, annual income, and so forth, or abstractions, such as intelligence, alienation, anxiety, stress, political power, and urbanization. It is possible to conceive of variables that are either concrete or abstract. However, since scientific observation requires that variables be measured, all research on variables begins by concretizing them. By operationalizing abstractions like those underlined in the hypotheses above, we turn them into variables. We begin to think of more quantitative questions: "How crowded must an animal be to aggress?" "What percentage of Americans think they are not making enough money?" "Is tolerance greater among college students than among high school students?" Such questions require other methods of observation.

We have seen Lorenz's findings on aggression in animals, and the results of the Kerner Commission report. Each of these sources suggested directions for more research, and both suggested a relationship between crowding and aggression. To learn more, we might next want to ask, "How frequent are different types of aggression when people are crowded?" We could look for an answer by studying a situation generally recognized as crowded (if we concretely describe the situation, we do not have to operationalize "crowded"), and count the instances of aggression. To do this, we must operationalize "aggression." If the crowded situation of interest is "living on Manhattan Island," we might define "aggression" as having been convicted of homicide, aggravated assault, or rape while living in Manhattan. If the crowded situation is the stands at the Superbowl, "aggression" might be defined as participating in a fistfight or shouting such aggressive slogans as "Kill 'em!"

These operational definitions are fine in theory, but it will be very difficult to get the criminal records of everyone in Manhattan, and it might be even more difficult to accurately determine the number of people in fistfights at the Superbowl. The difficulties include getting information on everyone (you can't see the whole crowd at once), avoid mistakes (it is sometimes hard to tell participants from bystanders in a fistfight), and getting *complete* information on anyone. It becomes necessary to draw conclusions from only some of the people in a crowded situation.

Populations and Samples

A *population* is any defined group of people, things, or events. Some examples are "registered Republicans living in Nebraska," "six-year-olds," "revolutions," "Christian church congregations," "city governments," "sixth grade reading texts," and "spectators at the 1979 Superbowl."

A *sample* is a group of some members of a population. Thus, the Republicans of Scottsbluff are a sample of Nebraska Republicans, the congregations in Los Angeles are a sample of all congregations, and so on. Note that to sample from a population, the population must be concretely defined. To take a sample of revolutions, for example, there must be a concrete definition of "revolution" so that you know whether the events sampled are actually members of the population of revolutions.

It is generally true that when one asks a question such as "How frequent are different types of aggression when people are crowded?" or any similar question of how much or how many, information cannot easily be obtained on the whole population about which the question is asked. It is necessary to draw conclusions about the population from a sample. The discipline of *statistics* has developed ways to describe and draw conclusions about populations using information about samples. You will see statistics at work when you read research in the social sciences; now it is sufficient to present some of the barest principles so that you can understand the nature of the scientific methods that rely on statistics.

To find out how frequent various types of aggression are under crowded conditions, we might enter a crowded situation and observe a sample of people for aggressive behavior, or interview a sample of people looking for evidence of aggressive feelings. We could then attempt to generalize from the sample to the whole population. I use a hypothetical piece of research as an example, for reasons that will soon become clear. In this hypothetical research, a sample of 500 adults living in Manhattan was obtained. Each person was interviewed and asked a number of questions, including some about the person's experiences with aggressive acts during the past year. Fourteen percent reported having been robbed or "mugged" during the past year (only one-third of these reported the event to the police), 20% said they had had their apartments burglarized, and 8% reported a series of annoying or obscene phone calls. A whopping 57% had "felt like physically attacking someone" during the past year (88% of males; 26% of females). (Remember, these percentages are all hypothetical!) We might conclude from these findings that the same percentages hold for all people living in Manhattan. If we draw this conclusion, we might say that the data from Manhattan are consistent with the theory that crowding increases aggression, since there seems to be a lot of aggression in crowded Manhattan. The hypothetical research described here is called a sample study.

Sample Study

A sample study is one in which some of the people, groups, or events are sampled from a population of interest, and an attempt is made to draw conclusions about the whole population. These studies usually begin with a question about how much, or how often, or how common something is. Researchers attempt to get an answer by carefully choosing a sample from the population, making observations, and using statistical methods to make inferences about the whole population.

The most common form of sample study involves a survey, using a questionnaire or an interview schedule as in the made up example. There are other ways of sampling, though. It is possible, for example, to measure the amount of aggressive behavior in a classroom by *observing* the behavior of a sample of the children, during a sample of the school days. The crucial thing about a sample study is that its goal is to *determine the frequency* of something by looking at a selected sample. We will see that in other methods of gathering evidence, samples are also drawn from populations, but the term *sample study* is used here in a restricted sense. By *sample study*, I mean only the pure case, a study whose only purpose is to determine the frequency of some variable (or variables) in a population.

The sample study has an advantage over naturalistic and retrospective methods in that it is quantitative. We know not only that there is *some* aggression under crowded conditions, but we begin to get an idea of how much of a particular kind. Only quantitative methods can clearly point out the magnitude of a problem. However, the information we get from a sample study is limited in two major ways. First, we must be sure that the sample used is *representative* of the population. To draw conclusions about the population, we must be sure that the people or events sampled do not differ in any important way from the people or events left out of the sample. A look at the problem of sampling the adults living in Manhattan will suggest the difficulty of getting a representative sample. We could list all the million-plus adults and choose randomly (by drawing their names from a giant hat, for example), but we are unlikely to get an up-to-date list. We could obtain a list of all the street addresses and sample those, but which residents do you interview in a multi-family dwelling? Even if you could decide this, you might make several trips before finding the person at home, and the other information may then be out of date. If you took an easy way out and concentrated only on certain neighborhoods, you would have to be sure that the level of violence and crowding in these neighborhoods was representative of violence and crowding all over Manhattan. These sampling problems are discussed in more detail in Chapter 3.

A second problem exists with sample studies, even if you are confident that the sample is representative. Social scientists usually want to understand the relationships between events. If 57% of Manhattanites "felt like physically attacking someone," what does this tell us? It certainly does *not* tell us that Manhattanites are unusually aggressive. Maybe 57% of suburbanites in Scarsdale have the same feelings. And even if we knew that 57% was unusually high, we could not conclude that this aggressiveness was related to crowding. The aggressiveness may be due to other important features of living in Manhattan: the noise level, the air pollution, the ethnic mix of the population, the types of work people do, and so on. (In fact, violent crime has increased in Manhattan over the past few decades while the population has declined.) Sample studies give information, but they do not help clarify the relationships between events.

It is because sample studies do not give satisfying answers to questions about the relationship between crowding and aggression that I found it necessary to invent a sample study to illustrate the method. Sample studies are useful for gathering information about one variable at a time, but social scientists generally want to study the effects of variables on one another. For this reason, sampling methods are usually used as part of more complex methods of gathering evidence. To study the relationship between crowding and aggression, for example, a researcher might take a series of questions about aggressive feelings and give them to samples of people living in cities of varying population density. If people in less crowded cities tended to give fewer aggressive answers, one might conclude that aggressiveness is related to population density (crowding). This research method is called the *correlational study*.

Correlational Study

The following is an example of a correlational study of the effects of crowding. Mitchell (1971) was interested in the effects of high density housing on people's physical and mental health and happiness. He operationally defined crowding in terms of the amount of space available per person in the housing units people lived in (more space = less crowding). In the city of Hong Kong, he found people living in the same city under vastly different conditions of crowding (anywhere between 20 square feet and hundreds of square feet per person in the housing units). Mitchell interviewed thousands of people, recording the density of their living space and their answers to questions about their health, their feelings, and their happiness. He also recorded information about income level (since crowding is related to low income, it is important to have this information; we do not want to blame the effects of poverty on crowding). Mitchell sampled the people of Hong Kong, but he was mainly interested in comparing parts of the sample with each other. He had a subsample of people living in very crowded conditions that he could compare with a subsample living in relatively un-crowded conditions in the same city. He was also able to compare people with similar incomes living at higher and lower densities. Thus, he could not only tell whether many people living in crowded conditions complained of nervousness (for example), but he could also tell whether these people were more likely to have the complaint than a comparable group of people (same city, similar income) living in less crowded conditions. Mitchell reported that with comparable groups of people, health, happiness, and mental health were the same in crowded and less crowded conditions.

Mitchell's method was the correlational study. A *correlational study* is one that measures two or more variables and attempts to assess the relationship between them, without manipulating any variable.

Correlational studies begin with an implicit or explicit question: *"Is there a relationship between X and Y?"* In Mitchell's study there were several parallel questions: "Is there a relationship between crowding and health? happiness? mental health?" The term "relationship" can be stated in another way. Mitchell is asking whether knowledge of the density of a person's living space tells anything about health, happiness, or mental health. If we know someone lives in a tiny apartment, can we make a better prediction about his/her happiness, say, than we could without this piece of knowledge? If Mitchell could establish, even for Hong Kong, that people in small apartments are generally less happy than people in large houses, this would mean that knowledge about density was useful for predicting happiness (at least in Hong Kong). The greater the density, the less the happiness. (Mitchell did not find this relationship).

Notice that a relationship like this gives information in both directions. If you know that "the greater the density, the less the happiness," you can predict that a person in a large apartment is probably happy, and also that a happy person probably has a large apartment. (You *cannot* conclude that the person is happy *because* of the large apartment.)

Relationships between variables often can be translated into simple statements such as "The more of X, the more of Y," or "The more of X, the less of Y." There are also more complicated relationships, such as "X is greatest at moderate levels of Y, and there is less X with very low or very high amounts of Y." All these statements have in common the ability to predict either of the variables based on knowledge of the other.

Correlational studies are distinguished from sample studies by the fact that more than one variable is measured, and information is collected about whether the variables are related. If Mitchell had determined that 20% of the people in Hong Kong had less than 40 square feet of living space, and that 22% rated themselves as "unhappy" or "very unhappy," he would have been doing a sample study that measured two variables. Only when he provides information that allows us to tell whether the unhappy people are the same people who are crowded does he give information about the *relationship* between crowding and happiness. Because he has provided this information, his study is correlational.

Correlational studies are distinguished by the fact that they *do not manipulate variables*. A correlational study of crowding and aggression observes and measures these two variables, but it does not either create or modify the crowding or the aggression. If you studied the effects of crowding on aggression by putting people in a crowded room and observing their responses, you would be manipulating crowding, and the study would not be correlational.

The correlational study is a very commonly used method in the social sciences, and it takes many forms, some of which do not, at first, bear much resemblance to Mitchell's study. Here are some examples:

(a) Baby girls (6 to 12 months) who vocalized frequently in a testing situation had higher IQs as adults than girls who did not vocalize (Cameron, Livson, & Bayley, 1967). Note that this study compares two variables (vocalization in infancy and IQ in adulthood) within a single group of subjects.

(b) In towns undergoing political change, political conflicts are much more likely to be rancorous ("dirty" tactics used on both sides) than in politically stable towns (Gamson, 1966). Here there are two groups, politically stable towns and politically unstable towns, and the frequency of the variable "rancorous conflict" is compared.

(c) It has been said that first-borns are prone to seek company when anxious. Therefore, Zucker, Manosevitz, and Lanyon (1968) predicted that first-borns caught in the great electrical blackout in 1965 would be more likely than later-borns to seek the company of others. This study also relates two variables: seeking company (did vs. didn't) and birth order (first vs. later). The study is correlational because it relates the variables (by comparing the frequency of company-seeking in first-borns and later-borns) without manipulating either variable. (The prediction was not strongly supported by the evidence.)

(d) College girls waiting to be subjects in an experiment in which they were to receive electric shocks were given the choice of waiting alone or in a group of others. First-borns were more likely to choose waiting in a group (Schachter, 1959). This study is much like (c), in that both studies compare first-borns and later-borns in their affiliative responses to anxiety. The major difference is that the researcher in this study did not wait for the anxiety to be produced naturally. He created a standard anxiety-producing situation to which he exposed his subjects. Thus, Schachter manipulated the situation. He did not, however, manipulate the *variables* he was studying (birth order and affiliation). Schachter *did* manipulate anxiety, but since everyone was in the same anxiety-producing situation, anxiety was presumed to be a constant (not a variable) in the study. Schachter could have manipulated anxiety. For example, he might have told half the subjects that they would be judging the lengths of lines, mentioning nothing about shock. We could assume that these subjects were less anxious than the others. Had the study run this way, Schachter would have been treating anxiety as a variable and he would have been manipulating it. He would have been conducting an *experiment*.

Correlational studies generally *test a hypothesis* about two variables *by observing and measuring the variables* to see if they are related. Correlational studies may bring subjects into a lab and have them do something there, as in example (d), *as long as they do not manipulate the variables involved in the hypothesis*. (When a variable is manipulated, the study is classified as an experiment.) Here's another example of the difference between a correlational study and one that manipulates variables. Hypothesis: Married couples who communicate well with each other are happier because of it. A correlational study to test this hypothesis might have couples play a game like the TV game "Password," in which one partner gives cue words and the other guesses a target word (Goodman & Ofshe, 1968). The number of cue words needed to elicit the correct answer could measure communication efficiency. The couples could be questioned independently about their married life, and an index of marital happiness, derived from their responses, could be correlated with communication efficiency. If couples who play the game well score high in happiness, the data are consistent with the hypothesis. The same hypothesis could be tested by manipulating the variable of communication. The researcher might take a sample of couples applying for marriage counseling (and therefore presumed to be relatively unhappy as couples) and give half the couples a training program in interpersonal communications skills while putting the other half on a waiting list. If the trained group scores higher on the index of marital happiness there is evidence to support the hypothesis. The couples are happier, presumably because they have learned communications skills. This study differs from the correlational method in that it has manipulated the variable of communication.

An advantage of the correlational study over the other methods discussed above is that it can establish a *relationship* between variables. This can be done only when each of the variables is measured in each individual being studied. Another advantage of the correlational study is that it can be used to evaluate the contribution of third variables. In Mitchell's study, for example, the relationship between crowding and happiness could be studied with income removed as a factor. This was possible because all three variables were measured, and people could be matched on income for purposes of comparison.

A limitation of correlational studies is that they cannot give conclusive information about the causes of the relationship between variables. Reconsider the two studies about whether good communication between marriage partners makes them happier. In the correlational study we find out that people who play "Password" well (i.e., communicate efficiently) are happy, but we don't know if good communication made them happy, or if happiness made them communicate better, or if their common interests were responsible for both their happiness and their success at communication. All we know from this study is that the couples who are happy tend to be the same ones who communicate well.

It is possible for correlational research to produce somewhat more definitive information about causation. Suppose that a number of couples was followed from the time they became engaged for the next five years. Some of the couples break up before marriage, some marry then get divorced, and others are still married after five years, with varying degrees of happiness. If the couples who communicated well at the beginning of the five year period tended to be those who got married, stayed married, and were happily married after five years, we could at least conclude that good communication was a useful *predictor* of marital happiness. Since we know that efficient communication *preceded* marital happiness, happiness could not have been the primary cause of success at communication. Still, it may be that some couples are more happily *engaged* than others, and that smooth sailing during the engagement period may cause both efficient communication and happy marriages. Other explanations of the communication-happiness relationship are also still possible—for example, common interests could be the cause of both efficient communication and happy marriages. There are even more complex and sophisticated forms of correlational research, which can further increase our confidence about causes. Still, *we cannot make conclusive statements about causes and effects on the basis of correlational studies.*

The study in which people are given training in communication skills provides more certain information about causes than one can usually get from correlational research. We can be reasonably sure that communication training was responsible for increased happiness, because couples who weren't trained did not get any happier. This study, which manipulates one variable to assess its effect on another variable, is an *experiment.*

Experiments: Within-subjects and Between-subjects

An experiment is a study in which the effect of one variable on another is measured by manipulating the first variable and observing the second.

The hypothesis in any experiment assumes a cause-effect relationship between variables. In the example about communication skills and marital happiness, communication is assumed to be a cause of happiness. (One could hypothesize the reverse, that happiness improves communication, but that would be the hypothesis of a different experiment.) It is possible to think of an experimental hypothesis as an if . . . then statement: "*If* the communications skills of a married couple are improved, *then* their marital happiness will improve." In general, experiments test hypotheses of the form "*If* you manipulate variable *I, then* you will observe a change in variable *D*."[2] That is, the "if" variable is the one manipulated in an experiment. This "variable *I*" is called the *independent variable*. The "then" variable is the one observed; it (variable *D*) is called the *dependent variable*. It is important to note that some hypotheses have independent and dependent variables and others don't. Let's reproduce some of the hypotheses listed on page 29, and try to translate them into if . . . then form to get a clearer understanding.

"Animals respond aggressively to crowding." This translates as: *If* an animal is crowded, *then* it will respond aggressively. This is a *causal hypothesis*, since it presumes that one variable causes another. In this case, crowding causes aggression, rather than the other way around. This hypothesis (or any causal hypothesis) can be the hypothesis for an experiment. The experiment would get an animal, crowd it, and observe the aggressiveness of its response.

"Most Americans think they are not making enough money." This hypothesis has only one variable, so it cannot be causal. It cannot be stated in if . . . then form, and it cannot be the hypothesis of an experiment.

"People with premarital sexual experience have more stable marriages." This hypothesis asserts a relationship between two variables, but it does *not* imply that one variable causes another. It is very different from the similar-sounding hypothesis "Premarital sexual experience makes for more stable marriages." Although both hypotheses relate the same variables, only the second hypothesis implies that they are causally related. The second hypothesis has independent and dependent variables; it asserts that marital stability is *dependent* on premarital sexual experience. The first hypothesis contains no such implication. It is quite

---

2. Some writers make a distinction between a hypothesis and an "expected finding," reserving the term "hypothesis" for a relationship between the terms of a theory, and referring "expected finding" to what would be expected in a particular study if the hypothesis is true. When I talk about the hypothesis in an experiment, I am referring to the prediction the experiment was designed to test—whether it is a "hypothesis" in the theoretical sense or only an "expected finding."

possible that people with premarital sexual experience have more stable marriages, and yet that sexual experience has no effect on marital stability. Both of these variables may depend on age at marriage. People who marry older have had more time to engage in premarital sex; they may also be more able to make a mature judgment about whom to marry. If this is in fact the nature of the relationship between premarital sex and marital stability, the first hypothesis would be true and the second false. The hypothesis "People with premarital sexual experience have more stable marriages" is *noncausal*; it does not identify either variable as dependent on the other. It would be inappropriate to test this noncausal hypothesis by manipulating a variable, even if one could be ethically manipulated. A hypothesis like this can be appropriately tested with a correlational study.

"Intelligence does not depend on race." The word "depend" suggests that the hypothesis is causal: race, somehow, is supposed to cause a difference in intelligence. Intelligence is supposed to be *dependent* on race. The independent variable is race, and intelligence is the dependent variable. In theory, this hypothesis could be tested by an experiment. In practice, of course, race cannot be manipulated. Since an experiment is impossible, we must settle for correlational studies, and correlational studies never definitively test causal hypotheses. The reason for this will become clearer in Chapter 3.

"Education makes people more tolerant of other beliefs." This is causal—"makes" gives it away. Tolerance is *dependent* on education; it is the dependent variable. The independent variable is education. An experiment could be done to test this hypothesis.

Several points are embedded in the above paragraphs.

An *experiment* has been defined as a study in which the effect of one variable on another is assessed by manipulating the first variable and observing the second.

In an experiment, the first (manipulated) variable is called *independent*, the second (observed) *dependent*.

The hypothesis in any experiment is causal, and can be written as: "If you manipulate variable I (independent), you will observe a change in variable D (dependent)."

Any causal hypothesis can, in principle, be tested by experiment.

The hypothesis of a correlational study may or may not be causal.

A correlational study can definitively confirm a noncausal hypothesis; it is less than definitive in supporting causal hypotheses.

There are many ways to conduct experiments, but two major types stand out. The following studies in the area of crowding and behavior exemplify these types and the essential differences between them.

Loo (1972) formed groups of six children (three male, three female) four and five years old, and observed their play in two 48-minute sessions. In one play session, the children were in a room with 265 square feet of space; in the other session, the room was reduced to 90 square feet. The children's behavior was rated on ten dimensions, including "aggressive behavior," which was scored when a child physically attacked another child or a toy, or was destructive of equipment, or behaved in other similarly specified ways. Fewer aggressive acts were observed in the high density condition (that is, there was less aggression with crowding).

In the other experiment, Freedman, Levy, Buchanan, and Price (1972) placed groups of adults in either large (about 300 square feet) or small (about 100 square feet) rooms to hear mock jury trials. The cases were designed to sound realistic, and to be weighted somewhat in favor of conviction. Aggressiveness was operationally defined as the severity of sentences given to the defendants. (The researchers found that there was no overall effect of crowding, but that all male groups were more aggressive in the crowded room, while all female groups were less aggressive.)

There are many differences between these studies, including the type of people studied, the way aggression was measured, and the nature of the aggression (physical vs. symbolic). However, both studies manipulated crowding and measured the effects on aggression. There is an important difference in the way crowding was manipulated. Loo had the same groups of children play twice, once in the small room and once in the large room. She compared children's aggressiveness in the small room with the aggressiveness *of the same children* in the large room. An experiment that measures an effect by comparing the same subjects' behavior under different conditions of the independent variable is a *within-subjects experiment*, or within-subjects design.

The study by Freedman et al. had each jury convene only once. Juries met in the large room *or* the small room, but not both. Thus, the effect of crowding was measured by comparing people who met in the large room with *other people* (presumably similar) who met in the small room. This study is called a *between-subjects experiment*, or a between-subjects design, because it measures an effect by comparing the performance of *different people* under crowded and uncrowded conditions. This type of experiment is also called a *comparison group design*, because one group (e.g., crowded people) is compared with another group (uncrowded) to measure the effect of the variable on which they differ.

A *between-subjects experiment*, or *comparison group design*, tests a hypothesis about variables by manipulating at least one variable, using two or more groups of comparable subjects. The comparable groups are made to differ on an independent variable, and observed differences between the groups on a dependent variable are attributed to the effects of the independent variable. In the Freedman et al.

study, groups meeting in large and small rooms did not give sentences of different severity; the authors concluded that aggressiveness was not attributable to crowding alone.

The assumption that the subjects in the large and small rooms are "comparable" is necessary in all between-subjects experiments. It would be difficult to compare groups if they differed from each other in important ways besides the independent variable. If, for example, Freedman and his colleagues had assigned women primarily to the small room and men primarily to the large room, any differences in aggressiveness between rooms might be due either to crowding or to the sex difference. Groups are assumed to be comparable if they are known to be similar in important respects or if one large group is divided by lot into subgroups for the purpose of comparison. More on this in Chapter 3.

A *within-subjects experiment* tests a hypothesis about variables by manipulating at least one variable, and drawing inferences by comparing the subjects' performances under the influence of that variable with their assumed or known performances under other conditions. As in all experiments, the manipulated variable is the independent variable, and changes in the subject's behavior are attributed to the independent variable. In Loo's study, children were observed in both large and small rooms. Changes in their aggressiveness scores from one setting to the other were attributed to the difference in density between the rooms. Comparable groups are not needed because each person is being compared to him/herself.

In a within-subjects experiment, the effect of a manipulated variable is assessed by looking at the changes it produces in a single subject, or in a series of subjects who are all exposed to the variable. This type of experiment occurs when doctors, having failed with all standard treatments, try out a new medicine on a hopeless case to see if it helps. Any effect is measured by comparing the patient's survival with what would have been expected without the treatment. If the treatment appears successful, it is tried with another patient and another, until it has been used with a series of patients. Each treatment is a within-subjects experiment, and the group of treatments together can be considered a within-subjects experiment.

The within-subjects method of experimentation has been used extensively by followers of B. F. Skinner, who have demonstrated relationships between behavior and its consequences (rewards and punishments) by intensive within-subjects study of single cases. Frequently these studies use *repeated* manipulation of the same variable to demonstrate that behavior changes back and forth depending on whether the variable is present or absent. For example, a child cries every night at bedtime. The parents decide to ignore the crying, rather than give the child any attention (talking to it, punishing it, etc.) Each night, the number of minutes of crying is noted, and within a week, the crying has stopped. (This is the end of one experiment.) At this point, the parents respond to one isolated instance of crying, and to another, and the crying increases in length. (This is the end of a second, if unintended, experiment.) The parents then systematically ignore the crying again, and after a week or two, it stops (a third experiment). If you consider the three parts together as one within-subject experiment, you can see how this method can provide very good evidence of the relationship between two variables (in this case, between attention and crying at bedtime).

Experiments, in general, have an advantage over correlational studies because they can directly test causal hypotheses. With an experiment, it is possible to look for causes by manipulating a variable hypothesized to be causal and observing whether the predicted effect occurs. Between- and within-subjects experiments have their relative advantages and disadvantages. In a within-subjects experiment, it is not necessary to assume that different people are the same for the purposes of the study. One can use people who *are* the same. Unfortunately, people change after being in an experiment. In Loo's experiment on crowding and behavior, for example, the effects of playing in a small room may have carried over to the large room situation, since the same children were involved. When this kind of carryover is anticipated, one solution is to use a between-subjects design, as Freedman and his associates did in their experiment. There are other solutions, which are discussed later.

After reading about research such as that by Loo, Freedman, and others, you may be wondering what happened to the question we started this chapter with: "What effects does crowding have on people?" It has been transformed in the process of trying to get scientific answers. It may be clear by now that the original question was much too broad to obtain a scientific answer. Naturalistic observations and retrospective case studies can examine broad questions, but they are most often used to *suggest hypotheses* and to *identify variables* that may be worth studying further. The other methods all require operational definitions of variables, and this requires them to deal more in details. By the time you heard about Freedman's research, "effects . . . on people" had been transformed into "aggression," and then into "severity of sentences handed out to defendants." "Crowding" had become a jury meeting in a small room rather than a large one. There are obviously many "effects on people" and many types of crowding that Freedman's research did not even attempt to investigate.

The process of scientific research is such that it is considered more valuable to have information on the effects of a small jury room on the severity of sentences than it is to have information on the effects of "crowding" in general. This is so because only with operationally defined variables can we be clear about what has been observed, and only with the more sophisticated methods of gathering evidence (correlational studies and, especially, experiments) can we define the relationships between variables and the influences variables have on each other.

When you begin to look for the scientific evidence on a question you are interested in, be prepared to find that the best studies available deal with only a small part of your topic. (The Appendix gives useful hints for refining a general question and for locating detailed studies relevant to your narrowed question.) To make meaningful generalizations, you will have to work backwards from particular, closely related pieces of research on what may seem like a minute part of the problem to research on related subjects of more general interest. Freedman's study of the mock juries, for example, was part of his attempt to determine some of the effects of crowding. His work included a number of experiments and correlational studies conducted in his laboratory, as' well as detailed reading and evaluation of the theories and research produced by other people. Freedman's conclusions about the effects of crowding and their implications for life in cities are summarized in his very readable book *Crowding and Behavior* (1975). His general conclusion is that crowding of itself has no specific effect on behavior; it only intensifies the effects of the feelings and social interactions that are already there. (As might be expected with a topic like this, Freedman's conclusions are quite controversial.)

In this chapter, you have read about the distinctions among six methods of gathering scientific evidence, and you have been exposed to some additional terms useful for distinguishing among the six methods and for understanding the significance of the distinctions. The essential characteristics of the six methods are summarized in Table 1.

Table 1. Six methods of gathering scientific evidence

Method	Question asked	Hypothesis	Variables	Comparison group
Naturalistic observation	What happens? (open-ended)	none	none	none
Retrospective case study	Why did E (event) occur?	none	none; sometimes one	none
Sample study	How often does X (variable) occur? What is its average value?	sometimes (noncausal)	one	none
Correlational study	Are X and Y (variables) related?	yes (causal or non-causal)	more than one; none manipulated	sometimes
Between-subjects experiment (comparison group design)	Does X (independent variable) have an effect on Y (dependent variable)?	yes (causal)	more than one; one is manipulated	yes
Within-subjects experiment	Does X (independent variable) have an effect on Y (dependent variable)?	yes (causal)	more than one; one is manipulated	no; people compared with themselves

The exercises at the end of this chapter provide practice in identifying hypotheses and variables and classifying reports of research according to the method used to gather the evidence. They specifically test your ability to use these key terms:

> naturalistic observation (defined on p. 25)
> retrospective case study (p. 27)
> sample study (p. 32)
> correlational study (p. 34)
> between-subjects experiment, or comparison group design (p. 40)
> within-subjects experiment (p. 40)
> hypothesis (p. 29)
> causal and noncausal hypotheses (pp. 29, 38–39)
> variable (p. 30)
> independent variable (p. 38)
> dependent variable (p. 38)

Before working the exercises, you may want to consult Figure 2. It gives a decision-making procedure for classifying scientific research according to which method was used to gather evidence.

Exercises

For each report of research described below:

(a) Classify it as a naturalistic observation, retrospective case study, sample study, correlational study, within-subjects experiment, or between-subjects experiment.

(b) If there is a hypothesis, state it, identifying it as causal or noncausal.

(c) Name all variables in the hypothesis, identifying the independent and dependent variables if the hypothesis is causal.

Write your answers in the spaces provided, and also write down any doubts or questions you may have about your answers.

(1) A Head Start program in Midwest City was used to test the effectiveness of Head Start. A group of disadvantaged preschoolers in Midwest City was chosen to enter the program. IQ tests were given during the first week of the program and again at the end of the school year. There was an average gain of seven IQ points. It was concluded that Head Start can increase children's IQ scores.

(a)

(b)

(c)

(2) Head Start increases IQ scores. A sample of preschoolers in Midwest City was given IQ tests at the start of a school year, and was then divided into two

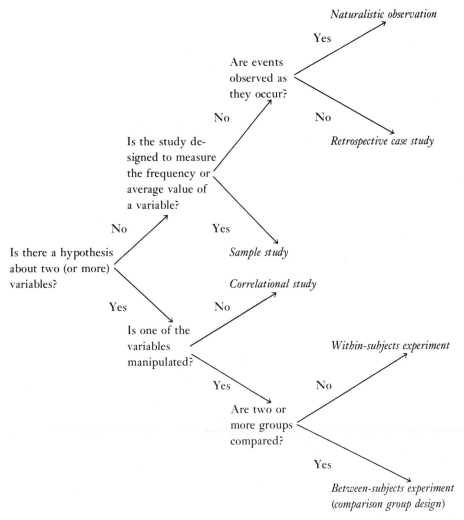

Figure 2. Decision-making procedure for distinguishing among six methods of gathering scientific evidence.

groups: for each pair of children with the same scores, one child was randomly assigned to the Head Start class, and the other was sent to a traditional nursery school. At the end of the year, the Head Start children scored seven points higher on IQ than the paired children in the nursery school.

(a)

(b)

(c)

(3) Head Start increases children's IQ scores. Children in Head Start in a ghetto neighborhood of Midwest City scored seven points higher on an IQ test than a group of children from the same neighborhood who went to regular nursery school.

(a)

(b)

(c)

(4) Students at Moreland University have an average SAT Verbal score of 520. This was the average score reported by a randomly selected group of 40 Moreland U. students.

(a)

(b)

(c)

(5) People who sit at the head of the table tend to become leaders in groups of people who have not met before. In a study using mock juries (Strodtbeck & Hook, 1961) subjects took seats at a table for twelve which had single seats at each end and five seats on each side. When subjects rated each other on the amount each had contributed to the group's final decision, subjects seated at the ends of the table got higher ratings than subjects seated at any other position. It was concluded that people turn to those at the head of the table for leadership.

(a)

(b)

(c)

(6) "A number of years ago I was given a female lamb taken from its mother at birth. My wife and I raised it on the bottle for the first ten days of life and then placed it out in the pasture with a small flock of domestic sheep. As might have been expected from folklore, the lamb became attached to people and followed the persons who fed it. More surprisingly, the lamb remained independent of the flock when we returned it to pasture. Three years later it was still following an independent grazing pattern" (Scott, 1945).

(a)

(b)

(c)

(7) A study compared 25 community leaders in a small Southern city with a group of randomly selected citizens matched with them for sex and age. All subjects were interviewed, and asked a series of questions about their background, to find differences that might explain community leadership. It was discovered that 17 of the leaders had been members of the YMCA as children, compared with only six of the randomly selected group.

(a)

(b)

(c)

(8) Subtle rewards can influence verbal behavior. Subjects were reinforced with a head nod whenever they said plural nouns during an interview. The frequency of plural nouns was higher in the last five minutes of the interview than in the first.

(a)

(b)

(c)

(9) In the male South European Emerald Lizard, aggressive behavior is elicited by the colors of the rival male. The inhibition against biting females depends on smell. When Lorenz (1966) colored a female lizard in male colors with crayons and put her in an enclosure with a male, the male attacked with open jaws. On reaching the female, he stopped abruptly and somersaulted over her. He then examined her carefully with his tongue and took no more notice of the male colors. For a long time afterward, "this chivalrous lizard examined real males with his tongue, that is to say he checked upon their smell before attacking them. Apparently it had affected him deeply that he had once nearly bitten a lady!" (Lorenz, 1966, pp. 118–119).

(a)

(b)

(c)

(10) To test a prediction that racial isolation led blacks to violence, Ransford (1968) conducted a study of blacks in the Watts section of Los Angeles after the 1965 riot. Ransford asked subjects if they had "ever done anything social" with white people they had contact with on jobs, in their neighborhood, and so on, "like going to the movies together or visiting in each other's homes." Subjects who had had such social contact with whites were less likely than other subjects to say they were "willing to use violence to get Negro rights."

(a)

(b)

(c)

(11) Wolfenstein (1951) attempted to outline changing conceptions of child-rearing in the United States over the period from 1914 to the date of her article. She used as data the bulletin *Infant Care*, published by the U.S. Department of Labor Children's Bureau in 1914, 1921, 1929, 1938, 1942, and 1945. Wolfenstein reported that the child in 1914 was seen as having many dangerous impulses (e.g., masturbation, thumb-sucking) that must be forcibly restrained (e.g., by tying feet to the crib to prevent self-stimulation from rubbing legs together). By 1945, impulses toward self-stimulation are seen as innocuous and less important. Infants were seen as being interested in exploring the world, rather than their bodies. Wolfenstein interprets the data as indicating that a "fun morality," more accepting of play, was emerging in American culture during this period.

(a)

(b)

(c)

(12) Schein (1960) interviewed released POW's from Chinese prison camps during the Korean War. He concluded that the key to Chinese success in eliciting false confessions and in persuading prisoners was a procedure that involved de-stroying social solidarity and interpersonal communication among the prisoners. The conclusion was based on evaluation of many prisoners' accounts.

(a)

(b)

(c)

(13) Zimbardo (1973) attempted to show (among other things) how a social structure can bring out brutality in presumably "normal" people. He assigned student volunteers to be either prisoners or guards in a simulated prison. The "prisoners" were arrested by real police, booked, fingerprinted, and brought to a "jail" where their care, feeding, and basic privileges were totally controlled by the "guards." In less than a week, some of the guards had become so sadistic and some of the prisoners so hateful that the simulation was cancelled for fear it would permanently harm the participants.

(a)

(b)

(c)

Answers to Exercises

(1) (a) Within-subjects experiment.
(b) Hypothesis: Head Start can raise IQ scores of disadvantaged preschoolers. (Because everyone in the study is a disadvantaged preschooler, economic and social situation and age are not variables in this study.) The hypothesis is causal.
(c) Independent variable: Head Start
    Dependent variable: IQ
This is an experiment because the children have been *assigned* to Head Start; the independent variable is manipulated. It is within-subjects because the effect on IQ is measured by looking within each child. When something's "effectiveness" is tested, a causal hypothesis is implied.

(2) (a) Between-subjects experiment.
(b) Hypothesis: Head Start increases children's IQ scores. (Essentially, this is the same hypothesis tested in example 1.)

(c) Variables are the same as in example 1.

Again, attendance at Head Start is manipulated, so this is an experiment. Here, however, the effect of Head Start is assessed by comparing the outcome of Head Start with the outcome of a comparison program (nursery school). Thus, we have a comparison group (between-subjects) design.

(3) (a) Correlational study.

(b) Hypothesis: Head Start increases children's IQ scores.

(c) Variables are the same as in examples 1 and 2. The researcher has stated a causal hypothesis, even though these correlational data cannot establish cause and effect. The study is correlational because the children were already in Head Start when the study began. This is an important difference between this study and studies 1 and 2. It may be that children enrolled in Head Start differ from their neighbors in many ways related to IQ. Possibly, children with the most intelligent, or most literate, parents are the only ones who get enrolled, because only these parents have the information that Head Start school is open. It may also be that Head Start enrolls mainly the kids on the same block as the school, and the block may be in an especially well-off or run-down part of the neighborhood. In other words, differences in IQ found in this study may be due to many factors related to home life, and unrelated to the Head Start program itself.

(4) (a) Sample study. The only purpose is to generalize from a sample to the whole population of Moreland U. students.

(b) There is no hypothesis. The study was apparently done to answer an open-ended question: "What is the average SAT Verbal score of students at Moreland U.?"

(c) There is a variable (SAT Verbal scores), but with only one variable in the study, it cannot be called either independent or dependent.

(5) (a) Correlational study.

(b) Hypothesis: People who sit at the head of a table tend to become leaders in groups of people who have not met before. Noncausal.

(c) Variables: sitting at the head of the table, leadership.

If you look closely, you will see that the variable of seating position at the table was *not* manipulated. Subjects were allowed to choose their own seats, rather than being arbitrarily assigned to seats. Thus, subjects—not the experimenter—were responsible for seating positions. This implies that differences in leadership *cannot* safely be attributed to seating position. It may be that the most assertive subjects chose the end seats, because they wanted attention from the group, or because they were prone to become leaders. Both leadership and seating position might have been determined by subjects' personalities.

The hypothesis is a bit ambiguous as to causality. It asserts that people who sit at the head of the table become leaders, but it does not assert that they become leaders *because* of where they sit. Hence, the hypothesis does not assert a causal relationship between the variables.

(6) (a) Naturalistic observation. (You might object that taking a lamb from its mother is manipulative, rather than naturalistic, and you would have a point. I call this a naturalistic observation, because from the time the Scotts got the lamb they proceeded to make fairly complete and concrete observations of its admittedly unusual situation, without manipulating variables, yet minimizing interference with the lamb's life.)
(b) There is no hypothesis.
(c) There are no variables explicitly being studied.

(7) (a) I would call this a *retrospective case study* on the grounds that the study seems to have proceeded from a fairly general question "What background produces leaders in this city?" Although researchers identified one variable, leadership, they did not clearly specify other variables with which they believe leadership correlates.

The researchers did, however, choose to look into the subjects' "background" for answers, and it can be assumed that they were asking for only selected background information. Since the study did relate leadership to a finite (and probably preselected) number of other variables, it seems also to be a *correlational study*. One could say that the researchers began with the idea that leadership depends on a person's background—a vague sort of hypothesis. The conclusion that YMCA membership is related to leadership is clearly correlational. Either answer, if adequate justification were given, seems appropriate.

(b) No hypothesis; if this is a retrospective case study. If you see it as correlational, you must assume an implicit hypothesis, such as "a person's background *determines* that person's leadership." This hypothesis is causal. The implicit hypothesis may also be noncausal: "People from different backgrounds are not equally likely to become leaders."

(c) In a retrospective case study, there are no variables "in the hypothesis." Leadership is apparently conceptualized as a dependent variable for which independent variables are being sought. If this is seen as a correlational study, the dependent variable is leadership, and the independent variable is "background" or some similar abstraction.

(8) (a) Within-subjects experiment.
(b) Subtle rewards can influence verbal behavior. Causal.
(c) Independent variable: subtle rewards
   Dependent variable: verbal behavior
Another, possibly more precise way to state this hypothesis would be: "Nonver-

bal reinforcement of a verbal response increases the frequency of that response." This is more precise because the nature of the dependent variable is much clearer when it is identified as the *frequency* of the response. This tells us exactly what kind of variability is being measured.

There is no comparison group in this study, so it is a within-subjects experiment. Since behavior is measured both before and after subtle rewards are given, the subjects are being compared with themselves.

(9) (a) Within-subject experiment. (This reads like a naturalistic observation, and it is, in the sense that more-or-less naturally occurring events are carefully described in concrete language. However, by coloring the female lizard, Lorenz has manipulated a crucial variable.)

(b) Hypothesis: "In the male South European Emerald Lizard, aggressive behavior is elicited by the colors of the rival male. The inhibition against biting females depends on smell." Both color and smell are involved in the hypothesis, but only color is manipulated. You could actually say that this is an experiment (within-subject) on the effects of color, and a naturalistic observation of the effects of smell. Thus, the hypothesis *of the experiment* is that "aggressive behavior is elicited by the colors of the rival male." The hypothesis is causal.

(c) Independent variable: colors of the male lizard
    Dependent variable: aggressive behavior

(10) (a) Correlational study. Although a survey method was used, and a sample was taken, the purpose was more than one of generalizing from a sample. From the start, the study was investigating the relationship between two variables. For this reason, it is not a sample study. It is not a retrospective case study, even though retrospective methods were used, because retrospective case studies do not have hypotheses in advance.

(b) Hypothesis: Racial isolation is a contributing cause of black violence. Causal.

(c) Independent variable: racial isolation
    Dependent variable: black violence

Because neither variable is manipulated, the study is correlational. Given Ransford's results, it is possible that willingness to use violence may produce racial isolation, rather than the other way around. It is plausible that blacks who are willing to voice approval of violence to a researcher might also turn off white acquaintances enough to qualify as "isolated." Thus, this correlational study cannot strongly support its causal hypothesis.

(11) (a) Retrospective case study.

(b) There seems to be no hypothesis. The study appears to have been conducted to answer a general question: "How have conceptions of child-rearing in the U.S. changed from 1914 to the 1950's?"

(c) Since there is no hypothesis, there are no variables in the hypothesis. The abstraction "conceptions of child-rearing" is really too vague to qualify as a variable (we don't even know along which dimensions these conceptions may vary), but other abstractions coming out of the study (such as "dangerous impulses" attributed to children, interest in exploring the outer world-vs.-own body, etc.) would qualify as variables. Since these variables were not anticipated by the author, I have classified the study as retrospective, rather than correlational.

(12) (a) Retrospective case study.

(b) No hypothesis. Schein seems to have been trying to explain how the Chinese were so successful, but he does not have a hypothesis beforehand.

(c) No variables "in the hypothesis." One could say that the variable "success in persuading" is being studied as a dependent variable, with the independent variable(s) to be determined. The interviews led Schein to suggest that social solidarity and interpersonal communication may have been potent independent variables.

This "case study" of a social structure was built up from interviews with a large number of the participants. Because the interviewees may have been in several different prison camps, it is not a case study in the technical sense of studying one particular time and location. Retrospective case study is the most appropriate category.

(13) (a) Between-subjects experiment.

(b) Hypothesis: Social structures (the social structure of a prison, to be more specific) can bring out brutality in "normal" people. The hypothesis is causal.

(c) Independent variable: social structure (of a prison)
Dependent variable: brutality

This is clearly an experiment, because the social structure was manipulated, and people were put into it. I call it a between-subjects experiment because the people who became brutal (presumably the "guards") can be compared to the other subjects ("prisoners"), who were exposed to different—you might say opposite—social pressures. Zimbardo's experiment as described could be called a within-subjects experiment, the striking feature of which was the *increasing* brutalization of the subjects. As time went on, people changed in comparison to themselves. The direction of causality in the hypothesis is clear. Zimbardo's point is that prison makes people brutal rather than brutality causing people to become prisoners or guards, as is often argued.

Problems

Try your skills at these problems; answers are not provided. For each report of research described below:

(a) Classify it as a naturalistic observation, retrospective case study, sample study, correlational study, within-subjects experiment, or between-subjects experiment.

(b) If there is a hypothesis, state it, identifying it as causal or noncausal.

(c) Name all variables in the hypothesis, identifying the independent and dependent variables if the hypothesis is causal. Write down any doubts you have about your answers.

(1) Rabin (1965) studied men's and women's motives for having children by asking them to complete sentences such as "Men want children because . . . ," "Women want children because . . . ," and so on. Two judges classified all responses under categories of motivation such as altruistic, narcissistic, and so forth. Almost half of the men's motives were narcissistic, involving proof of virility, perpetuation of self, and so on, while only nine percent of the female respondents mentioned "proof of femininity" as a motive for having children.

(a)

(b)

(c)

(2) A researcher attempted to decrease the aggressive behavior of a preschooler via a program of rewards for nonaggressive behavior. The child was given praise whenever he was able to interact with another child without any physically aggressive acts. At first, praise was given at the first sign of acceptable behavior, but as such behavior became more frequent, the reward was made contingent on longer and longer intervals of nonaggressive interaction. During this period, the frequency of the child's aggressive outbursts consistently decreased until it was almost zero.

(a)

(b)

(c)

(3) An investigator observing seating patterns in a bus station waiting room observed that people almost always sit at opposite ends of benches less than eight feet long, except when both ends of the benches are already occupied. He suggested that the mangement might be able to seat more people comfortably if they replaced the benches with separate chairs.

(a)

(b)

(c)

(4) On the basis of interviews with 112 commuting students at Suburban Community College, a researcher reported that only 8% were currently coming to school in car pools. Of those who were not pooling, 63% had considered the idea, but had rejected it. The most commonly stated reasons for not pooling were inconvenience of schedule (31%), lack of information about who was available to pool with (22%), and the feeling of a loss of independence (19%).

(a)

(b)

(c)

(5) A group of people who had used LSD twenty times or more was given a battery of psychological tests. Compared to the norms for these tests for the general population, the LSD group differed significantly in one respect: LSD users scored higher than the general population on a test measuring social introversion. It was concluded that the use of LSD tends to make people withdraw from social contacts.

(a)

(b)

(c)

(d) Why is the conclusion unacceptable on the basis of the evidence given? (This study was not really done; I invented it.)

(6) Janis and Mann (1965) tested the effectiveness of role-playing techniques in an attempt to change cigarette smoking behavior. Smokers were assigned either to play the role of someone who has just been informed she has lung cancer or to listen to a recording of such a role-playing session. Two weeks later, the number of cigarettes smoked daily had declined in the role-playing group compared to the subjects who only listened to role-playing.

(a)

(b)

(c)

(7) Antunes and Gaitz (1975) hypothesized that members of disadvantaged ethnic groups would "compensate" by having higher levels of social and political participation than persons of the same social class who are members of the dominant social group. They found that while blacks generally do participate more than whites of the same social class, Mexican-Americans tend to participate less than whites.

(a)

(b)

(c)

(8) In a study to determine the effect of anxiety on response to perceptual cues, people who scored either high or low on the Taylor Manifest Anxiety Scale were asked to observe two simultaneous events. Subjects faced a screen on which groups of dots appeared at irregular intervals. At each presentation, subjects were asked to report the number of dots. Subjects were also asked to press a key whenever they saw a light flash at the edge of the screen. The number of errors in

counting dots and in failure to respond to lights were measures of responsiveness. On both measures, the low-anxiety group scored better (fewer errors).
(a)

(b)

(c)

CHAPTER 3

Evaluating Scientific Evidence: I

You are now ready to begin evaluating scientific evidence. You have learned how to distinguish scientific evidence from nonscientific statements (Chapter 1) and how to discriminate among the major methods of gathering scientific evidence (Chapter 2). You may also have attempted to formulate a question that is answerable by scientific evidence and to find some of the evidence relevant to your question (using the strategy outlined in the Appendix). If so, this evidence may now be before you. The rest of this book is devoted to teaching the skills that will allow you, once you have found the evidence, to decide for yourself what conclusions to draw from it.

To get an idea of the dimensions of this task, consider a piece of research. Glock, Ringer, and Babbie (1967) theorized that the function of churches in our secular society is to compensate people for their social deprivations. This theory suggested the hypothesis that the more socially deprived people are, the more involved they will be in church activities. To test this hypothesis, the authors evaluated social deprivation and church involvement in a sample of Episcopalians from 234 congregations. Social deprivation was measured on a zero to eight point scale with people being given points for being female (two points), over 30 (one point), over 50 (one more point), unmarried (one point), childless (one point), and middle class (one point) or lower class (two points). The total points assigned to a person was the social deprivation score. Church involvement was measured on the basis of subjects' responses to questions about their participation in specific church activities. The researchers found that the higher a person's social deprivation score, the higher the index of church involvement. The results supported the hypothesis, and were taken as evidence for Glock's theory of the function of churches. (Glock and his colleagues presented more evidence than this, but this summary is enough for our purposes.)

The authors' conclusion is clear, but we should not accept these conclusions without first checking them ourselves. It is proper to ask two kinds of questions about a study before we accept its conclusions:

> 1. Do the data support the authors' conclusions with respect to the population sampled? (In this study, we ask whether social deprivation influenced church involvement among U.S. Episcopalians in 1952, the year the data were collected.)
>
> 2. If the conclusions are sound, do they generalize beyond the population sampled and the setting studied? (We must ask whether Glock's results generalize to other churches and to other years. Remember, Glock theorized about *all* churches, but only studied one.)

The first question involves what Campbell and Stanley (1963) have called *internal validity*. A study has internal validity to the extent that the data support conclusions about the hypothesis in the specific instance studied. We make judgments about internal validity by examining the procedural details of the specific study to decide whether the procedures used to measure and manipulate variables faithfully represented those variables. The Glock study, for example, has no internal validity unless the social deprivation scores actually measure social deprivation. If the assumption that people over 30 are more socially deprived than people under 30 (for example) is false, the operational definition of social deprivation is not measuring social deprivation, and it follows that conclusions about social deprivation cannot be drawn. The same kind of problem exists with the measure of church involvement. When people are asked about their participation in church activities, they sometimes say what they feel they should have participated in, rather than what they actually did. If this happens to any great extent, the "index of involvement" may be more an index of guilt about church activities, and conclusions about church involvement cannot be drawn. These illustrations should suggest that procedural details can make a difference in what a study is actually measuring. It is difficult to judge the internal validity of a piece of research.

The purpose of this chapter is to teach you which questions to ask so that you can make your own judgment of a study's internal validity. You will learn how to make appropriate criticisms of imperfect research (and in some areas of the social sciences almost all research is imperfect) and thus gain an appreciation of well-conducted research when it can be found. In the exercises and problems, you are given summarized research reports to analyze and evaluate in terms of the concepts presented here. (Chapter 4 provides practice in using the same skills to evaluate actual reports from professional journals.)

The second question mentioned above concerns whether the findings of a study can be generalized to other populations and settings. This involves *external validity*, and it only has meaning once the internal validity of a study has been established. A study has external validity to the extent that its results can be generalized to other situations in which the same variables operate. Thus, Glock's findings have external validity if they hold for other churches in other times, and for other types of social deprivation besides those Glock measured. As this example may suggest, external validity is best determined by comparing the findings of different pieces of research about the same variables. The evaluation of external validity is discussed in Chapter 5.

According to the working definition presented above, a study has *internal validity* when it is possible to draw conclusions about the hypothesis from the data. The problem of internal validity is one of moving from concrete observations to the abstractions they are supposed to be related to; from operational definitions to their corresponding variables. For example, Glock's study has no internal validity unless people's *reports* of their church activities reflect their actual involvement in the church. If these reports actually reflect a desire to look like a good Christian, or to please the interviewer, or to conform to behavioral standards in the community, the authors have measured not church involvement, but some *extraneous variable*.

An *extraneous variable* is a variable capable of explaining the findings of a study without invoking the hypothesis. In other words, the presence of an extraneous variable allows for *alternative explanations* of a set of observations: either the observed relationships are due to the variables in the hypothesis, *or* they result at least in part from an extraneous variable.

A researcher's central problem in demonstrating the internal validity of a piece of research is to achieve control over extraneous variables—there must be a way to rule out alternative explanations of the findings. For example, here is an alternative explanation of Glock's results: women in our society are supposed to be a religious influence in the family, so they may claim more church involvement than they actually have. Because the operational definition of deprivation gives women higher scores than men, this explains why people who score high on deprivation also score high on church involvement. This alternative can be ruled out if high social deprivation scores are related to high involvement scores when only women (or only men) are compared. In such groups, the relationship of social deprivation scores to church involvement scores cannot be due to sex differences.

The task of judging internal validity is the task of interpreting evidence. In Chapter 1, it was noted that "for observations to have scientific value, they must reliably concretize abstractions." Thus, useful evidence must be in concrete language. But there can be many ways that evidence may relate to the abstract variables we are really interested in. So the logical jump from concrete evidence to abstract variables is crucial to the scientific process. To evaluate a scientist's report of research, one must identify the scientist's conclusion from the evidence (the hypothesized explanation), and compare it with other possible conclusions (alternative explanations). Internal validity increases as these alternative explanations can be ruled out.

This chapter provides a guide for finding alternative explanations for social scientists' findings. It introduces some common extraneous variables and gives information about where to expect them and how they may be controlled. You will come across many new terms. Keep in mind that your purpose is not to memorize the terms but to get a feeling for the extraneous variables that exist in various types of research, so that you can suggest alternative explanations for research findings you read. Your primary goal is to learn to analyze and evaluate research reports.

This guide is organized around the six methods of gathering evidence presented in Chapter 2. Because each of these methods has its own procedures, each has its own characteristic extraneous variables. Consequently, your search for alternative explanations of the evidence will take different directions depending on the method used to gather the evidence. Some extraneous variables are almost universal problems in scientific research, while others cause difficulty primarily with particular research methods. The most basic research method (naturalistic observation) tends to raise the most universal problems, while the most refined method (experiment) has its own particular difficulties.

Naturalistic Observation: Problems Caused by the Presence of an Observer

Naturalistic observation is the most basic method of gathering scientific evidence, and it raises the most basic questions about validity. Naturalistic observation must introduce "minimal interference with events," yet there is no way to know for certain whether this requirement has been met. To find out how much an observer's activities have changed events, we would have to observe the events both with and without the observer, and see how much difference there is. This is, of course, a logical impossibility and therefore we can never be sure how much the research process has changed the people and events being studied. The methods of naturalistic observation have raised this issue, yet it is obviously crucial to all methods of social science research.

"On Stage" Effects

Experience has taught social scientists to identify situations in which the research process is most likely to interfere with events. One type of effect an observer can produce by merely being present has been called the *"on stage effect"* (Agnew & Pyke, 1969). This theatrical metaphor suggests that people may begin to "act" when they are aware there is an "audience." The problem of "putting on an act" can be expected to become more serious the more aware people are that there is an audience, the better they know what about them is being observed, and the more the subject of observation is personal or controversial. That is, the more difference it makes to people what impression they make, the more likely they are to act for the researcher. Below are some classic types of "on stage effects" and some methods used to control them.

1. People sometimes tell an observer what they think they "should" say. When people are asked about their values, many tend to report culturally acceptable values, even when they do not hold them. Such people's responses are influenced by their perceptions of *social desirability*. When people's adherence to a social norm is observed, it is reasonable to assume that the observer's presence may increase *apparent* conformity.

2. Sometimes people believe the observer to be somehow judging their personal adequacy or mental health. This belief, called *evaluation apprehension* (Rosenberg, 1965, 1969) obviously becomes stronger when the observer is labeled "psychologist." The effects of evaluation apprehension depend on the subject's perception of what mentally healthy people are supposed to do in the situation being studied.

3. Subjects of research occasionally try to make themselves look bad. This is perhaps due to a desire to sabotage the research or because the person feels something can be gained by looking bad. Some mental patients do this when they fear being released from a comfortable hospital stay (Braginsky & Braginsky, 1967).

4. People sometimes try to please a researcher by doing what they think she/he wants them to do. Someone who means to please may become attuned to subtle *"demand characteristics"* in the interaction (Orne, 1962) that give a clue to what the researcher is looking for. Orne originally argued that subjects could be expected to accept these cues and would try to do whatever they thought the researcher wanted. However, subjects might also use these cues to "sabotage" the study, or to outwit the researcher. There is evidence that this is a common attitude among people coerced into being research subjects, such as students who become subjects to fulfill a course requirement (Cox & Supprelle, 1971).

The "on stage effects" are called *artifacts* of research, because they are created by the researcher and are not normally part of the phenomenon the researcher wants to study. Thus, to the extent that people are acting differently because they are "on stage," any observations of variables in their behavior are also measuring extraneous variables. These extraneous variables—the desire to look "healthy," to please or outwit the experimenter, to say the acceptable thing, and so on—provide possible alternative explanations for observed behavior whenever there is reason to suspect that people are "acting."

The on stage type of artifact is produced when people are aware that they are being observed, and when they desire to make some sort of impression on the observer. This is most likely to occur under these conditions:

> When there is little purpose for the researcher's presence other than to observe the subject—that is, when the observer is *obtrusive*. This is frequently the case in survey research, where subjects not only know they are being observed, but usually know what about them is being observed because the questions are straightforward.

> When the researcher holds higher status than the subject. If the researcher holds higher status this should increase the subject's desire to influence the impression he/she makes. The problem is most serious when the researcher can control important events in the subject's life, such as when a teacher or professor studies a student, or a psychiatrist or psychologist observes a mental patient, or a corrections staff member studies a prison inmate.

METHODS OF CONTROL

Here are some methods social researchers use to handle "on stage" effects.

Unobtrusive measures. Webb, Campbell, Schwartz, and Sechrest (1966) wrote a book on ways to measure subjects' behavior without their knowing it is being measured. These unobtrusive measures may or may not involve invasions of individual privacy. Consider these examples: to compare the popularity of various exhibits at a museum, the carpets in each gallery are examined for wear. To measure the effect of social status as an inhibitor of aggression, Doob and Gross (1968) had either a late-model Chrysler or an old Rambler stop at a light and stay stopped when the light turned green. The length of time it took the car behind to honk measured the inhibition of aggression. To measure racial prejudice, two people, identifiable by voice as black and white, dialed telephone numbers (ostensibly wrong numbers). The callers explained they were calling from a pay phone on the parkway, where their car had broken down. They were trying to reach a garage and had run out of dimes. The people answering the phone were asked to please call the garage with the message. The number given was that of a researcher, who simply tabulated results (Gaertner & Bickman, 1972).

Deception. These last mentioned unobtrusive measures also involve deception. On stage effects can be controlled by deceiving the subject conquering the purpose of the research. Thus, any attempt by the subject to read and respond to the demand characteristics of the experiment is nullified; the study doesn't "demand" what it seems to. Deception is a particularly prominent feature of research in social psychology. Some problems occur when deception is used as a strategy. For one thing, its ethics are questionable. There is a serious debate, especially among psychologists, about when deception is ever justified in research, and some guidelines have been developed (American Psychological Association, 1973). It is generally agreed, at the very least, that deception should be avoided whenever it is possible to get acceptable data by any other strategy. Many also feel that it is better to give up on some research questions rather than deceive participants in the research. A second major problem with deceptions is a practical one. Since it is known that social researchers, particularly psychologists, use deception, potential subjects are sometimes suspicious even of research that involves no deception. Thus, subjects' expectations to be deceived may influence their behavior.

Demand characteristics control group. One way to control any artifact in research is to manipulate it experimentally, using a comparison group design. One group gets whatever demand characteristics are in the experiment as planned, and another group gets a different demand, intentionally produced. For example, in a study on persuasion, it is desirable to be sure that any effects result from the persuasive communication used in the study, not the subject's desire to please the speaker, or some other extraneous variable. To control for this possibility, an investigator might run one group in which the persuader is introduced in the usual way, and another group in which subjects are also told that the experimenter disagrees with the point of view about to be presented. In this second group (control group), demand characteristics are *added*, to counter the persuasion attempt. Comparing this group with the experimental group will help determine whether demand characteristics influence persuasion in the experiment. An *evaluation apprehension control group* can be set up along similar lines to control for this extraneous variable.

Special controls for social desirability. In research that collects data by interview or questionnaire techniques, it is possible to control for the social desirability effect by the use of carefully worded questions. If, for example, people are asked to choose between alternatives that have been previously rated as equal in social desirability, their choice must be based on the content of the questions, rather than on the social desirability of the answers.

More Persistent Changes Caused by Research

While on stage effects are serious problems for social research, the presence of a researcher can create more subtle and pervasive changes in the people being studied. This presence can, in some situations, cause people to change in ways that are more than just acting—that is, changes may occur that persist even when the subject is "off stage." Here are some examples.

1. Workers' productivity in an industrial plant at Hawthorne, Illinois, increased every time the workers were shifted to new, experimental working conditions. As they became used to the new conditions, production leveled off, only to increase when they were shifted again, even if they were shifted to conditions in which they had produced more slowly before (Roethlisberger & Dickson, 1939). The effect was attributed to the subjects' awareness that they were being given special treatment. The increased production was *real;* that is, it occurred even when no one was looking, and when there were no special rewards for it. The increased production (called the *"Hawthorne effect"*) could be best explained as a result of either the novelty of each new situation or the attention the workers got when their jobs were changed. Hawthorne-type effects are likely artifacts in studies using subjects who are suffering from boredom or lack of social contacts (e.g., chronic mental patients, assembly-line workers, residents of old age homes, schools for the retarded, etc.).

2. When a person expects a treatment or experience to change her/him, the person often changes, even when the "treatment" is known to be an inert or ineffective one. This effect is best known in research on drugs, in which the effect of the drug must be carefully separated from the effect of the fact that the patient is being given a prescription by a competent doctor. The "bedside manner" or the "power of suggestion" can heal too. This *placebo effect* has been offered as an explanation or partial explanation of voodoo death, religious healing, and psychotherapeutic cures.

3. Robert Rosenthal (1966) had people look at photographs and judge how successful the people in the photos appeared to be. The experimenters in Rosenthal's studies were told either that the mean rating of success would be about $+5$ or about -5 on a scale of -10 to $+10$. The experimenters who were given the positive expectancy obtained more positive ratings from their subjects than the experimenters given the negative expectancy. Rosenthal suggested that the *researcher's expectancy* may somehow change her/his behavior toward subjects, and that subjects may respond to these subtle cues, creating a self-fulfilling prophecy: the researcher's actions cause subjects to behave as expected. There is some evidence that one way a researcher can communicate an expectancy is through the tone of voice in which instructions are given (Duncan & Rosenthal, 1968; Duncan, Rosenberg, & Finkelstein, 1969). In Rosenthal's study, experimenters with positive expectancies tended, for example, to emphasize "plus ten" more than "minus ten" when reading the instructions that described the rating scale.

4. Jourard (1971) demonstrated that time spent in mutual self-disclosure of personal material by subject and experimenter could affect the rate of

learning of meaningless material by subjects. It seems that subjects' performance may be affected by their emotional reaction to an experimenter as a person. Jourard suggests further that in typical laboratory experiments, in which the experimenter attempts to be impersonal (to "control" emotional reactions), subjects may act in an atypical manner. If so, people's behavior under these conditions may be, in part, a response to the extraneous variable of a "cold" researcher. This source of distortion can be called a *personal relationship effect*.

All these artifacts, like the on stage effects, depend on some extraneous variable unintentionally introduced into the research—the element of novelty, a person's expectation of change, the researcher's expectation about the subject's behavior, or the impersonality of the researcher-subject relationship. Each extraneous variable, whenever it may be operating, suggests an alternative explanation of behavior. And it should be clear from the examples that these extraneous variables are not restricted to naturalistic observation.

METHODS OF CONTROL

Here are some methods used to achieve some control over these extraneous variables.

Blind measurement. If the researcher doesn't know what behavior is expected from the subject, it is impossible to communicate an expectancy and create a self-fulfilling prophecy. Blind measurement can be achieved by having subjects record their responses (on paper or electronically) in the absence of the researcher, or by having a team of researchers in which the researcher who makes the personal contact is not told what to expect.

Double-blind technique. This is an extension of the blind measurement technique. In a double-blind experiment, both the researcher *and* the subject are blind to the treatment (i.e., they do not know what treatment the subject is getting). This method was developed for drug research, but it has other applications. In a drug study, one experimenter assigns subjects to treatment conditions, and prepares the medication for all subjects. All preparations look, smell, and taste alike, although the contents are different. A second experimenter then administers the drugs to all subjects, without knowing who is getting what. This procedure controls for self-fulfilling prophecies by giving the researcher in contact with the subject the same expectancy for all subjects. It controls for the placebo effect by giving all subjects the same expectations of help. The effect of personal relationship is probably about the same for both treatment groups.

Placebo control group. This methodology was also developed for drug research, and it too has other applications. A placebo control group is treated exactly as an experimental group, except that instead of the experimental drug, a substitute is used that is physiologically inert (has no physical effects), but is indistinguishable from the drug by sight, smell, or taste. The purpose of the placebo is to separate the effect of the drug from the effect of expecting to be cured, talking to the doctor, and other aspects of the treatment situation that might help the patient, but do not depend on the specific medication given. Thus, any improvement in the drug treatment group above and beyond what is observed in the placebo group can be attributed to the drug. This procedure controls for the Hawthorne effect and the self-fulfilling prophecy, which both depend on the situation surrounding administration of treatment, rather than the specific treatment itself.

Something resembling the placebo control procedure can be used when nothing corresponds to a true placebo. In research on psychotherapeutic techniques, teaching methods, and treatment programs for juvenile delinquents, drug addicts, and so on, there is probably no completely inert treatment. In such research, various comparison groups have been used—people who want psychotherapy but are on the waiting list at the clinic, people getting an established, nonexperimental form of treatment, people meeting in a discussion group not designed as treatment, and so forth. While people in all these comparison groups might undergo change as a result of their treatment, no group is, strictly speaking, a placebo group. However, these comparison groups have the same function as a placebo group because they represent treatments that either are presumed to be relatively inert, or at least do not have the specific effects expected from the experimental treatment.

Warm-up period. If the kind and degree of personal relationship with the experimenter can affect subjects' behavior, it might help to have the experimenter spend some time getting to know subjects before starting the actual experiment. This procedure might diminish the Hawthorne effect, which seems partly due to the novelty of being observed by a researcher; it might also be expected to mitigate the effect of personal relationship. On the other hand, it might be argued that an experimenter may form a strong relationship with some subjects and not with others. If subjects' behavior is highly variable, it becomes harder to draw conclusions from the research. This argument suggests another control tactic.

The "canned" researcher. This is an invented name for a commonly used method of control. If the researcher-subject relationship is a source of difficulty, one solution would be to eliminate it. Any instructions to be given to the subject may be written out or presented on a prerecorded tape. (Note that while this procedure holds the researcher-subject relationship constant, it does not meet Jourard's (1971) criticism that "cold" experiments bring out atypical behavior in subjects.) If the subject never meets the experimenter personally, it is very difficult for the researcher to communicate expectancies by means of subtle nonverbal cues. Thus, the effects of self-fulfilling prophecy, demand characteristics, and so on are lessened. Also, it is certain that all subjects have received the same instructions, even down to tone of voice.

Table 2. Extraneous variables due to the presence of an observer

Extraneous variables	Alternative explanations	When a problem	Methods of control
ON STAGE EFFECTS			
Social desirability	Subject may be saying what he/she "should" believe	Survey research; controversial topics	Careful construction of questions; unobtrusive measurement
Evaluation apprehension (Rosenberg, 1965)	Subject may be trying to look good to someone judging "mental health," IQ, etc.	Survey research; when researcher has high status	Deception; unobtrusive measurement; special control group
Faking bad	Subject may be trying to sabotage research or look "sick" on mental evaluation	High status researcher; coerced subjects	Deception; unobtrusive measurement
Demand characteristics	Subject may be doing what he/she thinks researcher wants	High status researcher; volunteer subjects	Deception; unobtrusive measurement; special control group
MORE PERSISTENT CHANGES CAUSED BY RESEARCH			
Hawthorne effect (Roethlisberger & Dickson, 1939)	Workers produced more merely because of change in routine	Subjects lack social contacts or are bored	Comparison group with different treatment
Placebo effect	Subject may be changing because he/she expected to	"Therapy" settings where people expect to change	Warm-up periods; placebo control group; double-blind technique; "canned" researcher
Self-fulfilling prophecy (researcher expectancy)	Researcher may subtly communicate an expectancy that subject acts to fulfill	Researcher and subject in close contact	Blind measurement; double-blind technique; placebo control group; "canned" researcher; deception about expectancy
Personal relationship	Subjects may perform better because of a personal relationship to researcher (or worse without relationship)	A general problem	Warm-up period; "canned" researcher; comparison group with different relationship

In summary, researchers can produce two types of unwanted effects by their mere presence: on stage effects and the more persistent "real" changes in people that can result from the research process. These unwanted effects exist because researchers unintentionally introduce extraneous variables when they observe events. Table 2 presents the material in this section in condensed form.

This discussion is intended to help you to raise questions when you read scientific literature. If you have a good sense of how the research process can change people and events, you will be in a position to offer plausible alternative explanations for the findings of some of the research reports you read. Only when all reasonable explanations are collected can you make an educated judgment about how strongly a set of research results justifies an author's conclusions.

Retrospective Case Study: Problems of Selection, Distortion, and Memory

Retrospective case studies have two essential characteristics that allow for alternative explanations for their findings:

> 1. The researcher must *select* information worth collecting and reject other, possibly useful, information.
> 2. Retrospective studies collect data from the past, so they often rely on people's (faulty) memories.

These problems are not unique to retrospective case studies, but they appear most clearly in this research method.

Researcher Selectivity

When a researcher starts out with a theory (either implicit or explicit), it directs the questions that will be asked. Consider a psychoanalyst attempting to explain a patient's neurosis. The analyst conducts a retrospective study, looking for causes by gathering information from the patient's memory. Since psychoanalysts believe that neuroses have their roots in relationships with parents during early childhood, the analyst can be expected to show increased interest when the patient starts to talk about these relationships. The result will probably be that the patient produces many memories about early relationships with parents, and less information about other things that might also be related to the neurosis. The analyst's theory has led to the collection of evidence the theory considers important and to the neglect of other evidence. The theory has performed a valuable function by allowing the analyst to ignore irrelevant information, but it is always possible that some useful information was excluded from consideration—perhaps another explanation of the neurosis would appear if other questions were asked.

Thus, the researcher's selectivity has led to the *systematic neglect of certain information*.

This is almost a universal problem in social research, because all methods except naturalistic observation involve choices about which data to observe and which to ignore. The difficulty with making selections is that we do not know whether every possible fact has an equal chance of being observed. With human observers, it is safe to assume that the facts do *not* have an equal chance of being observed, because people have theories, or at least mental sets to look for certain kinds of facts. Often we, as observers, are not aware of the classes of information we are ignoring, and this is as true of scientists as it is of everyone else. When a researcher selects information to look at, the reader generally gets a *biased sample of information*.

The way to control this is not to try to eliminate the bias (how can one know when it is gone?) but to be explicit about it. Researchers do this when they identify variables and define them operationally. The reader then knows exactly which information was observed (information about the variables mentioned) and which was left out (everything else). The selectivity is still there, but the bases for the selection are known to all. In short, the way to handle the inevitable bias resulting from a researcher's selection of events is to use a research method other than retrospective case study. For this reason, retrospective case studies tend to be done early in the research history of a subject, before enough is known to decide which variables to study in depth. Later in the research history, when *theories* are developed, the researcher's bias can be made explicit. Theory dictates which events should be studied and which neglected; not all events are equally likely to be studied. Thus, a theory simplifies a researcher's job by defining some facts as irrelevant. A researcher with a theory need not observe everything, and can therefore be more careful about measuring what is considered most important. Theory is also valuable in that it makes explicit the bias that is inevitable whenever an observer chooses not to record everything. All this is in addition to the major values of theory: to advance understanding and give direction to research.

Other less desirable types of bias frequently operate in social research. Some of these suggest alternative explanations for research results. One type of bias, especially common in retrospective case studies, involves the influence of a research hypothesis on the way a researcher evaluates information after it is collected.

Researcher Distortion

If a researcher has a stake in a particular hypothesis, he/she may see evidence to support the hypothesis in spite of the best intentions. The evidence of research on attitude change suggests that anyone who spends many years of effort working on something is likely to come to believe in it, and this may affect what she/he sees. Thus, *researcher distortion* is a serious problem, especially with research in the social sciences where strongly held values are at stake. Consider an example: A psychologist who does group psychotherapy professionally wants to assess the effectiveness of her therapy. She believes that a diversity of personalities among the therapy group is counterproductive. She evaluates the progress of a diverse group of patients seen together and another diverse group of patients she is seeing in individual psychotherapy (control group). At the end of therapy, she reviews her notes, and rates patients "much improved," "somewhat improved," "no change," "somewhat worse," or "much worse," compared with when therapy began. Since she knows who was seen individually and who was seen in group, and she has a stake in the outcome, we might not want to trust her ratings as a measure of patient improvement. Suppose her observations were that the group patients did not improve (just as she expected). The psychologist might conclude that diversity in therapy groups is counterproductive, but we could offer an alternative explanation: Because of her bias, the psychologist did not see evidence of improvement in the group-treated patients and exaggerated the improvement of those in individual therapy. This distortion is most serious when the reliability of observations is questionable, as in most retrospective studies. However, even when variables are operationalized, distortion is possible.

METHODS OF CONTROL

If the psychologist is a conscientious scientist, she does not trust her own judgment, but brings in someone else to evaluate the patients. She would control the possible effects of her distortion by using blind measurement. With the judgment of a competent colleague who does not know her hypothesis, she can obtain more accurate information about each patient's progress. The judge would review a transcript of the therapist's notes, edited to remove information on whether the patient is being seen individually or in a group, and would make the same ratings the therapist might make. Whatever bias the colleague may have would not influence the results because this judge doesn't know which patients were seen individually and which in group, or that a difference between indivdual and group therapy is expected.

Control could go a step further. The researcher could *misinform* the judge about the hypothesis, or about her bias, or about the patients' progress (e.g., she could tell the judge that none of the patients seemed to be responding to treatment), and let the judge evaluate each patient. This procedure might be an improvement because it would counter any subtle communication of the researcher's bias that might prejudice the judge.

Reliance on Memory

In retrospective research, there is selectivity and distortion not only on the part of the researcher, but on the subject's part as well. What someone remembers is not only incomplete, it is systematically incomplete. Ordinary people, like scientists, have theories about the relationships between events, and what they judge as unimportant tends to be forgotten. These biases are usually unexpressed. Furthermore, memories can be distorted to fit the view that makes a person most comfortable at present. Suppose, for example, a researcher is interested in the predisposing factors in juvenile delinquency. A sample of delinquent boys is selected, and each is asked questions about his relationships with his parents. Most of the boys report that their fathers were frequently absent from the home and spent little time playing with them. Can their memories be trusted? It could well be that these delinquent boys are rebelling against their fathers' authority and are justifying their rebellion by remembering the times father was away and saying that father didn't care. It is hard to know what produced the boys' reports if their memories are the only evidence available. (This problem is not restricted to retrospective case studies—selective memory is a very serious problem in correlational research and even in experimental research when variables are measured by people's accounts of the past). Memories are most likely to be distorted when distortion can be used to justify one's actions and maintain or enhance one's self-esteem.

METHODS OF CONTROL

The only ways to control the effects of selective and distorted memory involve using other sources of information. In a study of the causes of delinquency, for example, it is possible to ask the delinquent boy and his parents the same questions about the period of his childhood. This way the amount of distortion between different memories will be known, even if it is impossible to know whose memory was most accurate.

In some retrospective research, it is possible to rely on *archival records* which do not depend on memory. The Kerner Commission study of urban riots (Chapter 2) used records of incomes and unemployment rates to determine the economic conditions of cities where riots occurred.

Another approach is to use a research method that does not rely on memory. In the study of delinquency, for example, it is possible to do a *prospective study*, in which a large number of children is *directly observed* before they become delinquents, to identify the differences between the children who do and don't turn out delinquent. Another alternative is experimental research. In the study of delinquency, a group of young children can be given whatever delinquents are

Table 3. Extraneous variables due to selection, distortion, and memory

Extraneous variables	Alternative explanations	When a problem	Methods of control
Researcher selectivity	Events may be due to causes researcher's theory does not consider important	Case studies; all research lacking operational definitions	Specify selectivity by operationalizing variables
Researcher distortion or bias	Researcher's evaluation of data may be colored by preconceptions	Researcher knows hypothesis; researcher has stake in hypothesis	Blind judges; misled judges
Selective or distorted memory (in subject)	Subject's memory may be distorted to fit his/her "theory" or current opinion	Retrospective research relying on memory; subject's self-esteem is at stake	Compare two memories; use archival records; prospective research

presumed to lack, to see if their rate of delinquency turns out to be lower than that of a control group.

In summary, researchers using retrospective methods can easily introduce extraneous variables into a study because people's selective attention and memory systematically distort reality. This section (summarized in Table 3) has shown how such distortion can suggest alternative explanations for the findings of retrospective studies.

Sample Study: Problems of Operational Definitions and Generalizing about Populations

Sample studies have three important characteristics not generally present in naturalistic observations and retrospective case studies.

1. Variables in sample studies are operationally defined.
2. Sample studies generalize about populations from information about samples.
3. Sample studies involve collecting the same information about a number of different people or events.

Since sample studies share these characteristics with correlational and experimental research, the validity problems that exist in sample studies are also present in the other forms of quantitative research.

Invalid Operational Definitions

Whenever operational definitions are used, the possibility exists that they are invalid. Unfortunately, there is no research design or procedure that will protect research from *invalid operational definitions*. In evaluating research, it is your job to think about the operational definitions used. Ask yourself if the definition of a variable being studied might be measuring something else. Here are some examples. Most intelligence tests require knowledge (often reading knowledge) of the language in which they are given—this means they are also measuring linguistic training. Juvenile delinquency can be defined in terms of convictions in court, but convictions are more frequent when defendants don't have private counsel—this means that the definition of delinquency is also measuring economic status. If a researcher using this definition of delinquency discovers that delinquents are educationally deprived, the findings may only mean that poor people get poor educations. In general, when an operational definition measures more than one thing at a time, whatever is said of one of the variables could, with justification, be said of the other(s) as well. Operational definitions that measure more than one thing at a time are said to be *confounded*, and the variables measured together are said to be confounded with each other. When an operational definition is confounded, any conclusion drawn about the variable it is supposed to measure may just as well be drawn about the extraneous variable confounded with it. In evaluating research, keep constantly aware that operational definitions are not necessarily the same as the variables they are supposed to measure. If you should even suspect confounding, offer an alternative explanation based on the extraneous variable buried in the operational definition.

Biased Samples

There are some difficulties associated with drawing inferences about populations based on information about samples, and they can best be illustrated by an example. Suppose a researcher wants to determine the birth control practices of married couples in Vermont. There are, let us say, 120,000 such couples and, to make things easier, let us also assume a list of their names and addresses is available. Still, 120,000 is too many couples to survey, and so a sample of 500 couples is taken. Skipping the important details for now, let's say that of the couples surveyed, 27% use the pill, 19% use sterilization (either partner), 17% use intrauterine devices, 17% use diaphragms, condom, and/or foam, 5% use rhythm, and the remaining 15% use no birth control. Is it safe to say, for example, that the pill is the most commonly used method of birth control among Vermont couples? Not necessarily. Here are some problems.

Samples rarely contain exactly the same proportions of anything as the population from which they are drawn. (If you doubt this, toss a coin 100 times, and see if you get 50 tails. You will probably get *about* 50 tails, but you will probably not get exactly 50.) If the sample is a good one, it is fair to conclude that *about* 27% of the couples in the Vermont population use the pill, and that *about* 19% use sterilization. To decide whether the pill is more commonly used, you would need to test the hypothesis that "about 27%" in this sample is greater than "about 19%." To do this, you would have to determine the likelihood that, given a population in which the pill and sterilization are used with equal frequency, a sample of 500 couples would include 27% using the pill and 19% using sterilization. If this is highly *unlikely*, you can be reasonably sure that the pill and sterilization are *not* used with equal frequency in the whole population. There are statistical procedures to determine this likelihood. In general, the larger the sample, the more certain you can be that an observed difference corresponds to a difference in the whole population. (The more often you toss a loaded coin, the more certain you can be that it's loaded.) When samples of 500 are taken out of a population of 120,000, they are likely to be *somewhat* different from each other and from the population, and the generalizations you can make from a sample can be expected to be slightly inaccurate. The larger the sample, the less inaccurate it will be. This error of inference is called *sampling error*.

Sampling error is an unavoidable problem when a scientist attempts to make inferences about a population from less than complete data. However, it need not lead us to question the internal validity of research for two reasons. First, if the sample is chosen carefully, so as to be representative of the population, the amount of sampling error can be placed within known limits. You may see such statements as "We can say with 95% confidence that Dewey will win within 3% either way of 53% of the popular vote." This means that 5% of the time the error will be greater and that 2½% of the time Dewey will not win a majority. Although such an error may embarrass the prognosticator, it is predictable. We know how much error to expect how often.

Second, and more important, when a sample is representative of a population, the error is equally likely to go in either direction. Data from representative samples vary *randomly* around the data that would be collected from the population; the findings are not systematically distorted by the measurement of an extraneous variable. Thus, while sampling error does limit the certainty of any inference about a population, it is a weak argument for questioning the validity of a researcher's conclusions.

The above comments were all predicated on the assumption that the sample of 500 Vermont couples was *representative* of all couples in the state. The serious problem with sampling involves being sure the sample is representative—that it is not systematically distorted by some extraneous variable. Suppose, for example, that the Vermont sample included only half the proportion of Catholics that exist in the state population. Such a sample is not representative; it is *biased*. A *biased sample* is one that contains a *systematic error:* it is consistently different from the population in a particular direction. In the present example, a sample with few Catholics probably underestimates the proportion of couples using rhythm and no birth control. A biased sample is one that consistently misrepresents the population from which it was drawn; data from such a sample differ from population data in a particular direction because of the presence of an extraneous variable. Name the extraneous variable, and an alternative explanation follows: "Rhythm was found to be the least popular birth control method in Vermont because the sample *underrepresented Catholics*, not because it is least popular."

METHODS OF CONTROL

The only way to be certain that a sample is representative is to use a truly *random sample*. This presumes a complete list of the population (which was available), and a systematic procedure that allows everyone in the population an equal chance of being chosen for the sample. This might be done by putting all the couples' names and addresses in a computer, assigning each couple a number, and using a program that generates random numbers. The first 500 numbers that correspond to numbers that had been assigned to couples would determine the people sampled. While this procedure is possible, it might exhaust the researcher's budget to pay for computer time and travel to the remote locations where all these people may live. Therefore, random samples, while they are theoretically ideal, are rarely used in large-scale sample studies.

A usual procedure is to choose a sample on some convenient basis, assuring that the sample is equivalent to the population with respect to several variables considered important to the research. For the Vermont birth control study, we might agree that it is important to make sure the sample and the population are similar in age distribution, religion, rural or urban residence, and number of children already born, since these factors probably influence birth control methods. If the researcher took a sample of people from rural areas, towns, and cities (in the same proportion as the state population), chose individuals in these locations on a random basis, and showed us that the sample was very close to the overall population of couples in terms of the other variables mentioned, we might be willing to accept the sample as representative. Other than true random sampling, there is no absolute rule for drawing a representative sample. All we can ask of a researcher is that the sample is representative of the population in those things that are probably relevant to the research question. If we are assured of that, we can proceed on the assumption that the error in this sample is no different from the error in a true random sample.

When evaluating a piece of research that uses sampling techniques, consider the population being sampled, and then think about the method used to draw the sample. If you can think of a way in which the sample may be systematically different from the population, ask yourself whether this bias could have influenced the results. If it could have, an alternative explanation is possible.

The above discussion has concerned the difficulties in concluding that data from a sample accurately represented the population *from which the sample was drawn*. To ask whether the findings are true of other populations is to raise another question, which is discussed in Chapter 5. In the Vermont example, limited questions are asked about whether one can be justified in drawing conclusions about adult married Vermonters. If one can, these conclusions still may not apply to the birth control practices of unmarried Vermonters or of people living elsewhere. I emphasize this point because researchers often take samples from much more restricted and less interesting populations than the adult married couples of Vermont. Most educational and psychological research uses conveniently available populations, such as "third grade pupils in the Horseheads Central School District" or "introductory psychology students at Moreland University, spring term, 1963." The question of internal validity often becomes the question of whether results hold true even for such restricted populations as these.

Sampling bias is possible even with such restricted populations. One common source of sampling bias is the use of volunteer subjects for experiments. Unlike the average person, the person who volunteers for psychological research is likely to want to please (demand characteristics), and may also be unusually well motivated to perform. Consequently, what is true of volunteer subjects may not be true of the population from which they are drawn. Thus, when volunteers are used, their desire to please (extraneous variable) may provide an alternative explanation of their behavior.

Uncontrolled Variation in Information

It may seem easy to collect the same information from (or about) different people, but this is not always so. In a sample study using interviews, respondents may say different things to different interviewers depending on the interviewer's sex, age, race, or other characteristics that act as extraneous variables in the research. Sometimes it is possible to avoid this problem by using a single interviewer or interviewers who are similar in terms of characteristics that may influence a person's response. Still, *holding the interviewer constant* is not always an ideal solution. Consider a survey on interracial attitudes. People will respond differently to black and white interviewers, but it would not help to use only one race of interviewers. Any difference between the responses of whites and blacks may be due either to their different attitudes or to their different reactions to being interviewed by, for example, a black (extraneous variable). In this case, control may be achieved either by eliminating the interviewer entirely (a mailed questionnaire could be used if its contents did not reveal its author's race), or by using both black and white interviewers to collect data from both black and white respondents. The latter solution may be preferable because it allows one to both hold the interviewer's race constant and to measure its effects. If black and white interviewers get the same results from similar respondents, it can be concluded that the interviewer's race made no difference. This method of using both races of interviewer has created an experiment within the sample study: Race of interviewer is manipulated to see its effects on respondents. The strategy of measuring the effect of a potential extraneous variable is discussed further on pp. 87–88.

Other problems exist in trying to get the same information from different people. It may go without saying that in a questionnaire everyone should be asked the same questions, but one cannot always assume that the questions are understood the same way by everyone. Some people may not understand because of limited vocabulary or reading ability, and it is not safe to assume their answers mean the same as those of other people. This problem can best be prevented by preliminary work by the researcher to make sure questions are understood.

The problem of "getting the same information" exists not only in interview and questionnaire situations, but in most forms of quantitative research, including laboratory experiments. In conducting an experiment on learning, for example, sounds from outside the lab may distract some subjects and constitute an extraneous variable that should be controlled because people are not all learning under the same conditions. You could do nothing, assuming that each subject is equally likely to be subjected to a distracting level of noise, or you could hold noise constant by placing the subject in a soundproof room, or putting plugs in his/her ears, or giving her/him a head set with a prerecorded tape of noise to listen to. When it is fairly easy to hold an extraneous variable constant by use of a standard procedure, this is the best method of control.

METHODS OF CONTROL

The information collected sometimes depends on who gathers it, or on how, when, or where it was collected. There are two main methods to control this problem.

Hold procedures constant. Ask questions in the same order, with the same wording; use one interviewer; always collect data in the same lab, at the same time of day, on the same apparatus, and so on.

Experimentally manipulate the variable causing responses to vary. The use of black and white interviewers in a survey of racial attitudes is the example used above. This method allows one to both control for and measure the effect of a potential extraneous variable.

When none of these controls is used, the researcher must assume (a better word is hope) that variations are random. The example of noise outside the learning lab is an illustration. With luck, this will influence the subjects in each group about equally. Even with luck, though, noise may so increase the variability between individuals as to hide any effect of the variables being studied.

The major validity problems of sample studies also exist in correlational and experimental research. All these quantitative methods operationalize variables, draw conclusions from samples to populations, and attempt to get the same information repeatedly. When evaluating quantitative research, watch out for:

> *Invalid operational definitions* (ones that measure a variable other than or in addition to what they are supposed to measure).
> *Biased samples* (samples that are systematically different in some way from the population they are drawn from).
> *Uncontrolled variation in information* (information that depends on who collected it, or how, when or where it was collected).

If you suspect any of these problems, name the extraneous variable(s) that might be responsible, and try to explain how the extraneous variable(s) might account for the researcher's findings.

Correlational Research: The Problem of Subject Variables

Correlational research assesses the relationship between variables without manipulating any variable. The essential problem with this procedure is that it is impossible to measure one variable at a time in existing populations. Any measure of occupational status, for example, is in part a measure of education, because in our society the status of an occupation is closely related to the amount of education required for it. To attempt to relate occupational status to any other variable (say intelligence or leadership ability) is difficult because any relationship that appears to exist may, in fact, be due to either occupation or education. Such variables as occupational status, education, intelligence, political party affiliation, and others, when they are measured as things a subject possesses before the research begins, are called *subject variables*, or *organismic variables*, and they pose the validity problem most characteristic of correlational research.

A *subject variable* or *organismic variable* is any characteristic that a research subject brings along to the research setting. For individuals, these characteristics include such attributes as sex, religion, education, and so on; for groups, they include group structure, communication patterns, and coalitions within the group. Some variables may or may not be organismic, depending on how they are treated in research. Anxiety is a good example. Consider an investigation of the effect of anxiety on learning. One method for this investigation would categorize people as highly anxious, moderately anxious, or nonanxious, using a pretest instrument such as the Taylor Manifest Anxiety Scale. The subjects would be given standard material to learn, and their performances compared. This correlational study measures the anxiety subjects bring with them to the study; anxiety is a subject variable. An experimental study of the effect of anxiety on learning might attempt to create anxiety experimentally (e.g., by misinforming some subjects that they are about to take an intelligence test), and measure the performance of anxious and control subjects on the same learning task. In such a study, anxiety is manipulated and is not treated as an organismic variable. Both studies use between-subjects *designs*, because they draw conclusions by comparing one group of people to another. Only the second study is a between-subjects *experiment* because only this study manipulates anxiety and assigns people to the anxious or nonanxious groups.

The variables in correlational studies tend to be organismic variables. The problem this creates is that other organismic variables are invariably correlated with those measured. Anxiety may be related to low self-esteem, insecurity in the presence of authority figures, emotional instability, or any number of other things. Therefore, if a correlational study shows anxiety to be related to learning, several alternative explanations are plausible. Learning may be affected by anxiety, by any of the correlated variables mentioned, by some other correlated variable, or by any combination of the above. *Measures of organismic variables are always confounded by other organismic variables. Whenever one variable in a hypothesis is organismic, all correlates of this variable are extraneous variables in the study, and each one can potentially be used to suggest an alternative explanation.*

METHODS OF CONTROL

The example of anxiety and learning suggests one possible way to eliminate this problem.

Use an experimental design with randomization. When a subject variable is the independent variable in a hypothesis and it is capable of manipulation, a *between-subjects experiment* manipulating the variable can minimize the threat to validity. It is worth examining how this works. In an experiment on the effect of anxiety on learning, the potential subjects are *randomly assigned* to two groups: one group is made anxious (experimental group) and the other is not (control, or comparison group). "Randomly assigned" implies the use of a systematic procedure that gives everyone an equal chance of being assigned to each group. Drawing names from a hat, flipping a fair coin, or using random numbers are some acceptable procedures. The two groups are treated identically except for the procedure used to create anxiety. This means that subjects are greeted the same way and are given instructions that differ only in one respect. Let's say the "anxiety group" is told that what they are about to do is an intelligence test, while the controls are told that the experimenter wants to compare two word lists to see if they are of equal difficulty (or some other presumably non-anxiety-arousing instruction). Both groups are given the same word lists to memorize, and their learning is tested in the same way. Thus, the only systematic difference between the two groups is in the part of the instructions that was intended to produce (or not to produce) anxiety.

What about organismic variables? These subjects, like the subjects in a correlational study, differ in the anxiety they had when they arrived, and also in self-esteem, relationships to authority, and every other variable that may be related to anxiety or learning. However, the subjects who began with high anxiety, say, were equally likely to be assigned to either group; so also were the subjects with low self-esteem, emotional instability, and so on. Thus, it would be unreasonable to conclude that the reason the people in the anxious group performed better was that they were trying to bolster their low self-esteem by performing well. There is no reason to believe that this group had lower (or higher) self-esteem than the other group. The process of assigning subjects at random to groups in a between-subjects experiment is called *randomization*, and we say that organismic variables (self-esteem, anxiety before the experiment began, etc.) are *randomized. Random assignment to conditions eliminates any bias that might systematically put similar people in the same group.* Contrast the randomized experiment with a correlational study of the same variables. In the correlational study, the highly anxious people probably have other personality characteristics in common as well (some possibilities have already been mentioned), and any of these could explain any observed difference in learning. In the experiment, personality characteristics are randomized. They are not systematically related to anxiety, because each personality type is equally likely to be in the anxious and nonanxious groups of the experiment. Thus, personality differences between groups are unlikely explanations of any differences in learning.

It is important to note that randomization does not eliminate all the personality differences between the two groups, but only ensures that each personality type or characteristic is *equally likely* to be in either group. On occasion, the people with low self-esteem, for example, will be put in the same group by the luck of the draw, but this does not happen systematically. The errors due to randomization in experiments resemble those produced by representative or random sampling in sample studies. Random error exists in both, but it is tolerable because it is not biased in either direction, and because its magnitude can be estimated with statistical techniques. In short, while randomization does not eliminate extraneous variables, and it does not keep them from varying, it does minimize their power to offer alternative explanations for research findings.

Randomization controls organismic variables only when they are independent variables, and when they can be manipulated. In many cases, these criteria are not met. For example, most of the variables of interest to sociologists and political scientists are either impossible or very difficult to manipulate. Think of doing an experiment to measure the effects of religion, social class, stigmatization, alienation, cultural conflict, or social disorganization. All are variables that subjects (people or societies) carry with them, and which pretty much must be studied as they are. A general strategy for controlling the effects of correlates of organismic variables that cannot be manipulated is matching.

Matching. This is the strategy of comparing individuals or groups who are equal in terms of an extraneous variable in order to rule this variable out as an explanation of a hypothesized relationship. Wrightsman (1969) used matching in a study done to discover whether supporters of George Wallace for President in 1968 upheld "law and order" as much in their daily lives as their candidate did in his campaign. In Nashville, the local government had passed an ordinance requiring all cars to display a tax sticker (cost: $15) beginning November 1, 1968, a few days before the election. Wrightsman's study was simple: he and his students went around to parking lots after the law went into effect and noted the presence or absence of tax stickers on cars with political bumper stickers. Wallace supporters (operational definition: Wallace sticker on car) obeyed the law significantly less frequently than Humphrey or Nixon supporters, or cars without bumper stickers. This is a correlational study. Neither variable (candidate supported, obedience to law) was manipulated. It follows that organismic variables entered the study with the subjects (cars), and that some of these may be related to the variables being studied. One such variable is socioeconomic status. Wrightsman reasoned that Wallace supporters in Tennessee tended to come from the working class, and they might, therefore, be less likely to have the $15 for the sticker. If this were true, the findings could be explained without reference to the Wallace supporters' lawfulness.

Wrightsman used matching to rule out this explanation. Wrightsman's observers were instructed to proceed by looking for a car in a parking lot with a political bumper sticker, recording the necessary information about the car, and then recording the same information about the car parked closest on its left that had no bumper sticker. It was reasoned that cars parked next to each other in the same lot would likely belong to people of similar socioeconomic status who were on similar errands. Thus, each car was matched with a single other car of presumably equal socioeconomic status. Wallace cars were less law-abiding than the cars parked on their left, while Nixon and Humphrey cars were more law-abiding than the cars parked on their left.

It is important to realize that matching controls only those variables that are matched. It may still be, for example, that Wallace supporters who used bumper stickers were more generally rebellious people than the average Wallaceite. Since Wallace was not an "establishment" candidate, affixing a Wallace sticker may have taken a streak of rebelliousness. The Humphrey and Nixon sticker-users may have been more typical of all supporters of their candidates. If this were true, Wrightsman's results would imply that it was rebelliousness that led some people both to use Wallace stickers and not to affix tax stickers. The conclusions would not apply to Wallace supporters in general. However far-fetched this hypothesis, the matching for socioeconomic status does nothing to rule out the alternative explanation based on rebelliousness.

Because matching controls only those variables that are matched, there is a practical limit to how many organismic variables can be controlled by matching. A researcher generally uses matching to control only those variables most likely to provide alternative explanations of the expected results. This is sometimes done even in experimental research, when a variable is so important that the researcher is unwilling to rely on randomization to equalize it. Such a situation might exist in research on learning, where intelligence is so important an organismic variable that subjects may be matched on it before being randomly assigned to experimental groups.

Occasionally, in an experimental study, a special sort of matching called the *yoked control* is used. Subjects are paired and then undergo treatments that are identical except for the independent variable. A good example is Brady's work with the "executive monkeys" (Brady, 1958). Two monkeys, strapped into identical apparatus, were either shocked or not shocked together. Although each monkey had a lever in front of him, only one lever had the power to turn off or prevent the shocks. (The monkeys with this lever—the "executives"—developed ulcers.) Another example comes from dream research. In studies in which subjects are deprived of dreaming, their sleep is also interrupted, so the two variables (dreaming and sleeping) are confounded. To control this, a second subject may be yoked with the dream-deprived subject so that whenever one subject starts to dream, both are awakened, regardless of whether the second subject is dreaming. Thus, both subjects are interrupted in sleep to the same extent, but only one is systematically dream-deprived.

The ultimate in matching, of course, is to *compare subjects with themselves.* This is possible in correlational research on such topics as emotional mood, intellectual development, and social change, all of which imply change over time within a single individual or society. Within-subjects experiments also control for subject variables by comparing subjects with themselves. More will be said below about this method for controlling organismic variables.

Statistical control of correlates of organismic variables. Similar in intent to matching are a number of procedures that attempt to accomplish matching after the fact. The researcher collects information about possible extraneous variables and then compares subjects who are equivalent in terms of these variables. Wrightsman used an elementary form of statistical control in his bumper-sticker study to deal with the extraneous variable of socioeconomic status. On the assumption that the age of a car was a good index of the socioeconomic status of its owner, Wrightsman recorded the model years of all cars observed. When Wallace supporters with new (less than four year old) cars were compared with Humphrey and Nixon supporters with new cars, the Wallaceites were less obedient of the law. The same relationship held when people with older cars were compared. By comparing groups of cars of the same age, Wrightsman was able to judge the relationship between political preference and obedience with socioeconomic status held constant. Since the relationship still held, one alternative explanation was ruled out.

In this procedure, Wrightsman did not match individual cars, but controlled status effects through data analysis. Status was measured (by age of car), and the data analysis was broken down according to status in the hope that, with status held constant, the hypothesized relationship would still hold.

More sophisticated methods of statistical control have been developed to deal with the problem of subject variables, and you will find them in reports of correlational research. The statistical procedures and rationales for such techniques as partial correlation (e.g., Friedman, 1972; Hays, 1963) and analysis of covariance (e.g., Kerlinger, 1973; Winer, 1962) are described in various books on research methodology, including those cited here.

Inclusion of extraneous variable(s) in the hypothesis. Randomization, matching, and the statistical controls discussed above all attempt to keep extraneous variables out of consideration. It is also possible to measure an extraneous variable specifically to assess its effect on the variables of the original hypothesis. Consider this example. An educator wished to study the effect of programmed instruction on performance in a college introductory psychology course. Since the researcher did not have the power to see that students were randomly assigned to programmed or nonprogrammed instruction, the study was correlational. The final exam performance in a section receiving programmed instruction was compared with that of another section receiving more traditional instruction. The programmed group scored higher on the final exam. It was later discovered that the students in the programmed section had higher verbal ability (as measured by Scholastic Aptitude Tests). Thus, their success on the final exam might have been due either to superior instruction or to superior verbal ability; the two variables were confounded.

Because the researcher had information on all three variables (type of instruction, verbal ability, and performance) for each subject, it was possible to examine the joint effect of the independent variable and the "third" variable on performance. This was done by dividing the students in each section into subgroups according to their SAT-Verbal scores, and by summarizing the results (see Table 4).

This table summarizes what we already know and gives additional information. The last column shows that the programmed instruction group scored higher on the final exam (80.8 to 73.1), and the bottom row shows that students with high verbal ability (SAT-Verbal over 500) did better than students of lower verbal ability (83.3 to 71.1). We can also see from the columns labeled "n" that more high-verbal students were in the programmed section (16 to 8, though each section had 25 students). This is information we already had. The special value of this table is that it also gives quantitative information on the effects of programmed instruction on each type of student (low and high verbal ability) separately. When we examine these data, we find that programmed instruction greatly improved the performance of low-verbal students, who scored 77, compared to 68 for similar students in the traditional class. However, programmed instruction was no help to the students with high verbal ability. In fact, these students performed slightly better in the traditional class (84 to 83). By measuring verbal ability, and including it as a variable for study, we have discovered that the effect of programmed instruction depends on the type of student being taught. The researcher started with a simple question about two variables—"Which instructional method is more effective?"—and was able to get an answer about three variables—"Programmed instruction is better with students of low verbal ability, but the method of instruction makes little difference with students of higher verbal ability." The joint effect of verbal ability and instructional method on performance is called an *interaction of variables*.

Table 4. Mean final examination scores of introductory psychology students of low and high verbal ability receiving two types of instruction (hypothetical data)

METHOD OF INSTRUCTION	SAT-Verbal Scores				GRAND MEAN
	500 OR BELOW	n [a]	OVER 500	n [a]	
Programmed	77.0	9	83.0	16	80.8
Traditional	68.0	17	84.0	8	73.1
All students	71.1	26	83.3	24	76.6

[a] "n" denotes the number of people in each subgroup. In the programmed instruction section, nine students had SAT-verbal scores of 500 or below and sixteen had scores over 500 and so on.

When the effect of one variable depends on the presence, absence, or amount of another variable, the two variables are said to interact. In the example, the effect of programmed instruction depends on the type of student. The reverse is also true: the performance of a given type of student depends on the type of instruction (at least for low-verbal students). An interaction exists whenever two or more independent variables, by virtue of acting at the same time, influence a dependent variable. In the programmed instruction example, both type of instruction and verbal ability are considered as independent variables which, when combined, have an influence on performance. That is, the effect of the two variables acting together is different from the sum of two separate effects. Programmed instruction increases performance, and so does verbal ability, but programmed instruction, when combined with high verbal ability, does nothing to increase performance.

Probably the most famous interaction is that of alcohol and barbiturates. Someone who is used to taking either drug knows what to expect when taking one alone, but the deaths of people who have taken both are proof that the interaction is different from the sum of the two drug effects. Each drug has an effect, and so does their interaction.

In the case of the drug interaction, each drug has an effect by itself, but the effect of the two taken together cannot be predicted from the effect of the single drugs alone. It is also possible for variables to interact even when it seems that neither of them has any effect by itself. Consider the example of a psychologist who tried out a new "energizing" drug on a sample of emotionally disturbed and mentally retarded children. The children's behavior changed after ingesting the drug, but the average change was zero. When the researcher divided the results between boys and girls, it became clear that the girls all became more active after taking the drug, while the boys became less active. When boys and girls were considered together, the increase and decrease canceled each other, and the net effect appeared to be zero. (This example and several others appear in a detailed article on the concept of interaction by Schaefer [1976].)

It is important to realize that the existence of an interaction changes the meaning of the information that was available before the interaction was examined. This is obvious in the example of the "energizing" drug, where the effect of the drug seems to be zero until the interaction with the child's sex is taken into account. The point applies equally well to the example of programmed instruction. Although it is true that, for the students studied, those receiving programmed instruction did better, this simple statement is misleading. The facile interpretation—that programmed instruction helps students learn better—is incorrect. If there is any causal relationship, it can only be for some (low-verbal) students. By explicitly studying the extraneous variable of verbal ability, something was learned about programmed instruction that would have been missed if verbal ability had been controlled by randomization or matching. The strategy of including additional variables in the hypothesis sometimes allows us to discover that the effect of an independent variable may depend on a variable that had previously been thought to be extraneous. Since extraneous variables commonly interact in this way with variables of more direct interest, the best way to handle "extraneous" variables is often to explicitly measure them to assess their importance. This strategy reaches its highest development when an extraneous variable can be experimentally manipulated to study its effects, as in the example of black and white interviewers on p. 81.

The strategy of including extraneous variables in the hypothesis is limited in that it controls only those variables that are included. Other organismic variables are left uncontrolled. In the programmed instruction study, for example, an important organismic variable is the teacher's instructional style. Type of instruction is confounded with the style and personality of the teachers involved, and this cannot be changed by measuring students' verbal ability.

Often, researchers begin with a hypothesis stated in terms of the interaction of variables. The critical period hypothesis in developmental psychology is an example. The effect of a life experience is held to be dependent on the stage of development during which it occurs. That is, the effect of experience depends on time. There are many other examples in the social sciences in which interactions are hypothesized. Such hypotheses can be tested either by correlational research, as in the programmed instruction example, or by experimental methods, if the independent variables can be manipulated. In any research of this type, the presence of an interaction changes the meaning of any effects of the variables that interact. The reasoning behind this is the same whether the interaction was predicted or not.

In summary, the chief problem in drawing conclusions from correlational research is that such research measures organismic variables. Any finding explained in terms of an organismic variable may alternatively be explained in terms of any other organismic variable that is correlated with the first, but was not studied. Four strategies are commonly used to solve this problem of inference:

> *randomization*—a between-subjects experiment allows organismic variables to vary randomly, and eliminates systematic error.
> *matching*—individuals can be matched with others (or themselves) so that the only important differences are in terms of variables in the hypothesis.
> *statistical control*—individuals can be matched after the fact to compare the effect of an independent variable on people who were initially comparable in terms of selected extraneous variable(s).
> *inclusion of extraneous variable(s) in the hypothesis*—an extraneous variable is measured and treated as an independent variable that may, either alone or

in interaction with other variables in the study, influence a dependent variable of interest.

Within-subjects Experiment: The Problem of "Time-tied" Extraneous Variables

The within-subjects experiment has already been mentioned as a technique for controlling organismic variables. By observing changes in a single individual, or group of individuals, the effects of a manipulated variable can be measured while achieving perfect control of organismic variables. A price is paid for this control, however. When a subject is observed over a period of time, to see when he/she changes, any variable that might have produced an observed change is confounded with the passsge of time. The independent variable might have changed the subject, but any other events during the same time period may also be responsible. In short, *"time-tied" extraneous variables* (Agnew & Pyke, 1969) *pose the characteristic validity problem of within-subjects experiments.*

Consider this example of a within-subjects experiment. A researcher is studying the effect of a new drug, Memoraid, on learning. Because some people learn faster than others, the researcher decides to use subjects as their own controls. Each subject will get a chance to learn both with and without the drug. On the first day, each subject is tested with a placebo (no drug), on a task involving the learning of a series of nonsense syllables. On the next day the subjects are given the real drug, and are asked to learn a new list of nonsense syllables. The subjects learn better the second time. The experimenter might be tempted to conclude that Memoraid improves learning. However, many time-tied extraneous variables are confounded with the drug's effect. Subjects may have learned something about memorizing nonsense syllables on the first day and applied the knowledge by learning better on the second day. Or, they may have become bored with nonsense syllables. This would mean that the drug has a stronger effect than the results indicate. Subjects may have gotten to know the experimenter better, and, feeling comfortable, may have performed better the second time. On the other hand, familiarity may have lowered their anxiety level, leaving them less motivated to perform well. It's also possible that time-tied changes took place in the apparatus used to collect data. The wires in the memory drum used to display the nonsense syllables may have become worn, and resistance in the circuits might have increased, causing the drum to move slower and giving subjects more time to learn on the second day. The laboratory might have been visited by noisy plumbers on the first day, or the weather might have been rainy, making the subjects mentally sluggish. And so on and so on.

The above problems are not unique to experimental research; they also exist in case studies, naturalistic observations, and correlational research. Suppose the effects of Memoraid were first discovered by a scientist who accidentally ingested some of the drug. Her/his evidence would have been based on a retrospective case study, without *any* effort at systematic control. The effects attributed to the drug could have easily been due to any number of time-tied variables.

METHODS OF CONTROL

Three common procedures for controlling time-tied extraneous variables are described below.

Use of a comparison group. A group of subjects could be observed over the same time period as the experimental subjects, but without exposure to the independent variable. In the Memoraid experiment, this could be accomplished by randomly assigning subjects to get either the drug *or* the placebo (control). This would transform the study into a between-subjects experiment. The between-subjects design does not have serious problems with time-tied extraneous variables.

Comparison groups can be used to control time-tied extraneous variables in nonexperimental research, and some special designs have been developed for this purpose. In the *multiple time-series design* (Campbell & Stanley, 1963; Gottman, McFall, & Barnett, 1969), a group that has been exposed to an independent variable is compared to a control group on several occasions both before and after exposure. Both groups are exposed to the passage of time, but if the independent variable makes a difference, they will change differently over time, and especially after the independent variable is introduced. More sophisticated procedures for making unambiguous inferences from correlational data over time include the cross-lagged panel design and methods of path analysis (e.g., Heise, 1969; Land, 1969).

Counterbalancing. In a counterbalanced design, two or more groups are used, one for each treatment condition. However, unlike the between-subjects experiment in which each group is exposed to different treatments, in a counterbalanced design, each group gets all treatments, but in different orders. To counterbalance the experiment on Memoraid and learning, one group would get the placebo on the first day, and Memoraid on the next day. The other subjects would get Memoraid first, and then the placebo. Thus, any effect of learning to memorize, or boredom, or noisy plumbers, or slow machines would be equally divided between subjects getting the drug and subjects getting the placebo. If any of these variables either aids or interferes with learning, it could not explain any difference between drug and placebo treatments. It is also possible to counterbalance the lists of nonsense syllables in this study. After all, one list may be easier to learn than the other. To control for this possibility, the two groups can be divided, with half of each group learning list A first, and then list B. The order would be reversed for the other half of each group. The counterbalanced design for the Memoraid experiment is given in Table 5.

ABA design (repeated experiments). In an ABA design, subjects are observed before and after an experimental treatment, as well as while they are getting the treatment. (A represents the condition in which the treatment is absent and B the condition in which it is present.) This experimental design is common to most studies in the field of behavior modification. For example, suppose a teacher wants to decrease the frequency of aggressive outbursts by one of the boys in the class. The teacher plans to reinforce nonaggressive behavior with praise, and remove the boy from his classmates when he acts aggressively toward them. First, a "baseline" is taken. That is, the child is observed for a while before the treatment begins, and the frequency of aggressive outbursts is tabulated. When treatment begins, the number of aggressive acts each day is recorded, and, it is hoped, it decreases. The experiment may go on, alternately starting and stopping the treatment a few times, to demonstrate a consistent relationship between onset of treatment and decreases in aggressive behavior. The subject has served as his own control.

Note that in this example, the within-subjects design is used with only one subject. Partly because of increased interest in behavior modification techniques, psychologists have been paying more attention to experimental designs for single subjects. As a result, more subtle methods of within-subject experimentation are constantly being developed (e.g., Hersen & Barlow, 1976).

The ABA design controls for some of the important time-tied variables. If a time-tied variable operated continually, its effect should increase with time, independent of treatments. In the Memoraid experiment, the effect of learning to learn, or boredom, or acquaintance of the subject and the experimenter should get stronger and stronger, rather than coming and going with the drug. If subjects were given a placebo at both ends of the experiment, and if they learned best in the middle (under the drug), the above mentioned variables could probably be discounted.

Table 5. A counterbalanced design

GROUP	First day treatment		Second day treatment	
	DRUG	SYLLABLE LIST	DRUG	SYLLABLE LIST
#1	placebo	list A	Memoraid	list B
#2	placebo	list B	Memoraid	list A
#3	Memoraid	list A	placebo	list B
#4	Memoraid	list B	placebo	list A

Both counterbalancing and the ABA design require that variables be manipulated. That is, these controls can be used only in experimental research. In correlational research, case studies, and naturalistic observations, the comparison group strategy is the only feasible way to rule out alternative explanations dependent on the passage of time.

Between-subjects Experiment: The Importance of Randomization

According to the working definition given in Chapter 2, a between-subjects experiment is a study comparing groups that differ in terms of an independent variable that has been manipulated by the researcher. This definition covers a variety of different research designs, with important differences between them. For example, the validity problems caused by subject variables can be minimized by using a between-subjects experimental design *with randomization*. But it is not uncommon for studies to be conducted that manipulate an independent variable but do not assign subjects at random to the experimental or control treatments. This often happens in psychotherapeutic or educational research, when some expert decides which treatments are most appropriate for which subjects. Such studies are often termed quasi-experimental (Campbell & Stanley, 1963), because they are experimental in some respects (manipulation of variables) but not others (randomization). When treatments are not randomly assigned, a study is open to criticism on the basis of uncontrolled subject variables. This is just as true when the independent variable is manipulated as when the study is correlational: subjects assigned to different treatments are systematically different in terms of whatever organismic variables may have caused someone to assign them to the particular treatment they got.

Even when subjects are randomly assigned to experimental treatments, the between-subjects experiment is not a foolproof design. "On stage" and other changes caused by research, as well as biases in judgment are problems for this method. Just as for other quantitative methods (sample study and correlational study), sampling bias and invalid operational definitions can pose serious threats to the validity of a between-subjects experiment.

The last sections of this chapter have outlined the major sources of alternative explanations for the results of quantitative research. Table 6 summarizes these sources, indicates when they are most likely to cause trouble, and describes some of the methods researchers use to rule out alternative explanations. This table, together with Tables 2 and 3, constitute a summary of the common sources of alternative explanations for the findings of social scientific research.

The exercises for this chapter emphasize the ability to identify alternative ex-

Table 6. Sources of alternative explanation in quantitative research methods

Source	Description	When a problem	Methods of control
Invalid operational definition	Operational definition measures another variable as well	Potential problem with all operational definitions	Prevent confounding
Sampling bias	Sample systematically different in some respects from population	Nonrandom sampling; volunteer subjects	Assure that sample is representative
Uncontrolled variation in information	Results depend on who collected them or how, when, or where collected	Whenever data are collected on several people or occasions	Hold procedures constant; manipulate the variable responsible
Organismic variables	Subject variables are measured and confounded with extraneous variables	When hypothesis contains an organismic variable	Randomization; matching; subject as own control; statistical control; manipulate extraneous variable
Time-tied variables	Independent variable's effects confounded with the passage of time	Research with no comparison group	Add comparison group; counterbalancing; ABA design

planations for research results and to suggest controls that would improve the research. Specifically, the questions in the exercises directly test your ability to use the following terms:

extraneous variable (defined on p. 63)
alternative explanation (p. 63)
randomization (p. 84)
holding procedures constant (p. 81)
matching (p. 85)
statistical control (p. 87)
subjects as their own controls (p. 86)
comparison group as a control (p. 92)
sampling bias (p. 79)

The main point of this chapter is to build your skill in reading scientific reports with a critical eye to alternative explanations for reported findings. The exercises provide the opportunity to practice evaluating reports of research. A procedure for seeking alternative explanations may be helpful to you, until you develop enough experience to look in the right places.

Begin by identifying the research method used in the study you are evaluating. Table 7 identifies the most common sources of alternative explanation for each research method, and suggests the place to begin looking for validity problems in a piece of research. By using the information in Table 7, you should be able to ask questions that will lead you to alternative explanations. With practice, you should become able to ask these questions and think of alternative explanations without consulting the table.

Table 7. Sources of alternative explanation in six methods of scientific research

Source	Research method					
	NATURALISTIC OBSERVATION	RETROSPECTIVE CASE STUDY	SAMPLE STUDY	CORRELATIONAL STUDY	WITHIN-SUBJECTS EXPERIMENT	BETWEEN-SUBJECTS
On stage effects (p. 65)	*	*	*	*	*	*
More persistent changes due to research (p. 67)	*	*	*	*	*	*
Researcher selectivity (p. 72)	—	**	—	—	—	—
Researcher distortion (p. 73)	—	**	*	*	*	*
Selective or distorted memory (p. 75)	a source of alternative explanation when research relies on memory data					
Invalid operational definitions (p. 77)	—	—	**	**	**	**
Sampling bias (p. 77)	—	—	***	*	*	*
Uncontrolled variation in information (p. 80)	—	—	*	*	*	*
Organismic variables (p. 82)	*	*	—	***	—(held constant)	**(if treatments are not randomized)
Time-tied variables (p. 91)	*	*	—	*(if subjects compared to selves)	***	—

*Asterisks indicate common sources of alternative explanation in a particular research method. The more asterisks, the more serious the problem. In looking for alternative explanations, start with sources given two or three asterisks, but do not ignore any column with an asterisk.

Exercises

The objective of this chapter and the following one is to help you learn to critically evaluate reports of empirical research. The exercises in this chapter provide practice on prepared summaries of (usually imaginary) research. In Chapter 4, you will apply your skills to actual published scientific reports.

The central skill in evaluating research is the skill of identifying plausible alternative explanations for researchers' findings. Because this ability is of greatest importance, the following "briefer" exercises and problems are provided for practice in offering alternative explanations. These are followed by other exercises that use all the skills of this chapter.

Briefer Exercises

For each research report summarized below, answer these questions in the spaces provided:

(a) What method was used to collect the data? (Use categories defined in Chapter 2.)

(b) What is the hypothesis (if any)? Identify the variables in the hypothesis, labeling the independent and dependent variables if the hypothesis is causal.

(c) Identify the findings (that is, what relationship of variables was observed?)

(d) Identify extraneous variables that suggest alternative explanations of these findings. State the alternative explanations, and suggest one method to control for each extraneous variable.

(1) To assess the effects of psychotherapy as opposed to drug therapy, the progress of schizophrenic patients receiving these therapies was observed. All subjects were diagnosed schizophrenic, and were assigned to the treatments considered appropriate by their attending physicians. Subjects in the drug therapy condition were receiving a variety of drug treatments, but none was receiving psychotherapy. Those in the psychotherapy treatment included only subjects for whom no drugs were prescribed. After six months' observation, improvement, as judged by outside consultant psychiatrists, was greater in the psychotherapy group. It was concluded that psychotherapy is more effective than drug therapy in the treatment of schizophrenia.

(a)

(b)

(c)

(d)

(2) To measure the effect of background music on retention of verbal material, volunteer subjects (drawn from an introductory psychology class on the basis of their interest) were randomly assigned to read a short story under one of three conditions: while listening to a recording of rock music (by the Grateful Dead), while listening to classical music (a recording of Beethoven's Second Symphony), or while listening to silence. All subjects wore head sets to screen out extraneous noises, and all were given the same multiple-choice test of their recall of details in the story. The group listening to silence remembered more details than either of the groups exposed to music, and it was concluded that music is a source of distraction leading to decreased retention.

(a)

(b)

(c)

(d)

(3) An organization of newsmagazine publishers commissioned a researcher to get evidence concerning any relationship between reading newsmagazines and being well-informed on current events. The researcher carefully chose a representative sample of 1000 adults, collecting data from each on the number of newsmagazines read in the past month. Each person sampled also took a short test on current events. A significant relationship was found: the more newsmagazines a person reads, the higher she/he scores on the current events test. It was concluded that reading newsmagazines makes a person well-informed.

(a)

(b)

(c)

(d)

(4) An experimental remedial math program was tested by using it on 30 fifth-graders all of whom were at least two years behind grade level in math. Subjects were all the fifth-graders who met this criterion in the school studied. After three months in the new program, the students had gained an average of eight months on their math achievement scores. Since this was a vast improvement over the three months' progress that might have been expected, the program was pronounced successful and instituted throughout the school system.

(a)

(b)

(c)

(d)

(5) An investigator hypothesized that males perform better under competitive conditions than females. To test this hypothesis, a group of college students, participating as a course requirement, was given a series of arithmetic problems under instructions that these were part of an intelligence test, and that their scores would be compared with those of other adults across the country (these instructions were intended to make the situation competitive). The males in this group did significantly better than females. A second group of students, satisfying the same course requirement, was given a series of nonsense syllables to learn, with instructions that the study concerned the relative ease of learning different kinds of meaningless material (these instructions were assumed to be noncompetitive). In this group, males and females performed equally well. The investigator concluded that males respond more favorably than females to competition (that is, the hypothesis was supported).

(a)

(b)

(c)

(d)

Answers to Briefer Exercises

(1) (a) Method: *between-subjects experiment*. Since subjects were assigned to either of two treatments, this study meets our definition of a between-subjects experiment. But note that subjects were given the treatments their physicians considered appropriate, and were *not* assigned to treatments at random. This makes the study less than fully experimental (a "quasi-experiment"), and leaves the study open to a variety of alternative explanations.

(b) Hypothesis: Psychotherapy and drug *therapy* are not equally *effective in treating schizophrenics*. The independent variable is therapy, since the type of therapy is what is varied. The dependent variable is effectiveness.

(c) Findings: Improvement was greater in the psychotherapy group than the drug therapy group.

(d) Extraneous variables and alternative explanations:

Changes caused by the research: Patients in psychotherapy spend more time with the doctor than patients receiving drugs. This fact may encourage the patient to "look good" to please the doctor (possibly in spite of a failure to improve). Patients might, for example, fail to report symptoms.

Biases: No information is presented on the biases of the participating doctors (or the outside consultants) for either form of therapy. Doctors' biases may work in the therapy situation as self-fulfilling prophecies. It is certainly true that doctors who do psychotherapy have a personal stake in the process that may make them work harder than they do when treating patients with drugs. The *doctor's effort*, rather than the specific treatment, may cause improvement. Consultants, if they know who got which therapy, could distort what they see to fit their preconceptions.

Invalid operational definitions: "Psychotherapy" and "drug therapy" are inadequately defined. Any number of different drugs and schools of therapy may be involved. An evaluation of "drug therapy" presumes that the doctors know what drug to prescribe (not always true, especially in psychiatry). We could be rejecting drug therapy on the basis of the inappropriate choice of a particular drug in several cases. Improvement is "as judged by outside consultant psychiatrists," and the possible biases in this definition have already been discussed.

Organismic variables: By allowing the doctors to choose the treatments (perfectly good medical practice), we have made the *treatment* into an organismic variable—subjects are already in a treatment before the researcher does anything. This leads to confounding because other, related, organismic variables may affect the outcome of treatment. There are several possibilities. For example, doctors may habitually assign the more serious cases to drug therapy, thinking that they cannot benefit from psychotherapy. Thus, the improvement of the psychotherapy patients may be due to the fact that they weren't as sick in the first place. (Extraneous variable: *Severity of illness*). It is also possible that the doctors assigned patients to psychotherapy when they sensed the *personal compatability* (extraneous variable) that may be necessary for successful therapy. Thus, their improvement may have been due to the doctors' screening, which allowed into psychotherapy only those patients who could be helped. Doctors could have screened their patients in many other ways (e.g., highly verbal patients tend to do better in psychotherapy, it is believed). Any organismic variable that differentiates the two groups may be responsible for the results.

Controls: Doctor-patient interaction can't be controlled entirely. In fact, it has been argued that the effect of psychotherapy may be due primarily to the relationship, rather than particular techniques. Biases might be lessened by assigning patients to doctors all of whom believe in the type of treatment they are asked to give, and by keeping the consultants blind to which patients receive what therapy. The problem of defining therapy can be handled by specifying which drug(s) and form(s) of psychotherapy are being studied. The results might not generalize to other treatments, but at least they would clearly apply to *some*. Organismic variables can best be controlled by random assignment to treatments. Doctors have sometimes agreed to this.

(2) (a) Method: *between-subjects experiment*.

(b) Hypothesis: *Music* affects the *retention of verbal material*. (Variables in italics.)

(c) Findings: People listening to silence retained more verbal material than people listening to two kinds of background music.

(d) Extraneous variables and alternative explanations:

Biases: There is a sampling bias involved in using volunteers. Volunteers usually are more interested, motivated to please, and willing to work than a cross section of the same population. This causes confounding and suggests an alternative explanation only if some of the factors associated with volunteering might offer an explanation of the results. There is no obvious reason to expect that volunteers, in particular, would do better or worse with music or without (though they might do better than average under *all* conditions). If, however, the researcher had expectations about how subjects would perform, volunteers, being motivated to do what the experimenter wants, might confirm the hypothesis even if music had no effect.

Invalid operational definition of "music": "Music," in this study, is operationally defined as either the Grateful Dead or Beethoven, and "no music" is defined as silence. Isn't there something in between? You might say this study is comparing the effect of *sound* and *no sound* on retention. We can't tell if the effects are produced by sound or by *musical* sound; the two are confounded. This could be controlled by having the "no music" group hear a recording of conversation, or of white noise, at the same decibel level as the recorded music.

Organismic variables: These are controlled, since the subjects were assigned to the three conditions at random.

(3) (a) Method: *correlational study.*

(b) Hypothesis: There is a relationship between *reading newsmagazines* and *being informed on current events.* The study started out to look for *a* relationship; only after the study was done was there any mention of a *causal* relationship. The hypothesis does not distinguish between independent and dependent variables.

(c) Findings: People who report having read a large number of newsmagazines are better informed about current events than people who report having read fewer newsmagazines. (Note that this statement is much different from the stated conclusion, which does not follow from this evidence.)

(d) Extraneous variables and alternative explanations:

"On stage " effects: Some subjects may lie to the researcher about how many magazines they read (it's hard to fake a current events test, unless you want to look stupid). This suggests an alternative explanation if (a) there is reason to expect that they may lie, and (b) their lying would change the results. These conditions may exist in this study. Suppose that some of the more educated subjects fear that they would look bad if they admitted how little they read. The same people may be informed about current events (maybe by watching the evening news), but without reading. The finding would then be a result of well-informed people trying to *appear* well-read, rather than any effect of actual reading of newsmagazines.

Organismic variables: In any correlational study, look for these. Here someone has used a correlation to "prove" a causal relationship; the reasoning is fallacious because any number of extraneous factors (organismic variables) might have produced the effect (of making some people better informed than others). Here are a few likely examples: People of higher *economic status* (extraneous variable) are well-informed (because they can have an impact on current events) and read more newsmagazines (because they can afford them). Or, people with more *education* are better informed (through their education) and read more magazines (because they like to); it may be, though, that it is their reading of *newspapers* that makes them well-informed. Or, maybe some people who must be well-informed about current events because their jobs require it read newsmagazines as a way to stay well-informed. And so on.

Controls: For organismic variables, you could use an experimental design or match or control statistically for extraneous variables. Since it would be hard to make people read newsmagazines (how could you be sure they read them?), it might make more sense to use matching or statistical after-the-fact control. I'd suggest controls for socioeconomic class, level of education, and the amount of exposure they have to sources of news other than magazines. If subjects matched on these variables knew more current events when they read more newsmagazines, I might start to believe that the magazines had something to do with it.

(4) (a) Method: *within-subjects experiment*. Subjects are compared only to themselves (and to what they are expected to do).

(b) Hypothesis: *Remedial Math Program X* improves the *math achievement* of fifth graders who are behind grade level.

(c) Findings: Fifth-graders who were behind grade level in math gained an average of eight months on a math achievement test in the first three months of a new remedial program.

(d) Extraneous variables and alternative explanations:

Changes caused by research: There is a very real possibility that *the act of instituting the new program* (extraneous variable), rather than the program itself, could influence results. Students and teachers may try harder just because the method is new, and this effort may pay off (the Hawthorne effect). The new method may also give the slow students more *attention* than they would otherwise get. If the teachers believe in the new method, they may put unusual effort into it, and produce a self-fulfilling prophecy. Finally, the teachers, knowing that they are being observed, may try harder, regardless of the method they are using. Most of these criticisms take the form that teachers and/or students might work harder in the experimental situation regardless of the program they are using. (*Control:* It would help to give the comparison group some *other* program which is also different from what the teachers have used in the past. This would allow you to tell whether one program was better, even when both are "new" and "experimental.")

Time-tied variables: These are the big sources of trouble in within-subjects experiments. How do you *know* that fifth graders in this school should improve three months in three months? It seems to make sense, but it may not be so. The fifth grade teachers may be exceptionally good (or the fourth grade teachers exceptionally bad), so that everyone accelerates in fifth grade, regardless of special programs. Or these fifth grade teachers may habitually give special attention to slow students, even when not using the new method. (*Control:* Use a comparison group. Really, these pupils should be divided in half, so that half the low-math fifth graders could be taught with a different system, for comparison.)

(5) (a) Method: *between-subjects experiment*. According to our classification system, this is an experiment because one of the variables (competitiveness) is manipulated. It is important to remember, though, that one of the independent variables (sex) is *not* manipulated. Thus, with respect to sex, the study is correlational.

(b) Hypothesis: *Males perform* better under *competitive conditions* than *females*. There are *two* independent variables here: sex (male vs. female) and competitiveness of situation (competitive vs. noncompetitive). The dependent variable is performance.

(c) Findings: Under competitive instructions, males outperformed females on arithmetic problems. Under noncompetitive instructions, both sexes learned nonsense syllables equally well.

(d) Extraneous variables and alternative explanations:

Changes caused by research: Regardless of the instructions given, subjects may have tried to please the experimenter by doing what amounts to the sex-typed behavior on the task. Males may have tried harder on the math, while females may not have tried so hard. Thus, sex stereotypes, rather than response to competition, may have been responsible for the results. Furthermore, this sort of situation would have been most serious in the "competitive" situation. If neither group makes a special effort with noncompetitive instructions, and only males try hard in math under competitive conditions (because they are supposed to be good at math), we would expect the reported results. Maybe on a verbal task, women would do better with competitive instructions. (Control: Equalize the tasks. It's easy to see here why a task that isn't sex-typed would be advisable—subjects would have no idea what is expected in terms of sex roles, and might respond to competitiveness, rather than to the nature of the task. One might also study the effect of sex-typing by manipulating this variable: you could assign male-stereotyped and female-stereotyped tasks under both competitive and noncompetitive conditions.)

Invalid operational definition of competitiveness: This operational definition is confounded because the competitive and noncompetitive groups differ not only in the instructions they were given but also in the type of material used to test their performance (an extraneous variable). Any sex difference attributed to competition may with equal reason be attributed to the type of task: men do better at math; women do better with verbal problems. You might also arrive at this explanation by considering:

Organismic variables: These may be a problem since one of the independent variables (sex) is organismic. If sex-related variables could explain the results, there is confounding. It turns out that such a problem exists. Males do better than females in mathematics, while females tend to excel on verbal tasks. In this study, the males did better on the mathematical task (the so-called competitive one) and the groups were equal on the verbal task (the "noncompetitive" one). This is consistent with what you might expect, even if the competitive instructions had no effect. (Control: The two tasks should have been equal in difficulty, and both should have been tasks on which men and women usually do equally well. Some pretesting of the tasks would have been necessary.) Note: we don't know how the two groups for this study were chosen. Were individuals assigned to groups at random? They came from one college course, but on what basis? One group may have been, for some reason, more verbal, more mathematical, or more competitive than the other.

Try the following problems; no answers are provided for them.

Briefer Problems

(1) To test the effect of marijuana on time perception, the following experiment was performed. Subjects were given a standard dose of THC (the primary psychoactive ingredient of marijuana), and were asked to estimate the duration of a light that appeared on a screen in front of them. The light appeared three times, for durations of 10, 30, and 60 seconds. Each subject was presented with each duration once, in a random order (a different random order was chosen for each subject). The dependent variable was defined as the percent overestimation of time found for each duration. An average overestimation of 17% was found for the 10 second duration, 22% for the 30 second duration, and 20% for the 60 second duration. It was concluded that marijuana has a significant effect on time perception, resulting in an overestimation of time.

(a)

(b)

(c)

(d)

(2) In another marijuana-time perception experiment, subjects were exposed to each of three dosages: Zero (placebo), low THC, and high THC (high and higher, if you will). Treatments were separated from each other by 24 hours, and all subjects first received the high dose, then the placebo, and then the low dose condition. All subjects in all conditions made a judgment of the duration of a light that was on for 30 seconds in all cases. The dependent variable was defined as percent overestimation of time, and was found to be 12%, 10%, and 20% for zero, low, and high doses, respectively. Statistical results were not significant,

and the investigator concluded that he had failed to support a conclusion that marijuana affected time perception.

(a)

(b)

(c)

(d)

(3) To support an argument in favor of long prison terms for felonies, a prison administrator produced data to indicate that the older a prisoner is when released from prison, the less likely he or she is to commit another crime within the next four years. Specifically, Glaser (1964) found that federal prisoners released at ages 18–21, 22–25, 26–35, and 36 and over were returned to prison or sentenced for felonylike offenses 48%, 40%, 34%, and 27%, respectively, within four years. The prison administrator argued that these data showed that keeping prisoners locked up longer made them less likely to commit new crimes.

(a)

(b)

(c)

(d)

(4) To compare the effectiveness of psychoanalytically oriented psychotherapy and behavior therapy, an experimenter randomly assigned neurotic patients to the psychiatric residents working under him on his hospital's staff. The residents were undergoing training in psychoanalytic techniques as part of their program, and were also given instruction in behavior therapy by an outside consultant, so that they could participate in the experiment. All patients were interviewed on admission to the hospital by the experimenter, who then assigned them to either behavior or psychoanalytic therapy. After six months of therapy, the patients were reinterviewed by the experimenter, and improvement was assessed by a checklist of symptoms filled out by the patient before and after therapy, and by the experimenter's rating of degree of improvement. Both groups improved significantly when patients' responses were used to measure improvement, but only the psychoanalytic group improved when the psychiatrist's ratings were used as the criterion. The investigator concluded that the results *favored psychoanalysis*, as patients' responses could have indicated denial of conflict, and that this possibility was more likely in behavior therapy patients.

(a)

(b)

(c)

(d)

(5) A researcher hypothesized that anxiety would inhibit people from making new social contacts. To test this prediction, a group of 20 people was convened for an afternoon wine-and-cheese party. Five of the 20 were observers, each assigned to observe three other people and to keep track of the number of times each person initiated conversation with someone else at the party. Observers were instructed not to initiate conversation with anyone. The number of conversations initiated was the measure of making new social contacts, and the score on the Taylor Manifest Anxiety Scale (administered two weeks before the party) was the measure of anxiety. Subjects scoring high on anxiety made significantly fewer social contacts than low-anxiety subjects, and this was taken as support for the hypothesis.

(a)

(b)

(c)

(d)

A more complete exercise follows, in which a bit more information is given about the study described, and in which you are asked to evaluate the study in more detail. Answers follow the exercise.

Complete Exercise

Answer the following questions about the research described below:
    (a) What method was used to collect the data? (Use the categories from

Chapter 2: naturalistic observation, retrospective case study, sample study, correlational study, within-subjects experiment, between-subjects experiment.)

(b) What is the hypothesis, if any? Is it causal or noncausal?

(c) Identify the variable(s) studied. If the hypothesis is causal, identify the independent and dependent variables. State the operational definition of each variable.

(d) Identify the findings (that is, what relationship of variables was observed?)

(e) Identify an extraneous variable that is controlled by holding it constant (e.g., by constant procedures, matching, statistical control, or comparing subjects to themselves).

Identify an extraneous variable that is randomized. (If there is none, say so.)

(f) Identify any extraneous variables that suggest an alternative explanation of the observed results. State the alternative explanation(s), and suggest one way to control for each extraneous variable involved.

(g) Identify the sample studied and the population from which it was drawn. If you detect any sampling bias, identify it.

(h) Identify any interactions of variables being studied.

The director of Hometown YMCA wanted to see if the "Y" program helps build leaders. He looked up the "Y" membership records, and found the names of all 52 boys aged 10–12 who were members in 1953. Using the school district's records of the same year, he randomly chose 52 boys of the same age, excluding from his sample any boy who was already on the "Y" list. He attempted to contact all of the 104 men (he could only locate 48 of the "Y" members and 41 of the nonmembers) and to determine their present occupations. Using a standard index of the socioeconomic status of occupations, a status rating was determined for each subject's present job. As the "Y" group had the higher average status rating, it was concluded that the "Y" builds leaders.

(a)

(b)

(c)

(d)

(e)

(f)

(g)

(h)

Answers to Complete Exercise

(a) Method: Correlational study (No variable was manipulated.)

(b) Hypothesis: Membership in the "Y" increases the chances of a boy's becoming a leader. Causal.

(c) Variables: Membership in "Y"; leadership.

Independent variable: Membership in "Y." Operational definition: being a boy, included on the membership list for 1953, and listed as between the ages of 10 and 12.

Dependent variable: Leadership. Operational definition: the score of subject's present occupation on an index of socioeconomic status of occupations.

(d) Findings: Members of the Hometown YMCA had higher status occupations than non-"Y" members of the same age and sex.

(e) Held constant: age of subjects when their status is assessed, sex of subjects, city they lived in at age 10–12.

Randomized: none. This was not a true experiment, and subjects were not randomly assigned to participate in the "Y" program or not to participate. Thus, there are a number of variables that may vary in an uncontrolled manner (see discussion of uncontrolled variables).

(f) Extraneous variables and alternative explanations:

Invalid operational definition of leadership: The researcher collected data about the socioeconomic status of the subject's present occupation, and drew a conclusion about leadership. While it is sometimes true that one can rise to a high status occupation because of one's leadership qualities, one can also attain this position through personal connections, special training, or an agreeable personality. These factors are all extraneous variables that might explain subjects' scores on "leadership." The definition of leadership is an especially serious problem, because of other difficulties described below.

Organismic variables: This is a classic case of correlations being used to prove causes. We do not know that leadership was caused by the "Y" program, because there may be any number of organismic variables, correlated with membership, that may be more important. Here are some that suggest alternative explanations of the results:

Parents' socioeconomic status: If the "Y" was mainly an organization serving the middle and upper classes in Hometown in 1953, the boys who joined had an advantage over the average public school boy, even before they entered the "Y." Their later success may have been due to family influence in the town, or to socialization into the behavior patterns that allow one to become successful in our society. This explanation is strengthened by the fact that the measure of "leadership" is really a measure of socioeconomic status.

Neighborhood: The "Y" probably mainly served boys who lived nearby. If the "Y" was in a fancy part of town, it received a selected sample of boys, even if it did not exclude the lower class. These boys had the advantages of social class already mentioned.

School attendance: The comparison group all went to public school, while we don't know if that is also true of the "Y" boys. If this is a town in which richer families sent their boys to private or parochial schools, then the "Y" group is being compared to a relatively disadvantaged population.

Alternative explanation: Boys who come from high socioeconomic status homes (and therefore are likely to join the Hometown "Y") are likely to obtain high socioeconomic status jobs. This may be accomplished through family connections, increased access to education, or through any number of personal qualities, with leadership only one.

Controls: An experimental design, assigning some boys to "Y"-type programs and others to no treatment, would be one solution to the problem of organismic variables. Because the long-term follow-up would be impractical, another solution is desirable. Subjects could be matched on a few potentially important extraneous variables (e.g., socioeconomic status of father's job, attendance at public school in all groups), and then compared again. (It might be necessary to throw out the data of some subjects who could not be matched.) Or data on these extraneous variables could be collected and entered into a data analysis that would control for them statistically.

The problem of measuring leadership is more difficult. It might be necessary to design a standard group situation in which people would behave in ways that can be rated in terms of whether leadership is shown. All subjects could then be called in to participate in this "experiment," and the results could be the measure of leadership. At any rate, some measure should be used that is based more directly on what the "Y" is trying to produce in its boys.

(g) Sample: 104 men; 52 who were members of the Hometown YMCA at ages 10–12 in 1953, and 52 of the same age who attended Hometown public schools in 1953, but were not "Y" members.

Population: Boys in Hometown who were 10–12 years old in 1953.

Sampling bias: One source of bias has already been mentioned. A sample of boys in public school is an unrepresentative sample of all the boys of that age in Hometown. This bias creates a problem because, while the comparison group was drawn only from the public school population, we do not know if this was also true of the "Y" group. Thus the sampling procedure confounds "Y" membership with type of school attended.

Another source of bias exists. Not all the subjects sampled actually appeared in the results. Four "Y" boys and nine in the comparison group could not be located. We do not know how these boys would have scored on "leadership." This could suggest an alternative explanation if the uneven split favors one group. Suppose that Hometown is a depressed area, and that the boys with high ambition and strong leadership qualities all left town. This would mean that the non-"Y" group was underrated in terms of actual leadership ability. On the other hand, it may be that the boys who left town were mainly shiftless wanderers. If so, the "Y" group was underrated by the data. Thus, the loss of subjects from the sample (called "attrition") may be hiding an uncontrolled extraneous variable. At least we know that only 13 of 104 subjects are affected, so we may conclude that this is not a serious problem with the research.

This study seems to generalize its findings beyond the population it studied. The conclusion that the "Y" builds leaders clearly implies more than the 1953 program for 10–12-year-old boys, and it almost certainly is meant to generalize beyond Hometown. Such generalizations would not even be justified from an unbiased sample. Neither are these generalizations necessarily wrong. They require more information about the effects of "Y" programs on other populations.

(h) Interactions of variables: None is being investigated.

Now try answering the same questions about the research described in the following problems. No answers are provided for these.

Complete Problems

For each of the reports below, answer the eight questions that were listed on pages 109–110.

(1) Braginsky, Braginsky, and Fitzgerald (reported in Braginsky & Braginsky, 1974) conducted a study to see whether deviant political attitudes influenced psychiatric diagnoses. In plainer language, they wanted to see if mental health professionals judge people "crazy" because of their political beliefs. Two videotapes were prepared in which a doctor interviewed an actor playing the roles of two patients. Each tape was divided into four segments, and the mental health professionals who viewed the tapes were asked to diagnose the patient and rate the severity of his illness after each segment. In one tape, the "patient" expressed a New Left political philosophy, and in the other, a middle-of-the-road set of politics. The first segment of both tapes was identical, and consisted of a presentation of complaints "typical of mildly neurotic persons." In the second segment, the "patients" expressed their political philosophies, and in the third, they expressed their ideas of political strategy (including "radical tactics" in the New Left tape). The contents of the final segment are not discussed in this summary report. The patients were rated equal in degree of pathology after the first segment of the tape, but as the interview went on, the New Left patient was seen as more and more severely disturbed, while the ratings of the middle-of-the-road patient remained unchanged. It was concluded that the expression of deviant politics does influence psychiatric diagnosis. The authors suggest that one function of diagnosis in our society may be to "weed out" social deviants.

(a)

(b)

(c)

(d)

(e)

(f)

(g)

(h)

(2) To measure the effect of team teaching on school performance and attitudes, Gamsky (1971) conducted a study on ninth graders learning English and History. The two teachers involved in teaching these subjects used a team-teaching approach for one ninth-grade class, and their traditional approach for the other class. The classes were randomly assigned to treatment conditions, and were asserted to be composed of comparable students. The team-teaching approach used consisted of dividing the class periods (the English and History periods were back to back) into 20 minute segments, including large group work taught by each teacher, as well as individual and small group work. Teacher aides were available to help with the small groups. The traditional teaching approach was not described in detail. At the end of the year, achievement scores in both subjects were equal for the two classes, but the team-taught class scored higher on some measures of attitude toward school. It was concluded that team teaching had some benefits in the attitudinal area.

(a)

(b)

(c)

(d)

(e)

(f)

(g)

(h)

CHAPTER 4

Evaluating
Scientific
Evidence:
II

Chapter 3 was designed to provide a guide for judging the internal validity of social scientific studies. In the exercises and problems, you practiced finding extraneous variables and the alternative explanations they suggest for observed data, and you learned how to identify and suggest controls for extraneous variables. You also distinguished between the samples of people studied and the populations from which the samples were drawn, and identified the interactions being studied. In short, Chapter 3 gave you the tools to evaluate the internal validity of a summarized scientific study.

To be able to use these tools to evaluate *real* scientific reports, as they appear in the academic and professional journals, you must learn how to find what you are looking for in a scientific report. This chapter offers some pointers about evaluating evidence as it appears in the journals.

There is no new language to learn, though you will surely be exposed to new language in the journal articles you read. It may be best to be guided through a scientific article before you try to understand one on your own. The discussion that follows uses as an example the article by Landauer and Whiting, "Infantile Stimulation and Adult Stature of Human Males" (1964), which follows.

INFANTILE STIMULATION AND ADULT STATURE OF HUMAN MALES[1]

Thomas K. Landauer
DARTMOUTH COLLEGE

John W. M. Whiting
HARVARD UNIVERSITY

Recent experimental research has shown that extraordinary stimulation of animals (particularly rats) during infancy has profound and enduring physiological effects. One of the more persistent and striking of these effects, an increase in rate of growth and size attained at adulthood, is of particular relevance to this paper. It has been summarized by Levine (1960:85), one of the leading researchers in the field, as follows: "In all respects, in fact, the manipulated infants exhibit a more rapid rate of development. They open their eyes earlier and achieve motor coordination sooner. Their body hair grows faster, and they tend to be significantly heavier at weaning. They continue to gain weight more rapidly than the nonstimulated animals even after the course of stimulation has been completed at three weeks of age. Their more vigorous growth does not seem to be related to food intake but to better utilization of the food consumed and probably to a higher output of the somatotrophic (growth) hormone from the pituitary." As will be discussed below, it seems reasonable to interpret these unusual early experiences as stressful to the immature animals.

Although the exact mechanism underlying the stimulating effects of these early experiences upon growth has not been established, it is known that a lasting change in the endocrine system does occur. Since growth is presumably inhibited by corticosteroid stress response hormones, one

might hypothesize that animals stressed in infancy are in some manner less responsive to stress following this early experience, since this would lead to a lower average level of circulating corticosteroids and allow more uninterrupted growth. There is some experimental evidence suggesting that this may indeed be the case. When adult rats are placed on an enclosed table top, those stressed in infancy show significantly *less* defecation, urination, crouching, and wall seeking behavior than non-stimulated controls. Furthermore, infant-stressed rats taken from a colony and wheeled down on a cart to a laboratory showed a significantly lower leukocyte count than stressed controls (Levine and Lewis:1962). Since both of the above types of response indicate the action of growth-inhibiting stress hormones, a mechanism for the effect of infant stress upon growth is suggested.

It should be pointed out, however, that the experimental animals when subjected to electric shock show a more rapid increase in circulating corticosteroids as well as a higher concentration of them at the end of a 15-minute interval (Levine and Lewis: 1962). This seems to be evidence against the above interpretation. Levine suggests, however, that "it is possible that the non-stimulated subjects, although slower in their initial responses, may show higher sustained levels." He concludes that animals stressed in infancy "are more reactive to distinctly noxious and threatening situa-

Reprinted from *American Anthropologist*, 1964, *66*, 1007–1028. Copyright 1964, American Anthropological Association. All rights reserved.

tions, but that the nonstimulated (in infancy) animal appears to react to a greater variety of environmental changes. The nonstimulated subject seems to require less extreme changes in the environment to elicit a physiological stress response, and in this sense they are hyperreactors."

METHOD AND MEASURES

Most of the animal studies showing the effect of infant stress upon growth have used body weight as a measure (for example, Reugamer and Silverman 1956; McClelland 1956; Denenberg and Karas, 1959). One study (Weininger 1956), however, showed that the animals in the experimental group that had been removed from their cages and stroked each day for three weeks following weaning had significantly longer skeletons ($p < .001$) and longer tails ($p < .01$) upon reaching adulthood than the unstimulated control group. Furthermore, since there was no indication that the greater weight reported in the other studies was due to obesity, these studies also suggest that greater skeletal length is a consistent effect of infant stimulation.

This assumption allowed us to use height as the dependent variable to investigate the possible relation between infant stress and human growth, quantitative data on adult human male stature being available for a considerably larger number of societies than any other index of growth.

The choice of apparently "stressful" infant care practices as the independent variable requires more explanation. In early rat studies (Hammett 1922; Greenman and Dehring 1931; Weininger 1956) the experimental treatment generally consisted of taking the rat pups from their cages and gently stroking them for ten minutes or so each day for several weeks. Many of these studies explicitly referred to Freudian theory and interpreted this treatment as "tender loving care." Weininger (1956), for example, refers to the effects of maternal ne-

glect reported by Spitz (1946), Goldfarb (1943, 1949), and Levy (1934) implying that the rat pups left with their mother were more "neglected" than those petted by the experimenter.

More recent studies, however, indicate that "petting" probably has a frightening or stressful effect. In these studies (Levine, Chevalier, and Korchin, 1956; Levine 1957; Levine 1958; Levine and Lewis 1959; Werboff and Havlena 1963), it has been shown that a mild electric shock, drug-induced febrile convulsion, jiggling in an oscillating cage, or separation from the mother by removal from the nest for 3 minutes a day, has an effect very similar to "petting." The behavior and/or growth of rat pups treated in these ways differs significantly from the control animals that are simply left in the home cages. This led to a reexamination of the effect of the "petting" procedure and it was observed that rat pups while being so treated often showed signs of disturbance such as defecating, urinating, and squealing. Thus, more recent experimenters have interpreted the petting procedure as stressful. We, therefore, decided to look for customs of infant care in humans that were unusually stimulating or stressful rather than those which indicated the degree of "tender loving care."

Our method of attacking the problem was, therefore, to study cross-culturally the relation between apparently stressful infant care practices and the stature of adult males. A few words must be said about the assumptions underlying our use of the cross-cultural method for the purpose of testing this hypothesis. In many cases the stature data and the data on infant experiences of a given society had to be obtained from different sources, and had been collected at different times. Even when the same source provided both kinds of data, the descriptions of infant care pertained to a different generation than did the measurements of height. However, if we assume that customs pertaining to treatment of infants probably do not often change radically during one of a few generations, then it is reasonable to assume that the adults whose heights were reported were treated as infants in much the same manner as infants described in contemporaneous ethnographies.

We first obtained as much data as possible on 80 societies about which appropriate information was readily available. Data were taken from societies in the Human Relations Area Files with a few supplementary cases. Each society in the sample was treated as a separate case. The customary ways of treating infants in a given society was one variable. The mean adult stature of males was the other. Thus, the sample of 80 societies actually represented data from a much larger number of individuals.

Sampling of societies was primarily determined by the availability of information, but the sample included a fairly representative cross-section of the world's geographical areas, racial stocks, and cultural groupings.

To begin with, quantitative data on adult male stature were obtained. Next, a person who did not know the hypothesis to be tested and had not seen the height data, abstracted information on infant care from ethnographic reports on each of the societies. From examination of these abstracts we made a list of discrete practices which we thought might be stressful, or unusually stimulating in some manner, and which occurred sometime in early infancy. These were as follows:

1. Piercing, e.g., piercing the nose, lips, or ear to receive an ornament; circumcision, innoculation, scarification, or cauterization.

2. Molding, e.g., stretching the arms or legs, or shaping the head (usually for cosmetic purposes).

3. Extreme Heat—hot baths or exposure to fire or intense sunlight.

4. Extreme Cold—cold baths or exposure to snow or cold air.

5. Internal Stressors—administration of emetics, irritants, or enemas.

6. Abrasions—rubbing with sand, or scraping with a shell or other sharp object.

7. Unusually intense sensory stimulation—massaging, rubbing, annointing, painting, or exposing to loud noises.

8. Binding—swaddling tight enough to be judged painful or other severe restrictions of movement.

For a first rough index a society was given one point for each occurrence of any one of these practices if we judged it to be only slightly stressful; two points for each occurrence which we judged to be severely stressful. These intensity scores were then multiplied by the number of times during the first two weeks of the infant's life they were reported to occur. The judgments were made independently by two judges whose total scores correlated with each other approximately .80. Total scores obtained by simply adding up these ratings for each society were then correlated with mean adult male height. The product moment correlation coefficient was .33, which would be expected on the basis of chance alone less than one time in 100.

The next step was to redo the analysis in a less crude way. First, it seemed reasonable to distinguish between piercing and all other types of stress on the grounds that if the skin was broken as in ear or nose piercing or circumcision, this should put the organism under continued stress until the wound healed. The painful after-effects of these operations are often reported in the ethnographic literature. We decided therefore to consider piercing as stressful if it occurred but once, but to consider other types as stressful practices only if they were performed daily for at least two weeks. On the basis of this assumption the only types of stress that occurred in enough societies to obtain a reasonable estimate of their effect were piercing, molding, cold, and binding.

Only three or less societies of our sample reported the daily occurrence for two weeks of any of the other types of stress. Furthermore, with the above restricted definition, only piercing and molding showed the predicted relation to stature. Both binding and cold stress showed a slightly (insignificant) negative relation. For these reasons further investigation was limited to only two classes of stressors—piercing and molding. A test of the effects of other types of stress must be carried out in some other manner.[2]

In our initial study, early infancy was arbitrarily defined as the first two weeks of life (primarily because it made sampling and data collection more convenient). It would seem more appropriate to choose a period corresponding to the observed "critical period" for beneficial effects of stress in lower organisms. Unfortunately, however, there is no adequate way to extrapolate from animal studies to determine what the analogous period might be in humans. If there is such a critical period in humans, its duration will have to be determined empirically (and we will present a small amount of suggestive evidence concerning this question below). Nonetheless, the animal studies make it abundantly clear that the effects of early stress can be very different, in some instances opposite, from those of later stress. It was therefore essential to delimit the time period to be considered in *some* (hopefully reasonable) way. The one to three week period for beneficial effects of stress in rats and mice appears to correspond very roughly with the usual time of weaning. Since the average time for weaning for humans, cross-culturally

speaking, is approximately two years (Whiting and Child 1953) we decided to change our age criterion for infant stress from the first two weeks to the first two years, in the hope that this criterion would prove more biologically meaningful.

A review of the initial study revealed a further weakness. There were a number of societies for which the data on stature was at best suspicious because only a handful of people had been measured or because we had accepted an undocumented assertion by an ethnographer. To correct this weakness, we omitted all societies for which we did not have a report of actual measurement on at least 25 individuals. This reduced the size of our original sample from 80 to 36.

RESULTS

Reduced Original Sample
Results of reanalysis of the reduced original sample are given in Table 1. Societies which stressed infants produced males who were over two inches taller in adulthood than societies in which such practices were absent. The difference is statistically reliable at the .002 level.

New Sample
Since we had chosen piercing and molding stressors, and the two year age criterion for the analysis of the reduced original sample at least partly on the basis of results from the full original sample, we might have been capitalizing on chance to an unknown degree. It was obviously desirable, therefore, to retest the hypothesis on a completely new and independent sample. For this purpose another 30 societies with appropriate

Table 1. Reduced original sample

Mean adult male stature—in.	Piercing or molding during first 24 months of life	
	Present (n = 17)	Absent (n = 18)
	65.18	62.69

t = 3.72, p < .002

information were obtained and rated in exactly the same manner.[3]

The results for the new sample are shown in Table 2. Again societies which practice molding or piercing had significantly taller adult males than those which practice neither. The difference in average height was again over two inches and highly reliable ($p < .001$).

Combined Sample

Since the two samples yielded such similar results, it seems safe enough to combine them. Table 3 shows the association of each of the two classes of stressors, shaping and molding, separately for the combined sample. Societies practicing one or the other or both had significantly taller males than societies practicing neither. (Mean difference, 2.5 in. $p < .001$). The average heights associated with piercing alone, molding alone, or both together were approximately the same, which suggests some sort of threshold effect in which any sufficient stress will produce the maximum effect.

Critical Period

As has been suggested above, the animal studies indicate that there is a "critical period" for the effects of stress. For example, Denenberg and Karas (1959) showed that both rats and mice handled during the first ten days of life were significantly heavier as adults than those not handled during this time (i.e. a control group not handled at all and a second experimental group handled between the eleventh and twentieth day). Our data provide some information on this problem with respect to

humans. Apparently, because molding and shaping are more effective when the bones are soft, this practice is invariably begun almost immediately after birth. There is, however, considerable variation in the age at which an infant is circumcized, scarified, or pierced for ornaments. Although the age estimates are rough and the number of cases at some of the intervals is small, Table 4 suggests that the first two years could indeed be the critical period for humans.

Tests of Alternative Explanations

It remains to determine whether the association between infant stress and adult stature may be interpreted as the result of a causal relation. Since the observation is purely correlational, cause cannot be determined with any certainty. The problem is that there may be some third variable which occurs by chance in association with stressful infant care practices that is the real cause of variation in stature; or, alternatively, that there is some characteristic of certain groups of people that makes them tall and at the same time likely to stress their children. Thus, if there is any factor that occurs in the same societies of our sample as do the stressful infant care practices, serious doubt would be cast on our findings if this factor can reasonably be interpreted as promoting growth. We therefore tried to discover whether any of the factors known or commonly thought to influence height could be producing the observed correlation.

By obtaining data on our sample relevant to several such factors—genetic stock, sunlight, and diet—we adduced evience that

Table 2. Retest sample

Mean adult male stature—in.	*Piercing or molding during first 24 months of life*	
	Present (n = 19)	Absent (n = 11)
	66.05	63.41

t = 4.68, p < .001

Table 3. Combined sample

	Type of stressor			
PIERCING:	ABSENT	ABSENT	PRESENT	PRESENT
MOLDING:	ABSENT	PRESENT	ABSENT	PRESENT
70				
			x	
69				
			x	
68				
		x	xxx	
67		x	xx	x
	x		xxx	
66	x	x	xx	x
		x	xxxx	x
65	x		x	x
	xxxx	xx		x
64	xxx	x	xx	x
	xxxxx			
63	xxx		x	x
	xx		x	
62	xx		x	
	xxx			
61				
60	xx			
	x			
59				
	x			
58				
Mean	62.9	65.6	65.8	65.0
Significance level	Absent Absent	Absent Present	Present Absent	
Absent Present	$p < .02$			
Present Absent	$p < .001$	$p > .10$		
Present Present	$p < .10$	$p > .10$	$p > .10$	

Each "X" represents a society on which the mean adult stature was available for at least 25 individuals. For the difference between the absence of both types of stressor and the presence of one and/or the other, $p < .001$. All significance levels were obtained by Scheffés (1959) method of multiple comparisons.

tends to reject some of the more obvious alternative explanations of the stress-height correlation.

In order to control genetic variables to some degree at least, we broke our sample down into the five major regions of the world—Africa, Eurasia, Insular Pacific, North and South America.[4] If the relation holds true for each of these regions, then it would be difficult to argue that our findings

Table 4. Age at first stress

Stature	Under 2 weeks	2 weeks to 2 years	2 to 6 years	6 to 15 years	Not before 15
>67"	67.5 S 893 Bambara 67.5 M 39 Lau	69.5 B 34 Shilluk 68.5 I 724 Yankee 68.0 I 70 Dutch			
67"	67.0 B 422 Somali 67.0 M 384 Maori 67.0 M 79 Marquesans	67.5 S 385 Tuareg 67.0 S 94 Mossi			
66"	66.5 E 1095 Navaho 66.5 SCM 1130 Yoruba 66.0 M 623 Azande	66.5 I 292 Serbians 66.5 E 82 Toda 66.0 C 331 Arabs (Pal.) 66.0 C 529 Riffians			66.5 712 Ganda 66.0 91 Comanche
65"	65.5 C 583 Iranians 65.5 M 30 Klamath 65.5 EM 44 Ojibwa 65.5 S 166 Hausa 65.0 CM 624 Ibo	65.5 I 579 Poles 65.5 I 5179 Bulgarians 65.0 C 50 Telugu	65.0 C 597 Kurd		
64"	64.5 M 1051 Kazak 64.5 M 57 Javanese 64.5 M 82 Eskimo (Cop.) 64.0 M 31 Araucanians 64.0 B 453 Aranda	64.0 M 199 Chukchee 64.0 M 408 Zuni	64.5 E 39 Kikuyu 64.5 C 40 Kuwait 64.0 E 50 Ulithi 64.0 E 42 Marshallese 64.0 B 473 Bhil	64.5 E 39 Hadramaut	64.5 C 47 Ashanti 64.0 100 Gond
63"	63.0 E 276 Hopi 63.0 M 187 Mosquito		63.5 E 250 Oraon 63.5 EB 73 Nama 63.5 C 270 Rwala 63.0 C 32 Bontoc	63.0 E 946 Lesu 63.0 EB 178 Malayans	63.5 CE 145 Tarascans
62"		62.5 EN 81 Orokaiva 62.0 E 213 Khasi	62.0 E 622 Ainu 62.0 S 67 Yaghan	61.5 S 74 Kung	62.5 197 Koryak 62.5 56 Aymara
61"					61.5 S 57 Lepcha 61.5 68 Carib
<61"				59.5 N 257 Semang 58.5 T 438 Andamans	60.0 N 41 Cuna 60.0 T 300 Kapauku
Number of societies:	20	16	12	6	11
Number of individuals:	8249	9250	2555	1932	1814
Mean Stature:	65.4	65.9	63.6	61.7	63.0

At the left of each society is entered the mean adult male stature and the number of individuals upon which it was based. At the right, the type of stress is indicated by the following were due to genetics. As can be seen from Table 5, even though the mean for stature differs from region to region, a similar effect of infant stress appears in each region of the world.

Sunlight (one of the main sources of vitamin D) was studied by using an estimate of the number of sunny days in a year. This estimate was derived from ethnographic reports supplemented by maps showing annual variations in climate (Goode's Atlas 1957; 14–15). Mean annual rainfall was the best inverse index of sunlight available.

Obviously, this measure should be taken as only a rough index of sunshine and hence of the growth-stimulating vitamin D.

The results of this attempt to estimate the effect of this variable upon stature are presented in Table 6. It will be seen from this table that males growing up in sunny climates average 1.9 inches taller than males growing up where it rains frequently. This is in itself an interesting and perhaps surprising finding. For the purposes of this paper, however, it is more important to note that stress has some effect

Table 5. Geographical-genetic region

Infant stress	Africa		Eurasia		Insular Pacific		North and South America	
	ABSENT	PRESENT	ABSENT	PRESENT	ABSENT	PRESENT	ABSENT	PRESENT
70								
		X						
69								
				X				
68				X				
		XX				X		
67		XX				XX		
	X			XX				X
66		XXX		X	X			
		X		XXX				XX
65		X	X	X				
	XX		XX	X		X		X
64			XX	X	XX	X		XX
	X		XX				X	
63			X		XX			XX
			X			X	X	
62			X	X			X	
	X		X				X	
61								
60					X		X	
				X				
59								
				X				
58								
Mean	64.1	66.7	62.8	65.6	62.8	65.4	62.6	64.5
Difference	2.6		2.8		2.6		1.9	
p	<.01		<.001		<.01		<.05	

Mean adult male stature in inches

Each "X" represents a society for which the mean adult male stature was available for at least 25 individuals. Significance levels are based on t tests.

Table 6. Mean annual rainfall

Mean adult male stature in inches (INFANT STRESS)	Equal or greater than 60 inches ABSENT	Equal or greater than 60 inches PRESENT	Less than 60 inches ABSENT	Less than 60 inches PRESENT
70				X
69				X
68				X
		XX		X
67		XX		X
			X	XXXX
66		X	X	XXX
				XXXXXX
65		X	X	X
			XXXX	XX
64	X	X	XX	XXX
		X	XXXX	
63	XXXX			X
	X	X	X	
62		X	XX	
	XX	X	X	
61				
60	XX			
	X			
59				
	X			
58				
Mean	61.6	64.9	63.9	65.9
Difference		3.3		2.0
p		<.001		<.001
Mean		63.2		65.0
Difference			1.8	
p			<.001	

Each "X" represents a society on which the mean adult male stature was available for at least 25 individuals. Significance levels are based on t tests.

upon stature in both sunny and rainy climates, particularly in the latter. Our findings therefore cannot reasonably be attributed to an effect of climate.

Controlling for the effect of diet upon stature was difficult since we could find no index of diet that, in our sample at least, correlated with adult stature. Although Marjorie Whiting (1958) in a cross-cultural study reported that both the caloric value and the percentage of protein in the average adult diet were positively correlated with adult male stature, these relations did not hold for our sample. An estimate of relative availability of protein based upon the staple crop (Whiting 1963) again showed no relation to adult stature. This failure to find a relation between diet and stature may be due to an inadequate estimate of diet. We think that it is also possible, however, that the relation between diet and growth is not as simple as it has sometimes been presumed. A review of the literature indicates that much of the evidence linking diet with stature is an inference from the frequently observed positive correlation between stature and socio-economic class (Tanner, 1962:137 ff.). Clearly, there are many consistent differences other than diet that distinguish the upper from the lower classes (perhaps, even including differences in stressful infant care practices). It may well be unwarranted to assume that the amount of calories or protein in the diet is the crucial factor.

A final alternative which we cannot at present adequately rule out is that these stressful infant care practices actually tend to kill infants who would otherwise grow up to be short. Much more elaborate data are required to deal with this problem adequately. However, we have seen no reports of deaths resulting from piercing or molding in our sources—the native theory in most cases regards the practices as beneficial to health and strength. Furthermore, the mortality of rats is decreased rather than increased by the analogous procedures (Levine 1962).

DISCUSSION

The dangers inherent in inferring causation from correlation have been well advertised and need not be belabored here. Certainly, we would be the last to claim that our data give conclusive evidence that infantile stress enhances growth. There are a large number of possible contaminating variables which might account for our findings and which we have not been able to investigate. To mention but a few, it is possible that parents who stress infants in the ways we have studied also rear them in some way which promotes growth, for example by providing them with better medical care, more sunshine, vitamins, etc., or have a

higher value on size which they implement by selective mating or in some other way. Conversely, it is possible that only societies which have strong, fast-growing children can afford the otherwise dangerous luxury of decorating them with scars and deformations. (This is related to the possibility, discussed above, that infant stress is itself a selective factor which spares primarily those who will grow tall.) Or, it may be that children stressed in infancy acquire a mediating characteristic which induces them to engage in some activity which in turn results in increased stature in the population. For example, men stressed in infancy might be more pugnacious with the result that only the large survive, or they might have an acquired sexual preference for large mates (perhaps produced by some Freudian mechanism involving the interaction of the stressor trauma, and the period of infantile sexuality in which it occurred.) None of these possibilities (or the many, many more which the fertile imagination can provide) can be ruled out a priori. This is the problem of correlational research.

However, evidence from the present study has two advantageous features, not ordinarily associated with correlational investigations, which make it somewhat more reasonable than usual to entertain the possibility of a causal relation. The first is that the extensive study of human growth has produced a very limited number of demonstrated correlates of stature and it has been possible, in the present study, to rule some of these out by statistical analysis. Second, and more importantly, the correlation observed in the present study for humans corresponds to an experimentally demonstrated effect in laboratory mammals, and the type of phenomenon—endocrine control of growth—is one in which interspecies generality is common. Therefore, it seems to us that the inference from our data of a causal relation between infant experience and human growth is sufficiently plausible to warrant serious consideration.

SUMMARY

In summary, we have reviewed some recent studies that have shown that rats and mice stimulated during an early period of life attain greater size at adulthood. We have indicated that there are plausible explanations for this effect involving changes in functioning of the adrenal-pituitary system. In exploring whether these results could be generalized to humans, we found that for two independent cross-cultural samples, in societies where the heads or limbs of infants were repeatedly molded or stretched, or where their ears, noses, or lips were pierced, where they were circumcized, vaccinated, innoculated, or had tribal marks cut or burned in their skin, the mean adult male stature was over two inches greater than in societies where these customs were not practiced. The effects of these practices appear to be independent of several other factors known to be associated with increased stature.

NOTES

[1] This paper in an abbreviated form was read at the American Anthropological Association meeting in November 1962 at Chicago. We thank J. Merrill Carlsmith, and Emily H. McFarlin for assistance in data collection.

[2] While we can speculate that the piercing and molding practices correlate with height while the others do not because they intuitively seem more severe and "stressful" than the others, there are really no solid grounds on which to judge what was and was not stressful for the infants involved in the study. Consequently, our interpretation of piercing and molding (laceration and deformation) as special cases of "stressful" treatment in general is open to some question, and must be regarded as tentative.

[3] In our search for these societies we were greatly aided by Dr. Edward E. Hunt, Jr. whose knowledge of the literature on world anthropometry was invaluable.

[4] We decided that since there has been so much controversy recently as to what constitutes a race, the regional division was a safer procedure. It should be noted that we counted only

aborigines of the new world. Yankees were classed with the Eurasians. If Coon's classification of races is used instead of the regional classification shown in Table 5, the effects of stress are significant at better than the .01 level for Caucasoids and Mongoloids, but, although the differences are in the same direction and of the same magnitude for the Australoids and Congoids, the number of societies representing these races was too small for the differences to reach statistical significance. Since there are only two Capoid societies in our sample and neither are stressed, no test is possible for this group.

REFERENCES CITED

Denenberg, V. and G. G. Karas
1959
Effects of differential infantile handling upon weight gain and mortality in rat and mouse. Science 130:629.

Goldfarb, W.
1943
The effects of early institutional care on adolescent personality. Journal of Experimental Education 12:106–129.
1949
Rorshach test differences between family-reared, institution-reared and schizophrenic children. American Journal of Orthopsychiatry 19:624–633.

Goode, J. Paul
1957
Goode's World Atlas. Tenth Edition. Rand McNally.

Greenman, M. J. and Dehring, F. L.
1931
Breeding and care of the albino rat for research purposes. Philadelphia, The Wister Institute of Anatomy and Biology. Second Edition.

Hammett, M. S.
1922
Studies of the thyroid apparatus. Endocrinology 4:221–229.

Levine, Seymour J.
1957
Infantile experience and resistance to physiological stress. Science 126:405.
1958
Noxious stimulation in infant and adult rats and

consumatory behavior. Journal of Comparative and Physiological Psychology 51:230.
1960
Stimulation in infancy. Scientific American
202:80–86.
1962
Psychophysiological effects of infantile stimulation. *In* Roots of behavior, E. L. Bliss, ed.
New York, Paul B. Hoeber.
Levine, Seymour J., J. A. Chevalier, and S. O.
Korchin
1956
The effects of early shock and handling in infancy on later avoidance learning. Journal of
Personality 24:475–493.
Levine, Seymour J. and G. W. Lewis
1959
The relative importance of experimenter contact
in an effect produced by extrastimulation in
infancy. Journal of Comparative and Physi-
ological Psychology 52:368–370.
Levy, D. M.
1934
Experiments on the sucking reflex and social be-
havior in dogs. American Journal of Or-
thopsychiatry 4:202–224.
McClelland, W. J.
1956
Differential handling and weight gain in the rat.
Canadian Journal of Psychology 10:19–22.
Reugamer, W. R. and F. T. Silverman
1956
Influence of gentling on physiology of the rat.
New York, Proceedings of the Society for
Experimental Biology 92:170–172.
Sheffé, H.
1959
The analysis of variance. New York, Wiley.
Spitz, Rene A.
1946
Hospitalism: a follow-up report. *In* Anna Freud
et al (eds.) Psychoanalytic study of the
child. New York, International University
Press 2:113–117.
Tanner, J. M.
1962
Growth at adolescence. Springfield, Ill., Charles
C Thomas, Second edition.
Weininger, O.
1956
The effects of early experience on behavior and
growth characteristics. Journal of Compara-
tive and Physiological Psychology 49:1–9.

Werboff, Jack and Joan Havlena
1963
Febrile convulsions in infant rats, and later be-
havior. Science 142:684–685.
Whiting, Marjorie G.
1958
A cross-cultural nutrition survey of 118 societies
representing the major cultural and geo-
graphic areas of the world. Unpublished
D.Sc. thesis, Harvard School of Public
Health.
Whiting, John W. M.
1963
Effects of climate upon certain cultural practices.
Unpublished manuscript.
Whiting, John W. M. and Irvin L. Child
1963
Child training and personality. Yale University
Press.

ETHNOGRAPHIC BIBLIOGRAPHY

AINU
Bachelor, John
1927
Ainu life and lore: echoes of a departing race.
Tokyo. Kyobunkkwan.
Koya, Y et al.
1937
Rassenkunde der Aino. Tokyo, Japanische Ge-
sellschaft zur Förderung der Wis-
senschaftlichen Forschengen.
Landor, Arnold H. S.
1893
Alone with the hairy Ainu: 3,800 miles on a
pack saddle in Yezo and a cruise to the
Kurile Islands. London, John Murray.
ANDAMANS
Man, Edward H.
1932
On the aboriginal inhabitants of the Andaman
Islands. London, The Royal Anthropol-
ogical Institute of Great Britain and Ire-
land.
Radcliffe-Brown, A. R.
1922
The Andaman Islanders: a study in social an-
thropology. Cambridge, England, Cam-
bridge University Press.
Temple, Richard C.
1903
The Andaman and Nicobar Islands. Census of
India, 1901 3:1–137. Calcutta, Office of the
Superintendent of Government Printing.

ARANDA

Basedow, Herbert

1925

The Australian aboriginal. Adelaide, F. W. Preece and Sons.

Campbell, T. D. and C. J. Hackett

1927

Adelaide University Field Anthropology: Central Australia No. 1. Introduction: descriptive and anthropometric observations. Transactions and Proceedings of the Royal Society of South Australia, 51:65–75.

Spencer, Walter B. and F. J. Gillen

1927

The Arunta: a study of a Stone Age people, London, Macmillan and Co., Ltd.

ARAUCANIANS

Hilger, M. Inez

1957

Araucanian child life and its cultural background. Smithsonian Miscellaneous Collections, Vol. 133. Washington, Smithsonian Institution.

Latcham, R. E.

1904

Notes on the physical characteristics of the Araucans. Journal of the Royal Anthropological Institute 34:170–180.

Titiev, Mischa

1951

Araucanian culture in transition. Occasional Contributions from the Museum of Anthropology of the University of Michigan, No. 16. Ann Arbor, University of Michigan Press.

ASHANTI

Rattray, R. S.

1923

Ashanti. Oxford, Clarendon Press.

1927

Religion and art in Ashanti. Oxford, Clarendon Press.

AYMARA

Rouma, Georges

1933

Quitchouas et Aymaras. Etude des populations autochtones des Andes Boliviennes. Bulletin Societe Royal Belge d'Anthropologie et de Prehistorie. Bruxelles, Vol. 48:30–296.

Tschopik, Harry, Jr.

1946

The Aymara. Bureau of American Ethnology Bulletin, No. 143, Vol. 2:501–573. Washington, Smithsonian Institution.

1951

The Aymara of Chucuito, Peru: 1. Magic. Anthropological Papers of the American Museum of Natural History, Vol. 44:133–308. New York.

AZANDE

Lagae, C. R.

1926

Les Azande ou Niam-Niam: L'organization Zande, croyances religieuses et magiquis, coutumes familiales. Bibliotheque-Congo, Vol. 18, Bruxelles, Vromant and Co.

Larken, P. M.

1926–7

An account of the Zande. Sudan Notes and Records, 9:1–55, 10:85–134. Khartoum, McCorquodale and Co., Ltd.

Seligman, Charles G. and Brenda Z. Seligman

1932

Pagan tribes of the Nilotic Sudan. London, George Routledge and Sons, Ltd.

BAMBARA

Dieterlen, Germaine

1951

Essai sur la religion Bambara. Paris, Presses Universitaires de France.

Montell, Charles

1924

Les Bambara du Segou et du Kaarta: etude historique, ethnographique et litteraire d'une peuplade du Soudan Française. Paris, Emile Larose.

Paques, Viviana

1954

Les Bambara. International African Institute, Ethnographic Survey of Africa, Western Africa, French Series, Part I. Paris, Presses Universitaires de France.

BHIL

Naik, T. B.

1956

The Bhils: a study. Delhi, Bharatiya Adimjati Sevak Sengh.

Risley, Herbert

1915

The people of India. (Second Edition) Calcutta-London, W. Crooke.

BONTOC

Jenks, Albert E.

1905

The Bontoc Igorot, Department of the Interior

Ethnological Publications, Vol. 1. Manila, Bureau of Public Printing.

BULGARIANS

Sanders, Irwin T.

1949

Balkan village. Lexington, University of Kentucky Press.

Vatev, S.

1904

Contribution a l'étude anthropologique des Bulgares. Bull. et Mem. Soc. Anthrop. de Paris, 437–458.

CARIB

Gillin, John

1936

The Barama River Caribs of British Guiana. Papers of the Peabody Museum of American Archaeology and Ethnology, Vol. 14, No. 2.

CHUKCHEE

Bogoraz-Tan, Vladimir G.

1904, 1907 and 1909

The Chukchee: Parts 1–3, Memoirs of the American Museum of Natural History, Vol. 11. Leiden, E. J. Brill, Ltd. New York, G. E. Stechert and Co.

Debets, G. F.

1949

Anthropological research on Kamchatka: a preliminary report. Kratdie Soobshcheniia, Instituta etnografii, Vol. 5:3–18. Moskova and Leningrad, Akademiia Nauk, S.S.S.R.

COMANCHE

Boas, F.

1895

Zur anthropologie der nordamerikanischen Indianer. Zeitschrift für Ethnologie 27:366–416.

Wallace, Ernest and E. Adamson Hoebel

1957

The Comanches: lords of the South Plains. Norman, University of Oklahoma Press.

COPPER ESKIMO

Jenness, Diamond

1922

The life of the Copper Eskimos. Report of the Canadian Arctic Expedition, 1913–1918, Vol. 12, Part a. Ottawa, F. A. Acland.

CUNA

Harris, R. G.

1926

The San Blas Indians. American Journal of Physical Anthropology, 9, 1.

Hrdlicka, Ales

1926

The Indians of Panama and their physical relation to the Mayas. American Journal of Physical Anthropology, 9:1.

Inglrdisd, Marvel Elya and Christinne H. Moran

1939

From the cradle to the grave: the story of the typical San Blas Indian maiden. Cristobal.

Stout, David B.

1947

San Blas Cuna acculturation: an introduction. Viking Fund Publication in Anthropology, No. 9. New York

Wafer, Lionel

1934

A new voyage and description of the isthmus of America. Oxford, The Hakluyt Society, Series 2, No. 73.

DUTCH

Coon, C. S.

1939

Races of Europe. New York, Macmillan and Co.

Keur, John Y. and Dorothy L. Keur

1955

The deeply rooted: a study of the Drents community in the Netherlands. Monographs of the American Ethnological Society, 25. Assen, Netherlands, at the Royal VanGorcum Ltd.

GANDA

Mair, Lucy P.

1934

An African people in the twentieth century. London, George Routledge and Sons.

Roscoe, Joghn

1911

The Baganda. London, Macmillan and Co.

GOND (HILL MARIA)

Grigson, Wilfred V.

1949

The Maria Gonds of Bastar. Introduction by J. H. Hutton. Reissued in 1949 (first published in 1938) with a supplement containing 80 pages of additional matter and 39 illustrations by the author and Verrier Elwin. London, Oxford University Press.

HADRAMAUT

Thomas, Bertram

1932

Anthropological observations in South Arabia. Journal of the Royal Anthropological Institute of Great Britain and Ireland 62:83–103.

HAUSA

Smith, Mary F.

1954

Baba of Karo: a woman of the Muslim Hausa. London, Faber and Faber Ltd.

Talbot, P. A. and H. Mulhall

1962

The physical anthropology of Southern Nigeria: a biometric study in statistical method. Occasional Publications of the Cambridge University Museum of Archaeology and Ethnology. Cambridge, The University Press.

HOPI

Hrdlicka, Ales

1935

The pueblos, with comparative data on the bulk of the tribes of the southwest and northern Mexico. American Journal of Physical Anthropology, 30:235–460.

Murdock, George P.

1934

The Hopi of Arizona. *In* Our primitive contemporaries, 324–358. New York, Macmillan Co.

Simmons, Leo W.

1942

Sun Chief: the autobiography of a Hopi Indian. Published for the Institute of Human Relations. New Haven, Yale University Press.

IBO

Forde, C. D. and G. I. Jones

1950

The Ibo and Ibibio speaking peoples of southeastern Nigeria. Ethnographic Survey of Africa, Western Africa, Part III. London, International African Institute.

Talbot, P. A. and H. Mulhall

1962

The physical anthropology of southern Nigeria: a biometric study in statistical method. Occasional Publications of the Cambridge University Museum of Archaeology and Ethnology. Cambridge, The University Press.

IRANIANS

Donaldson, Bess Allen

1938

The wild rue: a study of Muhammadam magic and folklore in Iran. London, Luzac and Co.

Field, Henry

1939

Contributions to the anthropology of Iran. Publications of the field Museum of Natural History, Anthropological Series, Vol. 29. Chicago.

Masse, Henri

1938

Croyances et coutumes Persanes. Paris, Librairie Orientale et Americaine.

JAVANESE

Geertz, Hildred

1961

The Javanese family a study of kinship and socialization. New York, The Free Press of Glencoe, Inc.

Kohlbrugge, J. H. F.

1901

Longeur et poids du corps chez les habitants de Java. L'Anthropologie, 12:277–282.

KAPAUKU

Bijlmer, H. J. T.

1939

Tapiro Pygmies and Pania Mountain Papuans. Results of the Anthropological Mimika Expedition in New Guinea 1935–1939. Nova Guinea. Vol. 3:113–184. Leiden.

Pospisil, Leopold

1958

Kapauku Papuans and their law. Yale University Publications in Anthropology, No. 54. New Haven, Yale University Press.

KAZAK

Field, Henry

1948

Contributions to the anthropology of the Soviet Union. Smithsonian Miscellaneous Collections, Vol. 110, No. 3:1–244. Washington, Smithsonian Institution.

Grodekov, N. I.

1889

Kirgizy i Karakirgizy Syr Dar'inskoi Oblasti. Vol. I, Juridical Life. Tashkent, The Typolithyography of S. I. Lakhtin.

KHASI

Guha, B. S.

1931

The racial affinities of the people of India. Census of India, Vol. I, Part III, Simla, Government of India Press.

Gurden, P. R. T.

1907

The Khasis. London, David Nutt.

1904

Note on the Khasis, Syntengs, and allied tribes inhabiting Khasi and Janital Hills district in Assam. Journal of the Asiatic Society of Bengal, Vol. 73, Part 3, No. 4:57–75.

KIKUYU

Briggs, L. Cabot
1958
The living races of the Sahara Desert. Papers of the Peabody Museum of Archaeology and Ethnology. Vol. 28, No. 2.

Kenyatta, Jomo
1953
Facing Mount Kenya: the tribal life of the Gikuyu. London, Secker and Warburg.

Routledge, W. S. and Katherine Routledge
1910
With a prehistoric people: the Akikuyu of British East Africa. London, Edward Arnold.

KLAMATH

Boaz, Franz
1895
Zun Anthropologie der nordamerikanischen Indianer. Zeitschrift für Ethnologie 28:391.

Spier, Leslie
1930
Klamath ethnography. University of California Publications in American Archaeology and Ethnology, Vol. 30. Berkeley, University of California Press.

KORYAK

Jochelson, Waldemar
1905–1908
The Koryak: Part 1, religion and myths of the Koryak. Part 2, Material culture and social organization of the Koryak. Jessup North Pacific Expedition Publication, Vol. 6 (American Museum of Natural History Memoirs, Vol. 10).

KUNG BUSHMEN

Bleek, D. F.
1928
Bushmen of Central Angola. Bantu Studies, Vol. III, No. 2.

Marshal, Lorna
1959
Marriage among the Kung Bushmen. Africa 29:335–364.

Thomas Elizabeth Marshall
1959
The harmless people. New York, Alfred A. Knopf.

KURD

Field, Henry

1961
Ancient and modern man in southwestern Asia: II. Coral Gables, Florida, University of Miami Press.

Masters, William M.
1953
Rowanduz: a Kurdish administrative and mercantile center. Unpublished Ph.D. thesis, University of Michigan.

KUWAIT ARABS

Dickson, H. R. P.
1951
The Arab of the desert: a glimpse into Badawin life in Kuwait and Saudi Arabia. London, George Allen and Unwin, Ltd.

Field, Henry
1961
Ancient and modern man in southwestern Asia: II. Coral Gables, Florida, University of Miami Press.

LAU

Hocart, Arthur M.
1929
Lau Islands, Fiji. Bernice P. Bishop Museum, Bulletin 62. Honolulu.

Thompson, Laura
1940
Fijian frontier. Studies of the Pacific, No. 4. San Francisco, Institute of Pacific Relations.
1940
Southern Lau Fiji: an ethnography. Bernice P. Bishop Museum Bulletin 162. Honolulu.

LEPCHA

Gorer, Geoffrey
1938
Himalayan village: an account of the Lepchas of Sikkim. London, Michael Joseph Ltd.

Morris, John
1938
Living with Lepchas: a book about the Sikkim Himalayas. London, William Heinemann, Ltd.

Risley, H. H.
1891
The tribes and castes of Bengal. Anthropometric Data, Vol. 1. Calcutta, Bengal Secretariat Press.

LESU

Powdermaker, Hortense
1933
Life in Lesu, the study of a Melanesian society in New Ireland. New York, W. W. Norton and Co., Inc.

Schlaginhaufin, O.
1914
Anthropometrische Untersuchungen an Einge-
borenen in Deutsch-Neuguinen. Abhandl.
und Besichte des Museums Dresden, 14.

MALAYS

Firth, Rosmary
1943
Housekeeping among Malay peasants. Mono-
graphs on Social Anthropology No. 7.
London, London School of Economics and
Political Science.

Heberer, G. and W. Lehmann
1950
Die Inland-Malaien von Lombok und Sum-
bawa. Gottingen, Muster-Schmidt.

Lehmann, W.
1934
Anthropologische Beobachtungen auf den
kleinen Sunda-Inseln. Zeitschrift für Ethnologie 66:268–276.

Wilkinson, R. J.
1920
Papers on Malay subjects. Life and customs,
Part I. The incidents of Malay Life. Singa-
pore, Kelly and Walsh.

MAORI

Buck, Peter (Te Rangi Hiroa).
1949
The coming of the Maori. Wellington, Maori
Purposes Fund Board, Whitcombe and
Tombs, Ltd.

Ritchie, Jane
1957
Childhood in Rakau: the first five years of life.
Victoria University Publications in Psychology, No. 10 (Monographs on Maori
Social Life and Personality, No. 3) Wellington, Victoria University College.

MARQUESANS

Handy, E. S. Craighill
1923
The native culture in the Marquesas. Bernice P.
Bishop Museum Bulletin No. 9. Honolulu.

Linton, Ralph
1939
Marquesan culture. In The individual and his society: the psychodynamics of primitive social organization, Abram Kardiner. New
York, Columbia University Press.

Sullivan, Louis R.
1923
Marquesan somotology with comparative notes

on Samoa and Tonga. Memoirs of the Bernice P. Bishop Museum, Vol. 9:139–249.
Honolulu.

MARSHALLESE

Kramer, Augustin and Hans Nevermann
1938
Ralik-Ratak. Ergebnisse der Südsee-Expedition
1908–1910, II. Ethnographie: Mikronesian,
Vol. II. Hamburg, Friederichsen, De
Gruyter and Co.

Wedgewood, Camilla H.
1942
Notes on the Marshall Islands. Oceania 13:1–23.

MOSQUITO

Conzemuis, Eduard
1932
Ethnographical survey of the Miskito and Sumu
Indians of Hondruas and Nicaragua. Smithsonian Institution.

Kirchoff, Paul
1948
The Caribbean lowland tribes: the Mosquito,
Sumo, Paya, and Jicaque. Smithsonian In-
stitution, Bureau of American Ethnology.
Bulletin No. 143, 4:219–229. Washington,
Smithsonian Institution.

Pijoan, Michel
1946
The health and customs of the Miskito Indians of
North Nicaragua: interrelationships in a
medical program. Mexico, Instituto In-
digenista Interamericano.

MOSSI

Mangin, Eugene
1921
Les Mossi, essai sur les us et coutumes du peuple
Mossi a Soudan occidental. Paris, Augustin
Challamel.

Tauxier, L.
1917
Le noir du Yatenga: Mossis, Niconicsses, Simos,
Yarses, Silmi, Mossis, Peuls, 225–273.
Paris, Emile Larose.

NAMA HOTTENTOTS

Schapera, Isaac
1930
The Khoisan peoples of South Africa: Bushmen
and Hottentots. London, George Routledge
and Sons.

Schultze, L.
1907
Aus Namaland und Kalahari. Jena, Gustav Fis-
cher.

1928
Zur Kenntnis des Körpers der Hottentotten und Buschmänner. Zoologische und anthropologische ergebnisse einer Forschungsreise im westlichen und zentralen Südfrika, 5:145–227.

NAVAHO
Kluckhohn, Clyde
1947
Some aspects of Navaho infancy and early childhood. Psychoanalysis and the Social Sciences 1:37–86. New York, International Universities Press.
Kluckhohn, Clyde and Dorothea Leighton
1946
The Navaho. Cambridge, Harvard University Press.
Leighton, Dorothea and Clyde Kluckhohn
1946
Children of the people. Cambridge, Harvard University Press.

OJIBWA (CHIPPEWA)
Densmore, Frances
1929
Chippewa customs. Bureau of American Ethnology, Bulletin No. 86. Washington, Government Printing Office.
Grant, J. C. B.
1930
Anthropometry of the Chipewyan and Cree Indians of the neighborhood of Lake Athabaska. Ottawa, National Museum of Canada, Bulletin No. 64, Anthropological Series No. 14.
Hilger, M. Inez
1951
Chippewa child life and its cultural background. Smithsonian Institution, Bureau of American Ethnology, Bulletin 146. Washington, Smithsonian Institution.

ORAONS
Ror, S. C.
1915
The Oraons. "Man in India" Office, Church Road Ranchi, India.

OROKAIVA
Reay, Marie
1953
Social control among the Orokaiva. Oceania 24:110–118.
Williams, Francis E.
1930
Orokaiva society. London, Oxford University Press.

PALESTINE ARABS
Field, Henry
1961
Ancient and modern man in southwestern Asia: II. Coral Gables, University of Miami Press.
Granquist, Hilma N.
1947
Birth and childhood among the Arabs: studies in Muhammadan village in Palestine. Helsingfors, Finland, Söderström and Co.

POLES
Benet, Sula
1951
Song, dance, and customs of peasant Poland. New York, Roy Publishers.
Coon, C. S.
1939
Races of Europe. New York, Macmillan Co.

RIFFIANS
Briggs, L. Cabot
1958
The living races of the Sahara desert. Papers of the Peabody Museum of Archaeology and Ethnology, 28, No. 2.
Coon C. S.
1901
Tribes of the Rif. Harvard African Studies, No. 9. Cambridge, Peabody Museum, Harvard University.
Westermarck, Edward
1926
Ritual and belief in Morocco. London, Macmillan and Co.

RWALA
Briggs, L. Cabot
1958
The living races of the Sahara Desert. Papers of the Peabody Museum of Archaeology and Ethnology. Vol. 28, No. 2.
Musil, Alois
1928
The manners and customs of the Rwala Bedouins. New York, The American Geographical Society, Oriental Explorations and Studies, No. 6.
Raswan, Carl R.
1947
Black tents of Arabia. New York, Creative Age Press.

SEMANG
Evans, Ivor H. N.
1937

The Negritos of Malaya. Cambridge, The University Press.

Schebesta, Paul
1927
Among the forest dwarfs of Malaya. London, Hutchinson and Co.

Skeat, W. W. and C. O. Blagden
1906
Pagan races of the Malay peninsula. New York, Macmillan and Co.

SERBS

Coon, Carleton S.
1949
Racial history. *In* Yugoslavia, Robert J. Kerner, ed. Berkeley, University of California Press.

Halpern, Joel M.
1956
Social and cultural change in a Serbian village. New Haven, Human Relations Area Files.

SHILLUK

Riad, Mohamed
1955
Some observations of a fieldtrip among the Shilluk. Wiener Völkerkundliche Mitteilungen, Vol. 3:70–78. Wien, Völkerkundliche Arbeitgemeinschaft in der Anthropologischen Gesellschaft in Wien.

Seligman, Charles G. and Brenda Z. Seligman
1932
Pagan tribes of the Nilotic Sudan. London, George Routledge and Sons, Ltd.

SOMALI

Briggs, L. Cabot
1958
The living races of the Sahara desert. Papers of the Peabody Museum of Archaeology and Ethnology, Vol. 28, No. 2.

Lewis, I. M.
1955
Peoples of the horn of Africa. Ethnographic Survey of Africa, North Eastern Africa, Part I, London, International African Institute.

Paulitschke, Phillip
1888
Beiträge zue Ethnographie und Anthropologie der Soma, Galla, und Harari. Leipzig, Eduard Baldamus.

TARASCANS

Beals, Ralph L.
1948
Cheran: a Sierra Tarascan village. Institute of Social Anthropology Publication No. 2. Washington, Smithsonian Institution.

Lasker, Gabriel W.
1953
Ethnic identification in an Indian Mestize community: II. Racial characteristics. Phylon 14:187–190.

TELUGU

Dube, S. C.
1955
Indian village. Ithaca, Cornell University Press.

Guha, B. S.
1931
The racial affinities of the people of India. Census of India, Vol. I, Part III. Simla, Government of India Press.

ZUNI

Parsons, Elsie Clews
1919
Mothers and children at Zuni, New Mexico. Man 19:168–173. (Article 86)

Stevenson, Matilda C.
1904
The Zuni Indians: their mythology, esoteric fraternities, and ceremonies. 23rd Annual Report of the Bureau of American Ethnology to the secretary of the Smithsonian Institution, 1901–02, 1–634. Washington, Government Printing Office.

In the social sciences, articles that report empirical research have a fairly standard organization. If you look at Landauer and Whiting's article, you will notice that it is divided into several sections and subsections. Sections are set off by headings in CAPITALS, and subsections are headed in *italics*. In a typical scientific report in the social sciences, there are four or five standard sections, and the author has some latitude for using subsections. Landauer and Whiting's article has the normal anatomy of four or five sections.

The first section of any article is generally called the INTRODUCTION. It is usually not labeled as such, since the first section is obviously the introduction; so it is with Landauer and Whiting. An introduction will tell you something about the general question being investigated. It first reports what previous researchers have found out about this question, then tells you what this particular study will try to find out, and usually ends with a formal statement of the hypothesis. Thus, the introduction puts the present study in a context of previous, related research.

The second section of a scientific study is usually called the METHOD section, and is so labeled. Landauer and Whiting call it METHODS AND MEASURES. This section gives specific, detailed information about how this particular study was conducted. The rule of thumb for *writing* this section (which you will not be doing) is to give the reader all the information he/she would need to repeat the study. Thus, in this section you will find information about who, exactly, the *subjects* (a common subheading) were, how the variables were operationalized, what *procedures* (a common subheading) were used to conduct the research, what *measures* (common subheading) were used to get the numbers that represent the variables, and what specialized equipment, if any, was employed.

The third section of a typical scientific article is call RESULTS, and offers a summarized report of the findings of the research. Sometimes only the findings relevant to the main hypothesis are reported in this section, but sometimes auxiliary data are reported here as well. In this section you will run across the technical language and notation of statistics, which are used to summarize and draw conclusions from data in the great majority of empirical articles in the social sciences.

The fourth section of a scientific article is usually labeled DISCUSSION (sometimes this section is combined with RESULTS). Here the implications of the results are stated and the author's conclusions appear. If the results supported the hypothesis, the author might note other hypotheses also supported by these data. If the results were a surprise, the author might offer possible explanations. In the discussion section the author evaluates those alternative explanations of the data which he/she considers plausible or at least worthy of mention.

Most articles in scientific journals include a SUMMARY (which appears at the end, labeled, or as a subsection of the discussion) or an ABSTRACT (which appears at the beginning, often in fine print, set off from the introduction). *This section, wherever it is, is the first thing to read in a scientific report* because it gives you an overview of the purpose of the research, its methods, its findings, and the author's conclusions. Often you can find the answers to several of the questions you want to answer without looking further than the ABSTRACT or SUMMARY. In Landauer and Whiting's article, a summary is found at the end.

The above is a brief view of the structure of scientific research reports; more detailed accounts are available elsewhere (e.g., American Psychological Association, 1974).

The *first question* to answer about scientific reports is: *What method was used* (from among the categories defined in Chapter 2) to collect the data? If you look first at the title, you can be pretty sure this study is correlational, because it is unlikely that the researchers manipulated either infantile stimulation or adult statute of human males. To be more certain, look at the SUMMARY. Here the authors report that they "found that for two independent cross-cultural samples. . . ." If cultures are being compared, the authors are studying infant stress as an organismic variable, and they are not manipulating it. The test of method in this case is in the way the independent variable is operationally defined. If it is defined by an experimental manipulation, you have an experiment; if it is defined by the measurement of something already there, the study is nonexperimental.

You can also identify the method used by looking in the METHOD section. The approach is the same, but it may take longer to find the answer. Once you see that the independent variable is operationalized in terms of cultural differences, you know the study is nonexperimental.

The *second question* to answer is: *What is the hypothesis,* if any? Is it causal or noncausal? The first place to look for the hypothesis is in the title of an article. The titles of scientific articles are noted for being dull but full of information. More often than not the hypothesis, and the major variables studied, are all packed into the title. Landauer and Whiting's title, "Infantile Stimulation and Adult Stature of Human Males," suggests, accurately, that the hypothesis concerns a relationship between infantile stimulation and adult stature. Titles will rarely lie when they are as dull as this. The title does not, however, tell us whether or not the hypothesized relationship is causal. Sometimes a title will talk about "the effect of" something, or "the influence of" something, and you can tell from this that the hypothesis is causal. In this study, we must read further to decide.

Look next at the abstract or summary. Landauer and Whiting's SUMMARY describes a relationship between early stimulation and adult size of rats and mice, and indicates that their study was done to explore "whether these results could be generalized to humans." This gives us the same information we found in the title. But the summary tells us more. In describing the studies of rats and mice, the authors refer to the greater size of stimulated animals as an "effect involving changes in the functioning of the adrenal-pituitary system." In size is an effect, the hypothesis must be of a *causal* relationship between stimulation and height. At the end of the SUMMARY, the authors confirm this by further discussing "the effects" of infantile stimulation practices in humans.

Careful reading of the title and summary allows us to identify the hypothesis: "Infant stress influences human growth." The hypothesis is causal.

We can also get this information from the article itself, although it will take more reading. In the first sentence of the article, the authors tell us that they are interested in "extraordinary stimulation of animals . . . during infancy" and its "profound and enduring physiological effects." Fine. But they must get more specific: which animals? what physiological effects? The authors cite "size attained at adulthood," in the second sentence, as relevant. This is the physiological effect. The title, and the fact that the article is in a journal called *American Anthropologist*, suggest that it is about people, not other animals, but it is only in the METHOD section that the authors state (second paragraph) they are interested in *human* growth. At this point, we can be sure that the study is about infant stimulation and human growth. The talk of physiological *effects* suggests that the hypothesis is causal, and this impression is reinforced in the method section, which begins by talking about "the effect of infant stress upon growth." Stress is the cause; growth the effect. The clincher is in the second paragraph of METHODS AND MEASURES, where height is discussed as a dependent variable. It is clear that the authors have more in mind than mere correlation; the hypothesis can be stated as "Infant stress influences human growth." Judging from the evidence with rats, we can suspect that Landauer and Whiting's hypothesis is, more specifically, "Infant stress *increases* human growth."

Third question: Identify the variables being studied. Then, if applicable, what is the independent variable? What is its operational definition? What is the dependent variable? What is its operational definition?

If you have the hypothesis stated clearly, you can identify the variables. They are, for Landauer and Whiting, infant stress and adult stature (independent and dependent variable, respectively).

Operational definitions take some digging, but they are invariably found in the METHOD section. We want to know, concretely, what was defined as (first of all) "infant stress." In Landauer and Whiting's article—and this is not at all uncommon—the operational definition is very long. The authors tell us that they had someone abstract information on infant care in 80 societies, and that they then identified eight practices they considered stressful, scored each society for the presence or absence of each stressful practice, and so on, at length. Most of the rest of the METHOD section is devoted to the operational definition of "infant stress." In the end, a simple statement of the operational definition of "infant stress" would be "piercing or breaking of the infant's skin and/or molding or stretching of part of the body (continuously for at least two weeks) during the first two years of life." More specifically, these stresses were rated as present or absent on the basis of reading the material in the Human Relations Area Files.

"Adult stature" turns out to be hard to operationalize when you can't go out and measure people. A search of the method section shows (last paragraph) that "adult stature" was finally defined as the average height of all of at least 25 individuals (males?) whose heights were reported in the Human Relations Area Files for the culture in question.

Generally, operational definitions are found in the METHOD section, many are long and involved, and you know you have found a complete operational definition when your search ends in a number to represent a variable, or else in a category system (e.g., piercing of the skin—present or absent).

Fourth question: Identify the findings. Findings always appear in the RESULTS section, although they are also summarized in the abstract or summary. Newcomers to research in the social sciences often have more trouble with this section than with any other part of scientific reports. Let me digress to give a brief guide to deciphering the statistics that typically appear in RESULTS sections.

In research in the social sciences, the phenomena are usually not so obvious that any one can tell at a glance what is happening. For this reason, statistics are used to get mathematical statements about the magnitude of the observed effects, and about the probability that these effects might have occurred by chance.

The most important thing to know about the use of statistics is the logic of statistical inference. Let's take Landauer and Whiting's research as an example. Suppose for a minute that child care practices have no effect at all on adult stature, and that height is really determined by variables like genetic stock, climate, diet, and so on. If this were true, and a sample of societies was divided in half according to whether or not infants are stressed, the average heights of the societies in the two groups would be distributed randomly. The average heights in the two groups of societies might be exactly the same, but it is more likely that there would be some (probably small) difference. Still, it could happen that in a particular sample, most of the tall societies would fall into the same group. The statisticians have calculated a number of different mathematical functions that tell exactly how likely it is that, by chance, a difference of a certain size would appear. For any difference that is observed, a researcher can perform the appropriate calculations and find out how likely it is that this difference would have occurred by chance. Landauer and Whiting report in Table 1 an average height difference of 2.49 inches between societies that do and don't use piercing and molding during the first 24 months of life. At the bottom of the table, they report "$t = 3.72$, $p < .002$." t is a statistic the authors calculated from their height data, for the purpose of determining the chances of observing a height difference as great as they found (2.49 inches) if the societies were in fact randomly divided and piercing and molding were unrelated to adult stature. "$p < .002$" signifies that the *probability* of observing such a large difference in the given sample of societies by chance is less than .002, or less than two in 1000. If it is very unlikely that the difference is due to chance, it is correspondingly more likely that it is due to child care practices (or at least to some variable related to child care practices).

This, in simple terms, is the logic of statistical inference. It is assumed that the variables under study are *not* related (this is called the "null hypothesis," and is generally what a researcher wants to be able to *reject* as a likelihood). If it can be shown statistically that what is observed is inconsistent with the null hypothesis, this is rejected in favor of the alternative, namely that the variables under study *are* related.

Researchers have many ways of telling you about whether their data confirm their hypotheses or not. The simplest way, and the one to look for first, is the value of "p" associated with the statistical test of a hypothesis. Usually, in the social sciences, if p is less than .05, the null hypothesis is considered unlikely enough to be rejected. Look for p values, and interpret them as follows:

If	Then the probability of the result occurring by chance is
$p = .02$	.02, or 2%
$p < .05$	less than .05; less than 5%
$p < .001$	less than .001; less than $1/10$ of 1%
$.01 < p < .025$	between 1% and 2½%
$p > .10$	greater than 10% (in this case, the null hypothesis cannot be rejected)

Sometimes you may see the notation "n.s." where you expect a value of p. This stands for "not significant," and means that p is too large to reject the null hypothesis.

In the text of a RESULTS section, there are many ways an investigator may tell you whether a hypothesis is confirmed. Read the texts, and translate words into p values as follows:

If the text says	It means
The results are statistically significant (or reliable) at the .01 level	$p < .01$
Alpha (α) was set at .05, and the result was significant	$p < .05$
The null hypothesis was rejected with 95% confidence	$p < .05$
The difference was statistically reliable at the .05 level	$p < .05$

All of the above mean that the null hypothesis was rejected, and that the variables (whose relationship is being tested) *are* related to each other. This should give you the idea.

Many of the different statistics used in research are ultimately converted into p values. Thus, if you have no background in statistics, you may do best to ignore the values of such statistics as t, F, r, chi-square (χ^2), W, rho, tau, U, T, and z, and look for p. By doing this, you are taking the author's word that the statistic is appropriate for the data. It is true that scientists do sometimes err in their choice of statistics, but this is not the place to give you the background you would need to draw your own conclusions about whether such an error has been made.

It is worth mentioning one of the limits to the usefulness of a p value. A low p implies that the null hypothesis can be rejected with strong (but not perfect) confidence. It implies that there is some nonzero relationship between the variables being compared. It does *not*, however, say anything about the *strength* of that relationship. We do not know from Landauer and Whiting's data whether piercing and molding increases adult stature by 2.49 inches, or by 0.03 inches, or by 7.21 inches. We only know that the effect is not zero.

There are some ways to judge the strength of a relationship from the results reported in a study. The simplest way is to look at the size of the sample that produced the reported p value. Common sense and statistics both tell you that the greater the effect of a variable, the easier it will be to prove that it exists. If infantile stimulation produces an average height increase of 0.12 inches, say, one would have to measure a huge number of people to establish with high probability that the increase is different from zero. If the effect is three inches, one will not have to measure nearly as many people to prove the difference is other than zero. In general, $p < .05$ can indicate a strong relationship if the number of individuals in the sample is less than, say, 50. With sample sizes in the hundreds, any respectable effect will yield a $p < .001$. As the sample size gets up toward the hundreds, the size difference observed in the samples begins to be a fairly good estimate of the difference in the population. The difference of 2.49 inches reported by Landauer and Whiting is not based on a large enough sample to conclude that infantile stimulation can change height by 2½ inches, even though the odds are 500 to 1 that there is *some* effect. In short, not every *statistically significant* relationship is a *strong* relationship.

The above is an admittedly oversimplified introduction to reading statistics, but it should serve to help you through the RESULTS sections of a great many articles in the social sciences. If you run into an article that uses language or statistics you still cannot understand (such as partial correlation, multiple regression, or factor analysis, to name some), you might look up the meaning of the language (in a text on research design or statistics), or ask an advanced student or a professor. Sometimes you may get by if you just try to read around the technical language; if you understand what the p values refer to, you have understood the most important single part of the RESULTS section.

Back to Landauer and Whiting's findings. The SUMMARY tells us that "in societies where the heads or limbs of infants were repeatedly molded or stretched . . . , the mean adult male stature was over two inches greater than in societies where these customs were not practiced." This is the major finding, and it confirms the hypothesis that infant stress and adult stature are related. The RESULTS section goes into much more detail, but presents the same major finding.

The SUMMARY also mentions that the relationship seems "independent of several other factors known to be associated with increased stature." This statement refers to some further findings reported in RESULTS. The authors found that the relationship held in each of four geographic regions and regardless of mean annual rainfall. These findings help support the authors' ultimate conclusions that it is infantile stress, rather than some correlated organismic variable, that is responsible for the increased height of males in some societies.

Fifth question: Identify an *extraneous variable that is controlled* by holding it constant. Identify an extraneous variable that is randomized (if there is one).

Controls for extraneous variables generally get first mention in the METHOD section. In experimental studies, look for carefully followed *procedures* during the manipulation of the independent variable. In all studies, look for care in the measurement of nonmanipulated variables. Landauer and Whiting take care, when they begin to measure stress, to get "a person who did not know the hypothesis" to abstract the information on infant care. Presumably, this holds constant any biases in selecting information from the files. Someone who knew the hypothesis might have abstracted differently for societies of tall men and for societies of short men. This possibility of bias is held constant. Landauer and Whiting also hold extraneous variables constant in other ways. Though they do not *match* societies beforehand, they do measure some extraneous variables in order to rule them out as alternative explanations. They have used a simple form of *statistical control* by comparing societies from the same geographical areas (presumably a measure of genetic similarity) and from areas of similar mean annual rainfall (presumably a measure of sunlight and of vitamin D intake). The hypothesis was retested by making separate comparisons of only those societies that were the same in terms of each variable being held constant.

It is also possible to hold extraneous variables constant by more advanced statistical methods, and Landauer and Whiting's study offers an example of how this could have been done. Suppose Landauer and Whiting had measured age at first stress (independent variable), adult stature (dependent variable), and mean annual rainfall (an extraneous variable). There would be three measures for each culture, with each measure related to the other two. If rainfall is closely related to both adult stature and infantile stress, the apparent relationship of the independent and dependent variable may only mean that people living in sunny climates tend to stress their infant boys (for some unknown reason). Stress may have no direct effect on stature. If rainfall is less strongly related to stress and stature, we can have more confidence that the relation of independent and dependent variable is a real one. When the three variables are all measured, the relationship of independent and dependent variable can be estimated with the extraneous variable's effect held constant statistically. A statistic used to do this is called a partial correlation, and the effect of the extraneous variable on independent and dependent variable is said to be "partialed out." The mathematics of partial correlations is beyond the scope of this chapter, but is presented elsewhere (e.g., Hays, 1963). The logic is the same as Landauer and Whiting used when they separated high-rainfall from low-rainfall societies, but since rainfall is measured, the partial correlation makes use of more of the available information about levels of sunlight.

In the Landauer and Whiting study, nothing was randomized. Randomization, by definition, can be used only in experimental research. In between-subjects experiments, organismic variables are randomized when subjects are randomly assigned to treatment groups. In correlational research, organismic variables are allowed to vary, but they are not controlled by randomization.

Sixth question: Identify any *extraneous variables* that suggest an alternative explanation of the observed results. State the alternative explanation(s) and suggest one way to control for each extraneous variable involved.

In a carefully written scientific report, the author will mention any important extraneous variables that were not controlled. It may have been impossible to obtain control, or the variable may have been overlooked until after the data were collected. In either case, interpretation of the results depends on the extent to which extraneous variables were controlled, and possible alternative explanations are generally discussed along with the results in the DISCUSSION section. (Occasionally, a writer may mention uncontrolled extraneous variables in the METHOD section, in the course of explaining the controls for other extraneous variables.)

Landauer and Whiting's article is an exception to the general rule about where discussion of uncontrolled extraneous variables is found. Some such variables are mentioned in the METHOD section (e.g., data obtained from different sources, at different times, and the problem of relating child care practices to the height of the previous generation), however, the most extensive discussion appears in the RESULTS section. In the subsection "Tests of Alternative Explanations," the authors discuss possible effects of genetic stock, climate, and diet (extraneous variables), and attempt to control for the first two (by comparing societies that are similar regarding each variable). There is a discussion of why diet was not controlled. At the end of the RESULTS section, the authors mention the possibility that infant stress may serve to kill off those individuals who would grow short, thus preventing them from reaching adulthood and being measured. This possibility cannot be directly ruled out by available data, and remains uncontrolled,

even though the authors give plausible reasons for discounting it. In the DISCUS-
SION section, Landauer and Whiting do what most scientists do: they try to draw
conclusions from their data—carefully, without extrapolating very far, and taking
into account possible alternative explanations. If you have understood their study
so far, you should be suitably impressed with the caution Landauer and Whiting
use in generalizing from their data.

IMPORTANT: Not all investigators are as thorough and cautious as Landauer and
Whiting. It is always worth your while to try to identify extraneous variables the
author has not thought of. To do this, refer to the discussion of extraneous variables in Chapter 3 (especially Tables 2, 3, and 6), and try to think of types of
variables that are likely to be left uncontrolled in the type of study you are reading. If you can think of a type of variable, try to come up with an example of that
type that leads to an alternative explanation of the results.

Use the same tables to suggest controls for the uncontrolled variables you find,
and then be specific about how you would use the method of control you suggest
in the particular study you are reviewing.

Seventh question: Identify the sample studied and the population from which it was
drawn. If you detect any sampling bias, identify it.

Information on the sample and the population sampled is almost always found
in the METHOD section and within the subsection "Subjects," if there is one. If the
METHOD section is not subdivided, the information usually comes very early in
the section. In Landauer and Whiting's article, there is a page of METHOD section
before the sampling procedure is revealed: "We first obtained data on 80 societies
about which appropriate information was readily available. . . ." By the end of
the METHOD section, they have narrowed the sample to those 36 of the 80 societies
for which the heights of at least 25 individuals have actually been measured. In
the RESULTS section, the authors mention that a second sample of 30 societies was
drawn. In all, the sample was 66 societies on which data were available in the
Human Relations Area Files, and for which the heights of at least 25 adults have
been measured. This sample was drawn from the population of societies indexed
in the Human Relations Area Files. It is not clear whether the sample is biased,
but it could be. For one thing, societies whose adults have been measured may be
an unrepresentative sample in ways we do not know. A more likely source of bias
exists if these 66 societies are not the only ones in the Area Files in which 25
adults have been measured. If the authors only looked at some societies to obtain
their sample, how did they choose? They do not mention any procedure to as-
sure randomness.

Landauer and Whiting appear to be generalizing beyond the population of
societies in the Human Relations Area Files to all human societies. This is obvious in the last sentence of the article, where they talk about "a causal relation be-

tween infant experience and human growth" without qualifying which humans they are talking about. Such a conclusion is justified only if the Human Relations Area Files cover a representative sample of all human societies. If not, generalization must be supported by data from other populations.

Eighth question: Identify any interactions being studied. As this is worded, you must look for the answer in the hypothesis or hypotheses of the research. If the hypothesis suggests that the effect of one variable depends on a second variable, and if this interrelationship of effects is being investigated, there are interactions being studied. If not, there are none being studied.

In Landauer and Whiting's article, the main hypothesis of an effect of infantile stress on adult stature did not suggest any interactions. The authors do, however, discuss one kind of interaction in the section under RESULTS called "Critical Period." They suggest that the effect of stress on children depends on the age of the children when stressed. Two variables, stress (present or absent) and age, interact to produce an effect on growth. Table 4 of the study presents data on this interaction. The findings are consistent with the idea that children stressed before age two grow taller than children stressed in similar ways after age two. Though this is not the main hypothesis of Landauer and Whiting's study, it is closely related to the main hypothesis, and it does concern an interaction of the effects of two variables.

With the information you have just read, and with the practice on Landauer and Whiting's article, you should be ready to try an article on your own. The scientific report entitled "On Being Sane in Insane Places," by D. L. Rosenhan, is the example for this chapter.

Rosenhan's article differs in some important ways from Landauer and Whiting's. First of all, it is not divided into INTRODUCTION, METHODS, RESULTS, and DISCUSSION, the way most scientific articles are. You will have to find the answers you want by reading through. Don't be too discouraged; even though the formal headings aren't what you expect, Rosenhan presents his material in the same logical order you expect from other scientific reports.

A second difference between Rosenhan's article and Landauer and Whiting's is that Rosenhan's article is clearly more than one piece of research (that is, different kinds of data were collected, in different ways, to test different hypotheses). For the purposes of this exercise, consider only the main study, the one in which pseudopatients were admitted to mental hospitals, and the hospital's response (diagnosis, treatment, length of stay, etc.) was observed. Omit the section called "The Experience of Psychiatric Hospitalization," which contains some interesting, but separate, data.

At the end of Rosenhan's article is a place for you to answer the questions about it. My answers follow.

ON BEING SANE IN INSANE PLACES

D. L. Rosenhan

If sanity and insanity exist, how shall we know them?

The question is neither capricious nor itself insane. However much we may be personally convinced that we can tell the normal from the abnormal, the evidence is simply not compelling. It is commonplace, for example, to read about murder trials wherein eminent psychiatrists for the defense are contradicted by equally eminent psychiatrists for the prosecution on the matter of the defendant's sanity. More generally, there are a great deal of conflicting data on the reliability, utility, and meaning of such terms as "sanity," "insanity," "mental illness," and "schizophrenia" (1). Finally, as early as 1934, Benedict suggested that normality and abnormality are not universal (2). What is viewed as normal in one culture may be seen as quite aberrant in another. Thus, notions of normality and abnormality may not be quite as accurate as people believe they are.

To raise questions regarding normality and abnormality is in no way to question the fact that some behaviors are deviant or odd. Murder is deviant. So, too, are hallucinations. Nor does raising such questions deny the existence of the personal anguish that is often associated with "mental illness." Anxiety and depression exist. Psychological suffering exists. But normality and abnormality, sanity and insanity, and the diagnoses that flow from them may be less substantive than many believe them to be.

At its heart, the question of whether the sane can be distinguished from the insane (and whether degrees of insanity can be distinguished from each other) is a simple matter: do the salient characteristics that lead to diagnoses reside in the patients themselves or in the environments and contexts in which observers find them? From Bleuler, through Kretchmer, through the formulators of the recently revised *Diagnostic and Statistical Manual* of the American Psychiatric Association, the belief has been strong that patients present symptoms, that those symptoms can be categorized, and, implicitly, that the sane are distinguishable from the insane. More recently, however, this belief has been questioned. Based in part on theoretical and anthropological considerations, but also on philosophical, legal, and therapeutic ones, the view has grown that psychological categorization of mental illness is useless at best and downright harmful, misleading, and pejorative at worst. Psychiatric diagnoses, in this view, are in the minds of the observers and are not valid summaries of characteristics displayed by the observed (3–5).

Gains can be made in deciding which of these is more nearly accurate by getting normal people (that is, people who do not have, and have never suffered, symptoms of serious psychiatric disorders) admitted to psychiatric hospitals and then determining whether they were discovered to be sane and, if so, how. If the sanity of such pseudopatients were always detected, there would be prima facie evidence that a sane individual can be distinguished from the in-

Reprinted with permission of *Science*, 1973, *179*, 250–259.

The author is professor of psychology and law at Stanford University, Stanford, California 94305. Portions of these data were presented to colloquiums of the psychology departments at the University of California at Berkeley and at Santa Barbara; University of Arizona, Tucson; and Harvard University, Cambridge, Massachusetts.

sane context in which he is found. Normality (and presumably abnormality) is distinct enough that it can be recognized wherever it occurs, for it is carried within the person. If, on the other hand, the sanity of the pseudopatients were never discovered, serious difficulties would arise for those who support traditional modes of psychiatric diagnosis. Given that the hospital staff was not incompetent, that the pseudopatient had been behaving as sanely as he had been outside of the hospital, and that it had never been previously suggested that he belonged in a psychiatric hospital, such an unlikely outcome would support the view that psychiatric diagnosis betrays little about the patient but much about the environment in which an observer finds him.

This article describes such an experiment. Eight sane people gained secret admission to 12 different hospitals (6). Their diagnostic experiences constitute the data of the first part of this article; the remainder is devoted to a description of their experiences in psychiatric institutions. Too few psychiatrists and psychologists, even those who have worked in such hospitals, know what the experience is like. They rarely talk about it with former patients, perhaps because they distrust information coming from the previously insane. Those who have worked in psychiatric hospitals are likely to have adapted so thoroughly to the settings that they are insensitive to the impact of that experience. And while there have been occasional reports of researchers who submitted themselves to psychiatric hospitalization (7), these researchers have commonly remained in the hospitals for short periods of time, often with the knowledge of the hospital staff. It is difficult to know the extent to which they were treated like patients or like research colleagues. Nevertheless, their reports about the inside of the psychiatric hospital have been valuable. This article extends those efforts.

PSEUDOPATIENTS AND THEIR SETTINGS

The eight pseudopatients were a varied group. One was a psychology graduate student in his 20's. The remaining seven were older and "established." Among them were three psychologists, a pediatrician, a psychiatrist, a painter, and a housewife. Three pseudopatients were women, five were men. All of them employed pseudonyms, lest their alleged diagnoses embarrass them later. Those who were in mental health professions alleged another occupation in order to avoid the special attentions that might be accorded by staff, as a matter of courtesy or caution, to ailing colleagues (8). With the exception of myself (I was the first pseudopatient and my presence was known to the hospital administrator and chief psychologist and, so far as I can tell, to them alone), the presence of pseudopatients and the nature of the research program was not known to the hospital staffs (9).

The settings were similarly varied. In order to generalize the findings, admission into a variety of hospitals was sought. The 12 hospitals in the sample were located in five different states on the East and West coasts. Some were old and shabby, some were quite new. Some were research-oriented, others not. Some had good staff-patient ratios, others were quite understaffed. Only one was a strictly private hospital. All of the others were supported by state or federal funds or, in one instance, by university funds.

After calling the hospital for an appointment, the pseudopatient arrived at the admissions office complaining that he had been hearing voices. Asked what the voices said, he replied that they were often unclear, but as far as he could tell they said "empty," "hollow," and "thud." The voices were unfamiliar and were of the same sex as the pseudopatient. The choice of these symptoms was occasioned by their apparent similiarity to existential symptoms. Such symptoms are alleged to arise from painful concerns about the perceived meaninglessness of one's life. It is as if the hallucinating person were saying, "My life is emtpy and hollow." The choice of these symptoms was also determined by the *absence* of a single report of existential psychoses in the literature.

Beyond alleging the symptoms and falsifying name, vocation, and employment, no further alterations of person, history, or circumstances were made. The significant events of the pseudopatient's life history were presented as they had actually occurred. Relationships with parents and siblings, with spouse and children, with people at work and in school, consistent with the aforementioned exceptions, were described as they were or had been. Frustrations and upsets were described along with joys and satisfactions. These facts are important to remember. If anything, they strongly biased the subsequent results in favor of detecting sanity, since none of their histories or current behaviors were seriously pathological in any way.

Immediately upon admission to the psychiatric ward, the pseudopatient ceased simulating *any* symptoms of abnormality. In some cases, there was a brief period of mild nervousness and anxiety, since none of the pseudopatients really believed that they would be admitted so easily. Indeed, their shared fear was that they would be immediately exposed as frauds and greatly embarrassed. Moreover, many of them had never visited a psychiatric ward; even those who had, nevertheless had some genuine fears about what might happen to them. Their nervousness, then, was quite appropriate to the novelty of the hospital setting, and it abated rapidly.

Apart from that short-lived nervousness, the pseudopatient behaved on the ward as he "normally" behaved. The pseudopatient spoke to patients and staff as he might ordinarily. Because there is uncommonly little to do on a psychiatric ward, he attempted to engage others in conversation. When asked by staff how he was feeling, he indicated that he was fine, that he no longer experienced symptoms. He responded to instructions from attendants, to calls for medication (which was not swallowed), and to dining-hall instructions. Beyond such activities as were available to him on the admissions ward, he spent his time writing down his observations about the ward, its patients, and the staff. Initially these notes were written "secretly," but as it soon became clear that no one much cared, they were subsequently written on standard tablets of paper in such public places as the dayroom. No secret was made of these activities.

The pseudopatient, very much as a true psychiatric patient, entered a hospital with no foreknowledge of when he would be discharged. Each was told that he would have to get out by his own devices, essentially by convincing the staff that he was sane. The psychological stresses associated with hospitalization were considerable, and all but one of the pseudopatients desired to be discharged almost immediately after being admitted. They were, therefore, motivated not only to behave sanely, but to be paragons of cooperation. That their behavior was in no way disruptive is confirmed by nursing reports, which have been obtained on most of the patients. These reports uniformly indicate that the patients were "friendly," "cooperative," and "exhibited no abnormal indictions."

THE NORMAL ARE NOT DETECTABLY SANE

Despite their public "show" of sanity, the pseudopatients were never detected. Admitted, except in one case, with a diagnosis of schizophrenia (10), each was discharged with a diagnosis of schizophrenia "in remission." The label "in remission" should in no way be dismissed as a formality, for at no time during any hospitalization had any question been raised about any pseudopatient's simulation. Nor are there any indications in the hospital records that the pseudopatient's status was suspect. Rather, the evidence is strong that, once labeled schizophrenic, the pseudopatient was stuck with that label. If the pseudopatient was to be discharged, he must naturally be "in remission"; but he was not sane, nor, in the institution's view, had he ever been sane.

The uniform failure to recognize sanity cannot be attributed to the quality of the hospitals, for, although there were considerable variations among them, several are considered excellent. Nor can it be alleged that there was simply not enough time to observe the pseudopatients. Length of hospitalization ranged from 7 to 52 days, with an average of 19 days. The pseudopatients were not, in fact, carefully observed, but this failure clearly speaks more to traditions within psychiatric hospitals than to lack of opportunity.

Finally, it cannot be said that the failure to recognize the pseudopatients' sanity was due to the fact that they were not behaving sanely. While there was clearly some tension present in all of them, their daily visitors could detect no serious behavioral consequences—nor, indeed, could other patients. It was quite common for the patients to "detect" the pseudopatients' sanity. During the first three hospitalizations, when accurate counts were kept, 35 of a total of 118 patients on the admissions ward voiced their suspicions, some vigorously. "You're not crazy. You're a journalist, or a professor [referring to the continual note-taking]. You're checking up on the hospital." While most of the patients were reassured by the pseudopatient's insistence that he had been sick before he came in but was fine now, some continued to believe that the pseudopatient was sane throughout his hospitalization (11). The fact that the pa-

tients often recognized normality when staff did not raises important questions.

Failure to detect sanity during the course of hospitalization may be due to the fact that physicians operate with a strong bias toward what statisticians call the type 2 error (5). This is to say that physicians are more inclined to call a healthy person sick (a false positive, type 2) than a sick person healthy (a false negative, type 1). The reasons for this are not hard to find: it is clearly more dangerous to misdiagnose illness than health. Better to err on the side of caution, to suspect illness even among the healthy.

But what holds for medicine does not hold equally well for psychiatry. Medical illnesses, while unfortunate, are not commonly pejorative. Psychiatric diagnoses, on the contrary, carry with them personal, legal, and social stigmas (12). It was therefore important to see whether the tendency toward diagnosing the sane insane could be reversed. The following experiment was arranged at a research and teaching hospital whose staff had heard these findings but doubted that such an error could occur in their hospital. The staff was informed that at some time during the following 3 months, one or more pseudopatients would attempt to be admitted into the psychiatric hospital. Each staff member was asked to rate each patient who presented himself at admissions or on the ward according to the likelihood that the patient was a pseudopatient. A 10-point scale was used, with a 1 and 2 reflecting high confidence that the patient was a pseudopatient.

Judgments were obtained on 193 patients who were admitted for psychiatric treatment. All staff who had had sustained contact with or primary responsibility for the patient—attendants, nurses, psychiatrists, physicians, and psychologists—were asked to make judgments. Forty-one patients were alleged, with high confidence, to be pseudopatients by at least one member of the staff. Twenty-three were considered suspect by at least one psychiatrist. Nineteen were suspected by one psychiatrist *and* one other staff member. Actually, no genuine pseudopatient (at least from my group) presented himself during this period.

The experiment is instructive. It indicates that the tendency to designate sane people as insane can be reversed when the stakes (in this case, prestige and diagnostic acumen) are high. But what can be said of the 19 people who were suspected of being "sane" by one psychiatrist and another staff member? Were these people truly "sane," or was it rather the case that in the course of avoiding the type 2 error the staff tended to make more errors of the first sort—calling the crazy "sane"? There is no way of knowing. But one thing is certain: any diagnostic process that lends itself so readily to massive errors of this sort cannot be a very reliable one.

THE STICKINESS OF PSYCHODIAGNOSTIC LABELS

Beyond the tendency to call the healthy sick—a tendency that accounts better for diagnostic behavior on admission than it does for such behavior after a lengthy period of exposure—the data speak to the massive role of labeling in psychiatric assessment. Having once been labeled schizophrenic, there is nothing the pseudopatient can do to overcome the tag. The tag profoundly colors others' perceptions of him and his behavior.

From one viewpoint, these data are hardly surprising, for it has long been known that elements are given meaning by the context in which they occur. Gestalt psychology made this point vigorously, and Asch (*13*) demonstrated that there are "central" personality traits (such as "warm" versus "cold") which are so powerful that they markedly color the meaning of other information in forming an impression of a given personality (*14*). "Insane," "schizophrenic," "manic-depressive," and "crazy" are probably among the most powerful of such central traits. Once a person is desig-

nated abnormal, all of his other behaviors and characteristics are colored by that label. Indeed, that label is so powerful that many of the pseudopatients' normal behaviors were overlooked entirely or profoundly misinterpreted. Some examples may clarify this issue.

Earlier I indicated that there were no changes in the pseudopatient's personal history and current status beyond those of name, employment, and, where necessary, vocation. Otherwise, a veridical description of personal history and circumstances was offered. Those circumstances were not psychotic. How were they made consonant with the diagnosis of psychosis? Or were those diagnoses modified in such a way as to bring them into accord with the circumstances of the pseudopatient's life, as described by him?

As far as I can determine, diagnoses were in no way affected by the relative health of the circumstances of a pseudopatient's life. Rather, the reverse occurred: the perception of his circumstances was shaped entirely by the diagnosis. A clear example of such translation is found in the case of a pseudopatient who had had a close relationship with his mother but was rather remote from his father during his early childhood. During adolescence and beyond, however, his father became a close friend, while his relationship with his mother cooled. His present relationship with his wife was characteristically close and warm. Apart from occasional angry exchanges, friction was minimal. The children had rarely been spanked. Surely there is nothing especially pathological about such a history. Indeed, many readers may see a similar pattern in their own experiences, with no markedly deleterious consequences. Observe, however, how such a history was translated in the psychopathological context, this from the case summary prepared after the patient was discharged.

This white 39-year-old male . . . manifests a long history of considerable ambivalence in close relationships, which begins in early childhood. A warm relationship with his mother cools during his adolescence. A distant relationship to his father is described as becoming very intense. Affective stability is absent. His attempts to control emotionality with his wife and children are punctuated by angry outbursts and, in the case of the children, spankings. And while he says that he has several good friends, one senses considerable ambivalence embedded in those relationships also. . . .

The facts of the case were unintentionally distorted by the staff to achieve consistency with a popular theory of the dynamics of a schizophrenic reaction (15). Nothing of an ambivalent nature had been described in relations with parents, spouse, or friends. To the extent that ambivalence could be inferred, it was probably not greater than is found in all human relationships. It is true the pseudopatient's relationships with his parents changed over time, but in the ordinary context that would hardly be remarkable—indeed, it might very well be expected. Clearly, the meaning ascribed to his verbalizations (that is, ambivalence, affective instability) was determined by the diagnosis: schizophrenia. An entirely different meaning would have been ascribed if it were known that the man was "normal."

All pseudopatients took extensive notes publicly. Under ordinary circumstances, such behavior would have raised questions in the minds of observers, as, in fact, it did among patients. Indeed, it seemed so certain that the notes would elicit suspicion that elaborate precautions were taken to remove them from the ward each day. But the precautions proved needless. The closest any staff member came to questioning these notes occurred when one pseudopatient asked his physician what kind of medication he was receiving and began to write down the response. "You needn't write it," he was told gently. "If you have trouble remembering, just ask me again."

If no questions were asked of the pseudo-patients, how was their writing interpreted? Nursing records for three patients indicate that the writing was seen as an aspect of their pathological behavior. "Patient engages in writing behavior" was the daily nursing comment on one of the pseudopatients who was never questioned about his writing. Given that the patient is in the hospital, he must be psychologically disturbed. And given that he is disturbed, continuous writing must be a behavioral manifestation of that disturbance, perhaps a subset of the compulsive behaviors that are sometimes correlated with schizophrenia.

One tacit characteristic of psychiatric diagnosis is that it locates the sources of aberration within the individual and only rarely within the complex of stimuli that surrounds him. Consequently, behaviors that are stimulated by the environment are commonly misattributed to the patient's disorder. For example, one kindly nurse found a pseudopatient pacing the long hospital corridors. "Nervous, Mr. X?" she asked. "No, bored," he said.

The notes kept by pseudopatients are full of patient behaviors that were misinterpreted by well-intentioned staff. Often enough, a patient would go "berserk" because he had, wittingly or unwittingly, been mistreated by, say, an attendant. A nurse coming upon the scene would rarely inquire even cursorily into the environmental stimuli of the patient's behavior. Rather, she assumed that his upset derived from his pathology, not from his present interactions with other staff members. Occasionally, the staff might assume that the patient's family (especially when they had recently visited) or other patients had stimulated the outburst. But never were the staff found to assume that one of themselves or the structure of the hospital had anything to do with a patient's behavior. One psychiatrist pointed to a group of patients who were sitting outside the cafeteria entrance half an hour before lunchtime. To a group of young residents he indicated that such behavior was characteristic of the oral-acquisitive nature of the syndrome. It seemed not to occur to him that there were very few things to anticipate in a psychiatric hospital besides eating.

A psychiatric label has a life and an influence of its own. Once the impression has been formed that the patient is schizophrenic, the expectation is that he will continue to be schizophrenic. When a sufficient amount of time has passed, during which the patient has done nothing bizarre, he is considered to be in remission and available for discharge. But the label endures beyond discharge, with the unconfirmed expectation that he will behave as a schizophrenic again. Such labels, conferred by mental health professionals, are as influential on the patient as they are on his relatives and friends, and it should not surprise anyone that the diagnosis acts on all of them as a self-fulfilling prophecy. Eventually, the patient himself accepts the diagnosis, with all of its surplus meanings and expectations, and behaves accordingly (5).

The inferences to be made from these matters are quite simple. Much as Zigler and Phillips have demonstrated that there is enormous overlap in the symptoms presented by patients who have been variously diagnosed (16), so there is enormous overlap in the behaviors of the sane and the insane. The sane are not "sane" all of the time. We lose our tempers "for no good reason." We are occasionally depressed or anxious, again for no good reason. And we may find it difficult to get along with one or another person—again for no reason that we can specify. Similarly, the insane are not always insane. Indeed, it was the impression of the pseudopatients while living with them that they are sane for long periods of time—that the bizarre behaviors upon which their diagnoses were allegedly predicated constituted only a small fraction of their total behavior. If it makes no sense to label ourselves permanently depressed on the basis of an occasional depression, then it takes better evidence than is presently available to label all patients insane or schizophrenic on the basis of bizarre behaviors or cognitions. It seems more useful, as Mischel (17) has pointed out, to limit our discussions to *behaviors*, the stimuli that provoke them, and their correlates.

It is not known why powerful impressions of personality traits, such as "crazy" or "insane," arise. Conceivably, when the origins of and stimuli that give rise to a behavior are remote or unknown, or when the behavior strikes us as immutable, trait labels regarding the *behaver* arise. When, on the other hand, the origins and stimuli are known and available, discourse is limited to the behavior itself. Thus, I may hallucinate because I am sleeping, or I may hallucinate because I have ingested a peculiar drug. These are termed sleep-induced hallucinations, or dreams, and drug-induced hallucinations, respectively. But when the stimuli to my hallucinations are unknown, that is called craziness, or schizophrenia—as if that inference were somehow as illuminating as the others.

THE EXPERIENCE OF PSYCHIATRIC HOSPITALIZATION

The term "mental illness" is of recent origin. It was coined by people who were humane in their inclinations and who wanted very much to raise the station of (and the public's sympathies toward) the psychologically disturbed from that of witches and "crazies" to one that was akin to the physically ill. And they were at least partially successful, for the treatment of the mentally ill *has* improved considerably over the years. But while treatment has improved, it is doubtful that people really regard the mentally ill in the same way that they view the physically ill. A broken leg is something one recovers from, but mental illness allegedly endures forever (18). A broken leg does not threaten the observer, but a crazy schizophrenic? There is by now a host of evidence that attitudes toward the mentally ill are characterized by fear, hostility, aloofness, suspicion, and dread (*19*). The mentally ill are society's lepers.

That such attitudes infect the general population is perhaps not surprising, only upsetting. But that they affect the professionals—attendants, nurses, physicians, psychologists, and social workers—who treat and deal with the mentally ill is more disconcerting, both because such attitudes are self-evidently pernicious and because they are unwitting. Most mental health professionals would insist that they are sympathetic toward the mentally ill, that they are neither avoidant nor hostile. But it is more likely that an exquisite ambivalence characterizes their relations with psychiatric patients, such that their avowed impulses are only part of their entire attitude. Negative attitudes are there too and can easily be detected. Such attitudes should not surprise us. They are the natural offspring of the labels patients wear and the places in which they are found.

Consider the structure of the typical psychiatric hospital. Staff and patients are strictly segregated. Staff have their own living space, including their dining facilities, bathrooms, and assembly places. The glassed quarters that contain the professional staff, which the pseudopatients came to call "the cage," sit out on every dayroom. The staff emerge primarily for caretaking purposes—to give medication, to conduct a therapy or group meeting, to instruct or reprimand a patient. Otherwise, staff keep to themselves, almost as if the disorder that afflicts their charges is somehow catching.

So much is patient-staff segregation the rule that, for four public hospitals in which an attempt was made to measure the degree to which staff and patients mingle, it was necessary to use "time out of the staff cage" as the operational measure. While it was not the case that all time spent out of the

cage was spent mingling with patients (attendants, for example, would occasionally emerge to watch television in the dayroom), it was the only way in which one could gather reliable data on time for measuring.

The average amount of time spent by attendants outside of the cage was 11.3 percent (range, 3 to 52 percent). This figure does not represent only time spent mingling with patients, but also includes time spent on such chores as folding laundry, supervising patients while they shave, directing ward cleanup, and sending patients to off-ward activities. It was the relatively rare attendant who spent time talking with patients or playing games with them. It proved impossible to obtain a "percent mingling time" for nurses, since the amount of time they spent out of the cage was too brief. Rather, we counted instances of emergence from the cage. On the average, daytime nurses emerged from the cage 11.5 times per shift, including instances when they left the ward entirely (range, 4 to 39 times). Late afternoon and night nurses were even less available, emerging on the average 9.4 times per shift (range, 4 to 41 times). Data on early morning nurses, who arrived usually after midnight and departed at 8 a.m., are not available because patients were asleep during most of this period.

Physicians, especially psychiatrists, were even less available. They were rarely seen on the wards. Quite commonly, they would be seen only when they arrived and departed, with the remaining time being spent in their offices or in the cage. On the average, physicians emerged on the ward 6.7 times per day (range, 1 to 17 times). It proved difficult to make an accurate estimate in this regard, since physicians often maintained hours that allowed them to come and go at different times.

The hierarchical organization of the psychiatric hospital has been commented on before (*20*), but the latent meaning of that kind of organization is worth noting again.

Those with the most power have least to do with patients, and those with the least power are most involved with them. Recall, however, that the acquisition of role-appropriate behaviors occurs mainly through the observation of others, with the most powerful having the most influence. Consequently, it is understandable that attendants not only spend more time with patients than do any other members of the staff—that is required by their station in the hierarchy—but also, insofar as they learn from their superiors' behavior, spend as little time with patients as they can. Attendants are seen mainly in the cage, which is where the models, the action, and the power are.

I turn now to a different set of studies, these dealing with staff response to patient-initiated contact. It has long been known that the amount of time a person spends with you can be an index of your significance to him. If he initiates and maintains eye contact, there is reason to believe that he is considering your requests and needs. If he pauses to chat or actually stops and talks, there is added reason to infer that he is individuating you. In four hospitals, the pseudopatient approached the staff member with a request which took the following form: "Pardon me, Mr. [or Dr. or Mrs.] X, could you tell me when I will be eligible for grounds privileges?" (or ". . . when I will be presented at the staff meeting?" or ". . . when I am likely to be discharged?"). While the content of the question varied according to the appropriateness of the target and the pseudopatient's (apparent) current needs the form was always a courteous and relevant request for information. Care was taken never to approach a particular member of the staff more than once a day, lest the staff member became suspicious or irritated. In examining these data, remember that the behavior of the pseudopatients was neither bizarre nor disruptive. One could indeed engage in good conversation with them.

The data for these experiments are shown in Table 1, separately for physicians (column 1) and for nurses and attendants (column 2). Minor differences between these four institutions were overwhelmed by the degree to which staff avoided continuing contacts that patients had initiated. By far, their most common response consisted of either a brief response to the question, offered while they were "on the move" and with head averted, or no response at all.

The encounter frequently took the following bizarre form: (pseudopatient) "Pardon me, Dr. X. Could you tell me when I am eligible for grounds privileges?" (physician) "Good morning, Dave. How are you today?" (Moves off without waiting for a response.)

It is instructive to compare these data with data recently obtained at Stanford University. It has been alleged that large and eminent universities are characterized by faculty who are so busy that they have no time for students. For this comparison, a young lady approached individual faculty members who seemed to be walking purposefully to some meeting or teaching engagement and asked them the following six questions.

1) "Pardon me, could you direct me to Encina Hall?" (at the medical school: ". . . to the Clinical Research Center?").
2) "Do you know where Fish Annex is?" (there is no Fish Annex at Stanford).
3) "Do you teach here?"
4) "How does one apply for admission to the college?" (at the medical school: ". . . to the medical school?").
5) "Is it difficult to get in?"
6) "Is there financial aid?"
Without exception as can be seen in Table 1 (column 3), all of the questions were answered. No matter how rushed they were, all respondents not only maintained eye contact, but stopped to talk. Indeed, many of the respondents went out of their way to direct or take the questioner to

Table 1. Self-initiated contact by pseudopatients with psychiatrists and nurses and attendants, compared to contact with other groups

Contact	Psychiatric hospitals		University campus (nonmedical)	University medical center Physicians		
	(1) PSYCHI-ATRISTS	(2) NURSES AND ATTENDANTS	(3) FACULTY	(4) "LOOKING FOR A PSYCHIATRIST"	(5) "LOOKING FOR AN INTERNIST"	(6) NO ADDITIONAL COMMENT
Responses						
Moves on, head averted (%)	71	88	0	0	0	0
Makes eye contact (%)	23	10	0	11	0	0
Pauses and chats (%)	2	2	0	11	0	10
Stops and talks (%)	4	0.5	100	78	100	90
Mean number of questions answered (out of 6)	*	*	6	3.8	4.8	4.5
Respondents (No.)	13	47	14	18	15	10
Attempts (No.)	185	1283	14	18	15	10

*Not applicable.

the office she was seeking, to try to locate "Fish Annex," or to discuss with her the possibilities of being admitted to the university.

Similar data, also shown in Table 1 (columns 4, 5, and 6), were obtained in the hospital. Here too, the young lady came prepared with six questions. After the first question, however, she remarked to 18 of her respondents (column 4), "I'm looking for a psychiatrist," and to 15 others (column 5), "I'm looking for an internist." Ten other respondents received no inserted comment (column 6). The general degree of cooperative responses is considerably higher for these university groups than it was for pseudopatients in psychiatric hospitals. Even so, differences are apparent within the medical school setting. Once having indicated that she was looking for a psychiatrist, the degree of cooperation elicited was less than when she sought an internist.

POWERLESSNESS AND DEPERSONALIZATION

Eye contact and verbal contact reflect concern and individuation; their absence, avoidance and depersonalization. The data I have presented do not do justice to the rich daily encounters that grew up around matters of depersonalization and avoidance. I have records of patients who were beaten by staff for the sin of having initiated verbal contact. During my own experience, for example, one patient was beaten in the presence of other patients for having approached an attendant and told him, "I like you." Occasionally, punishment meted out to patients for misdemeanors seemed so excessive that it could not be justified by the most radical interpretations of psychiatric canon. Nevertheless, they appeared to go unquestioned. Tempers were often short. A patient who had not heard a call for medication would be roundly excoriated, and the morning attendants would often wake patients with. "Come on, you m-----f-----s, out of bed!"

Neither anecdotal nor "hard" data can convey the overwhelming sense of powerlessness which invades the individual as he is continually exposed to the depersonalization of the psychiatric hospital. It hardly matters *which* psychiatric hospital—the excellent public ones and the very plush private hospital were better than the rural and shabby ones in this regard, but, again, the features that psychiatric hospitals had in common overwhelmed by far their apparent differences.

Powerlessness was evident everywhere. The patient is deprived of many of his legal rights by dint of his psychiatric commitment (21). He is shorn of credibility by virtue of his psychiatric label. His freedom of movement is restricted. He cannot initiate contact with the staff, but may only respond to such overtures as they make. Personal privacy is minimal. Patient quarters and possessions can be entered and examined by any staff member, for whatever reason. His personal history and anguish is available to any staff member (often including the "grey lady" and "candy striper" volunteer) who chooses to read his folder, regardless of their therapeutic relationship to him. His personal hygiene and waste evacuation are often monitored. The water closets may have no doors.

At times, depersonalization reached such proportions that pseudopatients had the sense that they were invisible, or at least unworthy of account. Upon being admitted, I and other pseudopatients took the initial physical examinations in a semipublic room, where staff members went about their own business as if we were not there. On the ward, attendants delivered verbal

and occasionally serious physical abuse to patients in the presence of other observing patients, some of whom (the pseudopatients) were writing it all down. Abusive behavior, on the other hand, terminated quite abruptly when other staff members were known to be coming. Staff are credible witnesses. Patients are not.

A nurse unbuttoned her uniform to adjust her brassiere in the presence of an entire ward of viewing men. One did not have the sense that she was being seductive. Rather, she didn't notice us. A group of staff persons might point to a patient in the dayroom and discuss him animatedly, as if he were not there.

One illuminating instance of depersonalization and invisibility occurred with regard to medications. All told, the pseudopatients were administered nearly 2100 pills, including Elavil, Stelazine, Compazine, and Thorazine, to name but a few. (That such a variety of medications should have been administered to patients presenting identical symptoms is itself worthy of note.) Only two were swallowed. The rest were either pocketed or deposited in the toilet. The pseudopatients were not alone in this. Although I have no precise records on how many patients rejected their medications, the pseudopatients frequently found the medications of other patients in the toilet before they deposited their own. As long as they were cooperative, their behavior and the pseudopatients' own in this matter, as in other important matters, went unnoticed throughout.

Reactions to such depersonalization among pseudopatients were intense. Although they had come to the hospital as participant observers and were fully aware that they did not "belong," they nevertheless found themselves caught up in and fighting the process of depersonalization. Some examples: a graduate student in psychology asked his wife to bring his textbooks to the hospital so he could "catch up on his homework"—this despite the elaborate precautions taken to conceal his professional association. The same student, who had trained for quite some time to get into the hospital, and who had looked forward to the experience, "remembered" some drag races that he had wanted to see on the weekend and insisted that he be discharged by that time. Another pseudopatient attempted a romance with a nurse. Subsequently, he informed the staff that he was applying for admission to graduate school in psychology and was very likely to be admitted, since a graduate professor was one of his regular hospital visitors. The same person began to engage in psychotheapy with other patients—all of this as a way of becoming a person in an impersonal environment.

THE SOURCES OF DEPERSONALIZATION

What are the origins of depersonalization? I have already mentioned two. First are attitudes held by all of us toward the mentally ill—including those who treat them—attitudes characterized by fear, distrust, and horrible expectations on the one hand, and benevolent intentions on the other. Our ambivalence leads, in this instance as in others, to avoidance.

Second, and not entirely separate, the hierarchical structure of the psychiatric hospital facilitates depersonalization. Those who are at the top have least to do with patients, and their behavior inspires the rest of the staff. Average daily contact with psychiatrists, psychologists, residents, and physicians combined ranged from 3.9 to 25.1 minutes, with an overall mean of 6.8 (six pseudopatients over a total of 129 days of hospitalization). Included in this average are time spent in the admissions interview, ward meetings in the presence of a senior staff member, group and individual psychotherapy contacts, case presentation conferences, and discharge meetings. Clearly, patients do not spend much time in inter-

personal contact with doctoral staff. And doctoral staff serve as models for nurses and attendants.

There are probably other sources. Psychiatric installations are presently in serious financial straits. Staff shortages are pervasive, staff time at a premium. Something has to give, and that something is patient contact. Yet, while financial stresses are realities, too much can be made of them. I have the impression that the psychological forces that result in depersonalization are much stronger than the fiscal ones and that the addition of more staff would not correspondingly improve patient care in this regard. The incidence of staff meetings and the enormous amount of record-keeping on patients, for example, have not been as substantially reduced as has patient contact. Priorities exist, even during hard times. Patient contact is not a significant priority in the traditional psychiatric hospital, and fiscal pressures do not account for this. Avoidance and depersonalization may.

Heavy reliance upon psychotropic medication tacitly contributes to depersonalization by convincing staff that treatment is indeed being conducted and that further patient contact may not be necessary. Even here, however, caution needs to be exercised in understanding the role of psychotropic drugs. If patients were powerful rather than powerless, if they were viewed as interesting individuals rather than diagnostic entities, if they were socially significant rather than social lepers, if their anguish truly and wholly compelled our sympathies and concerns, would we not *seek* contact with them, despite the availability of medications? Perhaps for the pleasure of it all?

THE CONSEQUENCES OF LABELING AND DEPERSONALIZATION

Whenever the ratio of what is known to what needs to be known approaches zero, we tend to invent "knowledge" and assume that we understand more than we actually do. We seem unable to acknowledge that we simply don't know. The needs for diagnosis and remediation of behavioral and emotional problems are enormous. But rather than acknowledge that we are just embarking on understanding, we continue to label patients "schizophrenic," "manic-depressive," and "insane," as if in those words we had captured the essence of understanding. The facts of the matter are that we have known for a long time that diagnoses are often not useful or reliable, but we have nevertheless continued to use them. We now know that we cannot distinguish insanity from sanity. It is depressing to consider how that information will be used.

Not merely depressing, but frightening. How many people, one wonders, are sane but not recognized as such in our psychiatric institutions? How many have been needlessly stripped of their privileges of citizenship, from the right to vote and drive to that of handling their own accounts? How many have feigned insanity in order to avoid the criminal consequences of their behavior, and, conversely, how many would rather stand trial than live interminably in a psychiatric hospital—but are wrongly thought to be mentally ill? How many have been stigmatized by well-intentioned, but nevertheless erroneous, diagnoses? On the last point, recall again that a "type 2 error" in psychiatric diagnosis does not have the same consequences it does in medical diagnosis. A diagnosis of cancer that has been found to be in error is cause for celebration. But psychiatric diagnoses are rarely found to be in error. The label sticks, a mark of inadequacy forever.

Finally, how many patients might be "sane" outside the psychiatric hospital but seem insane in it—not because craziness resides in them, as it were, but because they are responding to a bizarre setting, one that may be unique to institutions which harbor nether people? Goffman (4) calls the process of socialization to such institutions "mortification"—an apt metaphor that includes the processes of depersonalization that have been described here. And while it is impossible to know whether the pseudopatients' responses to these processes are characteristic of all inmates—they were, after all, not real patients—it is difficult to believe that these processes of socialization to a psychiatric hospital provide useful attitudes or habits of response for living in the "real world."

SUMMARY AND CONCLUSIONS

It is clear that we cannot distinguish the sane from the insane in psychiatric hospitals. The hospital itself imposes a special environment in which the meanings of behavior can easily be misunderstood. The consequences to patients hospitalized in such an environment—the powerlessness, depersonalization, segregation, mortification, and self-labeling—seem undoubtedly countertherapeutic.

I do not, even now, understand this problem well enough to perceive solutions. But two matters seem to have some promise. The first concerns the proliferation of community mental health facilities, of crisis intervention centers, of the human potential movement, and of behavior therapies that, for all of their own problems, tend to avoid psychiatric labels, to focus on specific problems and behaviors, and to retain the individual in a relatively nonpejorative environment. Clearly, to the extent that we refrain from sending the distressed to insane places, our impressions of them are less likely to be distorted. (The risk of distorted perceptions, it seems to me, is always present, since we are much more sensitive to an individual's behaviors and verbalizations than we are to the subtle contextual stimuli that often promote them. At issue here is a matter of magnitude. And, as I have shown, the magnitude of distortion is exceedingly high in the extreme context that is a psychiatric hospital.)

The second matter that might prove promising speaks to the need to increase the sensitivity of mental health workers and researchers to the *Catch 22* position of psychiatric patients. Simply reading materials in this area will be of help to some such workers and researchers. For others, directly experiencing the impact of psychiatric hospitalization will be of enormous use. Clearly, further research into the social psychology of such total institutions will both facilitate treatment and deepen understanding.

I and the other pseudopatients in the psychiatric setting had distinctly negative reactions. We do not pretend to describe the subjective experiences of true patients. Theirs may be different from ours, particularly with the passage of time and the necessary process of adaptation to one's environment. But we can and do speak to the relatively more objective indices of treatment within the hospital. It could be a mistake, and a very unfortunate one, to consider that what happened to us derived from malice or stupidity on the part of the staff. Quite the contrary, our overwhelming impression of them was of people who really cared, who were committed and who were uncommonly intelligent. Where they failed, as they sometimes did painfully, it would be more accurate to attribute those failures to the environment in which they, too, found themselves than to personal callousness. Their perceptions and behavior were controlled by the situation, rather than being motivated by a malicious disposition. In a more benign environment, one that was less attached to global diagnosis, their behaviors and judgments might have been more benign and effective.

References and Notes

[1] P. Ash, *J. Abnorm. Soc. Psychol.* 44, 272 (1949); A. T. Beck, *Amer. J. Psychiat.* 119, 210 (1962); A. T. Boisen, *Psychiatry* 2, 233 (1938); N. Kreitman, *J. Ment. Sci.* 107, 876 (1961); N. Kreitman, P. Sainsbury, J. Morrisey, J. Towers, J. Scrivener, *ibid.*, p. 887; H. O. Schmitt and C. P. Fonda, *J. Abnorm. Soc. Psychol.* 52, 262 (1956); W. Seeman, *J. Nerv. Ment. Dis.* 118, 541 (1953). For an analysis of these artifacts and summaries of the disputes, see J. Zubin, *Annu. Rev. Psychol.* 18, 373 (1967); L. Phillips and J. G. Draguns, *ibid.* 22, 447 (1971).

[2] R. Benedict, *J. Gen. Psychol.* 10, 59 (1934).

[3] See in this regard H. Becker, *Outsiders: Studies in the Sociology of Deviance* (Free Press, New York, 1963); B. M. Braginsky, D. D. Braginsky, K. Ring, *Methods of Madness: The Mental Hospital as a Last Resort* (Holt, Rinehart & Winston, New York, 1969); G. M. Crocetti and P. V. Lemkau, *Amer. Social. Rev.* 30, 577 (1965); E. Goffman, *Behavior in Public Places* (Free Press, New York, 1964); R. D. Laing, *The Divided Self: A Study of Sanity and Madness* (Quadrangle, Chicago, 1960); D. L. Phillips, *Amer. Sociol. Rev.* 28, 963 (1963); T. R. Sarbin, *Psychol. Today* 6, 18 (1972); E. Schur, *Amer. J. Sociol.* 75, 309 (1969); T. Szasz, *Law, Liberty and Psychiatry* (Macmillan, New York, 1963); *The Myth of Mental Illness: Foundations of a Theory of Mental Illness* (Hoeber-Harper, New York, 1963). For a critique of some of these views, see W. R. Gove, *Amer. Sociol. Rev.* 35, 873 (1970).

[4] E. Goffman, *Asylums* (Doubleday, Garden City, N.Y., 1961).

[5] T. J. Scheff, *Being Mentally Ill: A Sociological Theory* (Aldine, Chicago, 1966).

[6] Data from a ninth pseudopatient are not incorporated in this report because, although his sanity went undetected, he falsified aspects of his personal history, including his marital status and parental relationships. His experimental behaviors therefore were not identical to those of the other pseudopatients.

[7] A. Barry, *Bellevue Is a State of Mind* (Harcourt Brace Jovanovich, New York, 1971); I. Belknap, *Human Problems of a State Mental Hospital* (McGraw-Hill, New York, 1956); W. Caudill, F. C. Redlich, H. R. Gilmore, E. B. Brody, *Amer. J. Orthopsychiat.* 22, 314 (1952); A. R. Goldman, R. H. Bohr, T. A. Steinberg, *Prof. Psychol.* 1, 427 (1970); unauthored, *Roche Report* 1 (No. 13), 8 (1971).

[8] Beyond the personal difficulties that the pseudopatient is likely to experience in the hospital,

there are legal and social ones that, combined, require considerable attention before entry. For example, once admitted to a psychiatric institution, it is difficult, if not impossible, to be discharged on short notice, state law to the contrary notwithstanding. I was not sensitive to these difficulties at the outset of the project, nor to the personal and situational emergencies that can arise, but later a writ of habeas corpus was prepared for each of the entering pseudopatients and an attorney was kept "on call" during every hospitalization. I am grateful to John Kaplan and Robert Bartels for legal advice and assistance in these matters.

[9] However distasteful concealment is, it was a necessary first step to examining these questions. Without concealment, there would have been no way to know how valid these experiences were; nor was there any way of knowing whether whatever detections occurred were a tribute to the diagnostic acumen of the staff or to the hospital's rumor network. Obviously, since my concerns are general ones that cut across individual hospitals and staffs, I have respected their anonymity and have eliminated clues that might lead to their identification.

[10] Interestingly, of the 12 admissions, 11 were diagnosed as schizophrenic and one, with the identical symptomatology, as manic-depressive psychosis. This diagnosis has a more favorable prognosis, and it was given by the only private hospital in our sample. On the relations between social class and psychiatric diagnosis, see A. deB. Hollingshead and F. C. Redlich, *Social Class and Mental Illness: A Community Study* (Wiley, New York, 1958).

[11] It is possible, of course, that patients have quite broad latitudes in diagnosis and therefore are inclined to call many people sane, even those whose behavior is patently aberrant. However, although we have no hard data on this matter, it was our distinct impression that this was not the case. In many instances, patients not only singled us out for attention, but came to imitate our behaviors and styles.

[12] J. Cumming and E. Cumming, *Community Ment. Health* 1, 135 (1965); A. Farina and K. Ring, *J. Abnorm. Psychol.* 70, 47 (1965); H. E. Freeman and O. G. Simmons, *The Mental Patient Comes Home* (Wiley, New York, 1963); W. J. Johannsen, *Ment. Hygiene* 53, 218 (1969); A. S. Linsky, *Soc. Psychiat.* 5, 166 (1970).

[13] S. E. Asch, *J. Abnorm. Soc. Psychol.* 41, 258 (1946); *Social Psychology* (Prentice-Hall, New York, 1952).

[14] See also I. N. Mensh and J. Wishner, *J. Personality* 16, 188 (1947); J. Wishner, *Psychol. Rev.* 67, 96 (1960); J. S. Bruner and R. Tagiuri, in *Handbook of Social Psychology*, G. Lindzey, Ed. (Addison-Wesley, Cambridge, Mass., 1954), vol. 2, pp. 634–654; J. S. Bruner, D. Shapiro, R. Tagiuri, in *Person Perception and Interpersonal Behavior*. R. Tagiuri and L. Petrullo, Eds. (Stanford Univ. Press, Stanford, Calif., 1958), pp. 277–288.

[15] For an example of a similar self fulfilling prophecy, in this instance dealing with the "central" trait of intelligence, see R. Rosenthal and L. Jacobson, *Pygmalion in the Classroom* (Holt, Rinehart & Winston, New York, 1968).

[16] E. Zigler and L. Phillips, *J. Abnorm. Soc. Psychol.* 63, 69 (1961). See also R. K. Freudenberg and J. P. Robertson, *A.M.A. Arch. Neurol. Psychiatr.* 76, 14 (1956).

[17] W. Mischel, *Personality and Assessment* (Wiley, New York, 1968).

[18] The most recent and unfortunate instance of this tenet is that of Senator Thomas Eagleton.

[19] T. R. Sarbin and J. C. Mancuso, *J. Clin. Consult. Psychol.* 35, 159 (1970); T. R. Sarbin, *ibid.*, 31, 447 (1967); J. C. Nunnally, Jr., *Popular Conceptions of Mental Health* (Holt, Rinehart & Winston, New York, 1961).

[20] A. H. Stanton and M. S. Schwartz, *The Mental Hospital: A Study of Institutional Participation in Psychiatric Illness and Treatment* (Basic, New York, 1954).

[21] D. B. Wexler and S. E. Scoville, *Ariz. Law Rev.* 13, 1 (1971).

[22] I thank W. Mischel, E. Orne, and M. S. Rosenhan for comments on an earlier draft of this manuscript.

Questions about "On Being Sane in Insane Places"

(a) What method was used to collect the data? (Use Chapter 2 categories.)

(b) What is the hypothesis, if any? Is it causal or noncausal?

(c) Identify the variables being studied. If the hypothesis is causal, what is the independent variable? What is its operational definition? What is the dependent variable? What is its operational definition?

(d) Identify the findings (what relationship of variables was observed?)

(e) Identify an extraneous variable controlled by holding it constant. Identify an extraneous variable controlled by randomization.

(f) Identify any uncontrolled extraneous variables. For each, give an alternative explanation of the observed results, based on the uncontrolled variable. Suggest a way to control for each uncontrolled variable.

(g) Identify the sample studied and the population from which it was drawn. If you detect any sampling bias, identify it.

(h) Identify any interactions being studied.

Answers

(a) *Method:* Within-subjects experiment.

The essence of the study was this: people complained of psychiatric symptoms (to gain admission) and then acted sane. The responses of the hospital staffs were observed. The experimenter deliberately created a situation (i.e., manipulated a variable) by having people identified as psychiatric patients act sane, and observed responses (dependent variables). There is no other group to compare with the one observed here.

(b) *Hypothesis:* Nowhere in Rosenhan's article is there a clear statement of a hypothesis, though it's obvious that there is one and that it involves the relationship of variables. One way to state Rosenhan's hypothesis is this: When a diagnosed psychiatric patient behaves normally, it has no effect on his/her diagnosis. In slightly different words, it is: Normality will not be recognized as such when it occurs in a hospitalized psychiatric patient. The hypothesis is causal. Rosenhan is saying that once someone is in the role of patient, sane behavior will *not cause* hospital staffs to treat the person as a sane person.

(c) *Variables:* normality (or normal behavior) and hospital's response (or recognition of normality). "Reports of hearing voices" is not a variable here. It's true that all pseudopatients simulated psychotic symptoms to get into the hospital, but the experiment wasn't done to see if symptoms could get them in. The question was whether sanity could get them out. The way to test this was to get sane people admitted as patients.

Independent variable: Normality (normal behavior). The operational definition is a long one. The last four paragraphs of the section "Pseudopatients and Their Settings" provide the operational definition of normality, since they describe what the pseudopatients did after they were admitted. These paragraphs can be summarized as follows: Pseudopatients gave their accurate life histories, except for name, vocation, employment, and the alleged symptoms. They ceased simulating symptoms when they arrived on the ward, and acted and interacted as they normally would, with the exception of taking extensive notes. They were cooperative, and sought release from the hospital.

Dependent variable: Hospital's response (recognition of normality). Whatever you call it, the dependent variable was whether or not the pseudopatients were ever recognized, or diagnosed, as sane. Rosenhan seems to use several operational definitions, some more concrete than others (see the section "The Normal Are Not Detectably Sane"). The more concrete operational definitions are diagnosis at discharge and length of stay in the hospital. Less concrete ones are questions raised about pseudopatients' simulations and "indications in the hospital records that the pseudopatient's status was suspect." The section "The Stickiness of Psychodiagnostic Labels" contains several examples of the hospital's response, but these are based on nonsystematic observation and cannot really be called operational definitions or measures of any variable.

(d) *Findings:* Again, there are a number of findings, some quantitative, and others qualitative. They are reported in two sections of the article: "The Normal are Not Detectably Sane" and "The Stickiness of Psychodiagnostic Labels." Some of the major findings are: all were discharged with a diagnosis of schizophrenia "in remission"; length of hospitalization averaged 19 days; there is no evidence in the pseudopatients' records that their status was suspect. Other findings concerned staff response to pseudopatients' note-taking, other patients' responses to the pseudopatients, and so on.

(e) *Extraneous variables held constant:* Some aspects of the pseudopatients' behavior were held constant. They reported the same symptoms, they all said the symptoms were gone, and all began reporting this at the same point in their hospitalization. All the pseudopatients (almost) did not take any medication, despite prescriptions. The general behavior of the pseudopatients was reportedly fairly well controlled, with respect to the ways in which they responded to ward staff, at least. Also, staff knowledge of the existence of pseudopatients was controlled by telling them nothing.

Extraneous variables controlled by randomization: None, in this design. There is no comparison group, so subjects cannot be assigned randomly to groups.

(f) *Uncontrolled extraneous variables:* Rosenhan discusses some of these. One is the *amount of time the staff had* to detect sanity. There are no data on whether detection might increase with time or with doctor-patient contact. While it's true that in 7 to 52 days the staff *should* have had enough time, Rosenhan's data show that doctors didn't spend much time with the patient. Thus, failure to detect sanity may have been due to a hospital social structure that discourages professional contact, instead of any inability of the professional staff to diagnose if they *do* make contact. This is an alternative explanation. Rosenhan would probably counter-argue that as all pseudopatients' discharge diagnoses were "schizophrenia in remission," the physicians must have felt capable of making a professional diagnosis at discharge. Still, the doctors were wrong.

Rosenhan also mentions the *tendency of doctors to err in the direction of caution*—to diagnose an illness if there is doubt. Rosenhan tries to rule out this variable by conducting an experiment-within-an-experiment; psychiatric staffs were told to expect a pseudopatient, and their diagnoses and suspicions were recorded. Many patients were "diagnosed" incorrectly as pseudopatients. Rosenhan did not make the proper test of this extraneous variable. Suppose he had told the hospital staff to expect pseudopatients and then actually had some admitted. It would be instructive to see if the pseudopatients could be correctly identified. If they could be discovered, then we would know that sanity can be recognized in a mental hospital, if only the doctors would look for it there.

Let us see if we can identify any extraneous variables Rosenhan has not discussed. We might look for comparison groups that should have been included (since the design is within-subjects). What should Rosenhan have controlled for? You might not think of these, but Lieberman (1973) came up with two interesting suggestions. First, Lieberman noted that ward conditions are designed to make insane people more manageable. The *effect of the ward environment* is extraneous to the question of whether sanity can be diagnosed. The results are explained on the grounds that staff may think nothing of sane behavior because patients often appear more sane than they actually are. Lieberman suggested that Rosenhan attempt to take insane people out of the hospital, to see if the people on the outside can detect insanity.

Lieberman also suggested that the pseudopatients were "not just sane persons; they were sane persons *feigning insanity*." The results may only mean that the doctors can not tell the insane from the sane feigning insanity (alternative explanation). A comparison group could have pseudopatients feign a regular medical problem (presumably one for which diagnosis relies heavily on self-report, as it does for schizophrenia). If the doctors were unable to diagnose normality in these patients, the cause of misdiagnosis must lie in the pseudopatients' dissimulation, and not in the diagnostic category "schizophrenia."

(g) *Sample and Population:* The sample consisted of twelve hospitals in five East and West Coast states, and their psychiatric staffs. The population sampled seems to be U.S. hospital psychiatric facilities, both public and private, and their staffs.

Rosenhan's conclusions are meant to apply to hospitals and their psychiatric staffs everywhere, and by implication to all mental health professionals. He says, "We now know that we cannot distinguish insanity from sanity," and this "we" would seem to mean anyone presumably qualified to make that distinction.

Sampling bias: Twelve hospitals in five states on the East and West Coasts were used, and Rosenhan tells us that they differed from each other on several dimensions. Still, we do not know the basis for choosing these twelve hospitals. As we are not told they were chosen at random from some psychiatric directory, we must presume that they were chosen for convenience (e.g., to the pseudopatients' homes). It is impossible to know whether this bias has seriously affected the results. My guess (and it is just that) is that sampling bias is not a serious problem with this study. Even so, the sampling procedure was not ideal.

(h) *Interactions:* None. Only two variables were investigated in the main study.

If you are interested, you might want to answer these same questions about the other studies Rosenhan reports. The one on the responses of psychiatric staffs, professors, and hospital doctors to people's questions (summarized in Rosenhan's Table 1) is an interesting piece of research.

CHAPTER 5

Reviewing
a Body
of Literature

In introducing chapter 3, I mentioned two questions that should be asked about a piece of research before accepting its conclusions. The first was whether the conclusions were supported by the data for the people or events studied. This was the question of internal validity, and Chapters 3 and 4 were devoted to it. By now, you should be fairly skilled at looking for alternative explanations and evaluating the internal validity of single scientific studies.

The second validity question has been left unasked until now. It was the question of whether the conclusions of a study apply to any people or events beyond the particular ones that were studied. This question is one of overriding importance, since our interest in research is rarely restricted to the specific situation studied. We are not so much interested in the stories of Rosenhan's pseudopatients as we are in the broader question of whether psychiatric diagnoses have anything to do with the patient, or whether they are only responses to the abnormal setting of the psychiatric facility. Our interest is in the variables, not the specific details of a piece of research. But by reading a single study, we cannot be sure to what extent the findings depend on the particular way the variables were measured. In Rosenhan's study, we can only guess whether the patients would have been treated differently if they had entered the hospitals with some other set of symptoms, and we cannot be sure whether they would have been discovered if the hospital staffs had been warned to expect pseudopatients. The answers to these questions are critical, but we cannot get the answers from Rosenhan's study alone.

Thus, a major reason for evaluating a group of studies is to determine the strength of evidence supporting or refuting a general statement about the relationships between variables. Two studies of the same variables may differ in many ways: their operational definitions of either variable, the subject population studied, and any number of procedural details in the ways the studies are conducted.

The act of drawing conclusions from a study involves a process of generalizing beyond these particulars to the broader question about the variables. The process is risky because there is no way to tell by examining a single study whether some apparently unimportant detail of its procedure is responsible for its findings, or whether its results would generalize to other subject populations. These determinations are best made by observing whether similar findings emerge from studies that use different procedures and different populations. External validity is best evaluated by comparing studies that deal with the same general question in different ways.

An example of this was presented in Chapter 2, with some studies dealing with the relationship between crowding and aggression. The idea that these two variables are related derives from a theory of territoriality in animal behavior. This theory holds that animals maintain and defend territories against invaders of the same species (sometimes also of the same sex). The territoriality hypothesis implies, among other things, that when members of the same species are crowded together in a small space, the incidence of aggression will increase. Thus, research relating crowding and aggression provides one way to test the territoriality hypothesis. Still, there are many ways to study the relation of crowding to aggression. One may study it in any species, in animals of various ages and either sex. One may look at crowding in living spaces over the length of a lifetime or crowding in a narrow passageway over a matter of seconds. Finally, aggression may be measured in any form from physical violence to negative comments about a person's ideas. If a relationship between crowding and aggression is found that holds across species, types of crowding, and types of aggression, we would have general support for the existence of the relationship, and also support for the territoriality hypothesis (though not conclusive support until the other implications of territoriality are investigated).

More often than not, hypotheses in the social sciences are not supported over such a wide range of situations and subjects. Studies of the "same" relationship find different, even contradictory, results. One of the ways in which theories evolve is through testing their implications and finding that the predictions do not always come true. If it is possible to define the difference between the situations where the theory works and the situations where it doesn't, a step has been taken toward refining and improving the theory.

When you set out to evaluate the scientific support for a generalization, you can expect that the original statement may have to be reformulated to account for negative evidence. Often this is done by identifying variables not previously considered important, but which seem to make the difference between when the old theory works and when it doesn't.

The purpose of this chapter is to give you some skills you will need to draw appropriate conclusions after you have read several scientific reports that provide data about the same general question. You will be using the skills you have already developed, but you will also need to have some way to compare the results of different studies, because they will not always point to the same conclusion.

A good general procedure for comparing studies is to summarize each article you read on a separate page, using an outline such as the one provided in Table 8. It will be helpful if your outlines are set up so that they can be placed side by side when you want to compare the articles.

If you look at Table 8, you will see that most of the information called for involves answers to the questions you have been answering in the last two chapters. Here are some brief notes about summarizing articles.

Leave space for several *independent and dependent variables* in your outline, as it is common for studies to test several hypotheses at once. Make careful note of the operational definitions used, since the same variable may be operationalized differently in two different studies. A frequent reason why studies get different results is that they do not define the same variables in the same way.

There is a space for *findings* in the summary table because research on the same question does not always lead to the same result. Try to write the findings down in operational terms, because this will make it easier to identify differences among studies.

Make careful note of *alternative explanations* of the results of each study. If you are lucky, data from other studies may help rule out some alternative explanations. On the other hand, if all the research is open to the same alternative explanation, you have identified an important conclusion about the research.

The *population sampled* is important to note. A finding that holds for one population may or may not be true of another population. The *only* way to know is by looking at research using other populations. If research using different populations uncovers the same results, you can have some confidence in the generality of the findings. If results do not generalize across populations, you can look to differences between the populations for possible explanations of the results.

It is important to note *interactions* reported in research. One study may find a general relationship between two variables while another may suggest that this general relationship depends on a third variable. An example of this is found in research on sex differences in conformity. Some early research indicated that females were more prone to conformism than males (e.g., Carrigan & Julian, 1966; Janis & Field, 1959). This finding is in accord with much popular mythol-

Table 8. Format for summaries of empirical research reports

Author(s), *date*—other bibliographic information should be noted here.
Method (classify according to categories in Chapter 2)

Hypothesis (list more than one, if there are several)

Independent variable(s)/Operational definition(s)
 (1)

 (2)

 (3)

Dependent variable(s)/Operational definition(s)
 (1)

 (2)

 (3)

Findings (What relationship of variables was observed?)

Controlled extraneous variables (note the ones you consider important)

Uncontrolled extraneous variables/alternative explanations
 (1)

 (2)

Sample/population sampled

Sampling biases

Interactions studied

Conclusion(s) of author(s)

ogy. However, more recent research has shown that the relationship between sex and conformity is not so simple. A person's susceptibility to group pressure depends on how much he/she knows about the subject matter (Sistrunk & McDavid, 1971), and most of the early research tried to induce conformity in areas that men were more likely to know about than women. When the variable of male interest versus female interest was used as an independent variable in a study of sex differences in conformity, the "sex difference" turned out to be entirely due to the type of item the experimenters were trying to get conformity to (Sistrunk & McDavid, 1971). Because of these results, the earlier research had to be reinterpreted. For this reason, it is important to note any interactions that are studied, and the effects of the interacting variables.

The last part of the summary table calls for a brief statement of the *author(s)' conclusion(s)*. Conclusions are general statements about variables that are made on the basis of the operationally stated findings. Rosenhan concluded, on the basis of his study with the pseudopatients, that "the normal are not detectably sane" and "we cannot distinguish sanity from insanity." It is important to distinguish conclusions from findings because it is possible to accept an author's findings while disputing the conclusions that are presumed to follow. In the controversy over Rosenhan's article, there has been little or no criticism of the findings—many critics do not even doubt that they could be reproduced in other hospitals—but there is loud disagreement about Rosenhan's conclusions. Try to state the author(s)' conclusion(s) clearly; yours may ultimately be different.

On the following pages, there are reprints of three studies dealing with the general question of bystander intervention in emergencies. In an emergency, is help more likely if there is a crowd of bystanders, or do crowds inhibit helping behavior? More specifically, all the studies investigate the effect of the number of bystanders in an emergency on the likelihood that at least one will do something to help.

Read the studies and summarize all three, using the format provided. My summaries begin on page 200. With summaries, we can then discuss how to draw conclusions from the three studies, and how to write a report evaluating the studies and giving your own conclusions.

When you read the studies, keep in mind that you are interested in the relationship between the numbers of bystanders and the likelihood of one of them helping. Try, as you read, to screen out information that is irrelevant to this question.

BYSTANDER INTERVENTION IN EMERGENCIES: DIFFUSION OF RESPONSIBILITY[1]

John M. Darley
NEW YORK UNIVERSITY

Bibb Latané
COLUMBIA UNIVERSITY

Ss overheard an epileptic seizure. They believed either that they alone heard the emergency, or that 1 or 4 unseen others were also present. As predicted the presence of other bystanders reduced the individual's feelings of personal responsibility and lowered his speed of reporting ($p < .01$). In groups of size 3, males reported no faster than females, and females reported no slower when the 1 other bystander was a male rather than a female. In general, personality and background measures were not predictive of helping. Bystander inaction in real-life emergencies is often explained by "apathy," "alienation," and "anomie." This experiment suggests that the explanation may lie more in the bystander's response to other observers than in his indifference to the victim.

Several years ago, a young woman was stabbed to death in the middle of a street in a residential section of New York City. Although such murders are not entirely routine, the incident received little public attention until several weeks later when the New York Times disclosed another side to the case: at least 38 witnesses had observed the attack—and none had even attempted to intervene. Although the attacker took more than half an hour to kill Kitty Genovese, not one of the 38 people who watched from the safety of their own apartments came out to assist her. Not one even lifted the telephone to call the police (Rosenthal, 1964).

Preachers, professors, and news commentators sought the reasons for such apparently conscienceless and inhumane lack of intervention. Their conclusions ranged from "moral decay," to "dehumanization produced by the urban environment," to "alienation," "anomie," and "existential despair." An analysis of the situation, however, suggests that factors other than apathy and indifference were involved.

A person witnessing an emergency situation, particularly such a frightening and dangerous one as a stabbing, is in conflict. There are obvious humanitarian norms about helping the victim, but there are also rational and irrational fears about what might happen to a person who does intervene (Milgram & Hollander, 1964). "I didn't want to get involved," is a familiar comment, and behind it lies fears of physical harm, public embarrassment, involvement with police procedures, lost work days and jobs, and other unknown dangers.

In certain circumstances, the norms favoring intervention may be weakened, leading bystanders to resolve the conflict in

Reprinted from *Journal of Personality and Social Psychology*, 1968, *8*, 377–383. Copyright 1968 by the American Psychological Association. Reprinted by permission.
1. This research was supported in part by National Science Foundation Grants GS1238 and GS1239. Susan Darley contributed materially to the design of the experiment and ran the subjects, and she and Thomas Moriarty analyzed the data. Richard Nisbett, Susan Millman, Andrew Gordon, and Norma Neiman helped in preparing the tape recordings.

the direction of nonintervention. One of these circumstances may be the presence of other onlookers. For example, in the case above, each observer, by seeing lights and figures in other apartment house windows, knew that others were also watching. However, there was no way to tell how the other observers were reacting. These two facts provide several reasons why any individual may have delayed or failed to help. The responsibility for helping was diffused among the observers; there was also diffusion of any potential blame for not taking action; and finally, it was possible that somebody, unperceived, had already initiated helping action.

When only one bystander is present in an emergency, if help is to come, it must come from him. Although he may choose to ignore it (out of concern for his personal safety, or desires "not to get involved"), any pressure to intervene focuses uniquely on him. When there are several observers present, however, the pressures to intervene do not focus on any one of the observers; instead the responsibility for intervention is shared among all the onlookers and is not unique to any one. As a result, no one helps.

A second possibility is that potential blame may be diffused. However much we may wish to think than an individual's moral behavior is divorced from considerations of personal punishment or reward, there is both theory and evidence to the contrary (Aronfreed, 1964; Miller & Dollard, 1941; Whiting & Child, 1953). It is perfectly reasonable to assume that, under circumstances of group responsibility for a punishable act, the punishment or blame that accrues to any one individual is often slight or nonexistent.

Finally, if others are known to be present, but their behavior cannot be closely observed, any one bystander can assume that one of the other observers is already taking action to end the emergency. Therefore, his own intervention would be

only redundant—perhaps harmfully or confusingly so. Thus, given the presence of other onlookers whose behavior cannot be observed, any given bystander can rationalize his own inaction by convincing himself that "somebody else must be doing something."

These considerations lead to the hypothesis that the more bystanders to an emergency, the less likely, or the more slowly, any one bystander will intervene to provide aid. To test this proposition it would be necessary to create a situation in which a realistic "emergency" could plausibly occur. Each subject should also be blocked from communicating with others to prevent his getting information about their behavior during the emergency. Finally, the experimental situation should allow for the assessment of the speed and frequency of the subjects' reaction to the emergency. The experiment reported below attempted to fulfill these conditions.

PROCEDURE

Overview

A college student arrived in the laboratory and was ushered into an individual room from which a communication system would enable him to talk to the other participants. It was explained to him that he was to take part in a discussion about personal problems associated with college life and that the discussion would be held over the intercom system, rather than face-to-face, in order to avoid embarrassment by preserving the anonymity of the subjects. During the course of the discussion, one of the other subjects underwent what appeared to be a very serious nervous seizure similar to epilepsy. During the fit it was impossible for the subject to talk to the other discussants or to find out what, if anything, they were doing about the emergency. The dependent variable was the speed with which the subjects reported the emergency to the experimenter. The major independent variable was the number of people the subject thought to be in the discussion group.

Subjects

Fifty-nine female and thirteen male students in introductory psychology courses at New York University were contacted to take part in an unspecified experiment as part of a class requirement.

Method

Upon arriving for the experiment, the subject found himself in a long corridor with doors opening off it to several small rooms. An experimental assistant met him, took him to one of the rooms, and seated him at a table. After filling out a background information form, the subject was given a pair of headphones with an attached microphone and was told to listen for instructions.

Over the intercom, the experimenter explained that he was interested in learning about the kinds of personal problems faced by normal college students in a high pressure, urban environment. He said that to avoid possible embarrassment about discussing personal problems with strangers several precautions had been taken. First, subjects would remain anonymous, which was why they had been placed in individual rooms rather than face-to-face. (The actual reason for this was to allow tape recorder simulation of the other subjects and the emergency.) Second, since the discussion might be inhibited by the presence of outside listeners, the experimenter would not listen to the initial discussion, but would get the subject's reactions later, by questionnaire. (The real purpose of this was to remove the obviously responsible experimenter from the scene of the emergency.)

The subjects were told that since the experimenter was not present, it was necessary to impose some organization. Each person would talk in turn, presenting his problems to the group. Next, each person in turn would comment on what the others had said, and finally, there would be a free discussion. A mechanical switching device would regulate this discussion sequence and each subject's microphone would be on for about 2 minutes. While any microphone was on, all other microphones would be off. Only one subject, therefore, could be heard over the network at any given time. The subjects were thus led to realize when they later heard the seizure that only the victim's microphone was on and that there was no way of determining what any of the other witnesses were doing, nor of discussing the event and its possible solution with the others. When these instructions had been given, the discussion began.

In the discussion, the future victim spoke first, saying that he found it difficult to get adjusted to New York City and to his studies. Very hesitantly, and with obvious embarrassment, he mentioned that he was prone to seizures, particularly when studying hard or taking exams. The other people, including the real subject, took their turns and discussed similar problems (minus, of course, the proneness to seizures). The naive subject talked last in the series, after the last prerecorded voice was played.[2]

When it was again the victim's turn to talk, he made a few relatively calm comments, and then, growing increasingly louder and incoherent, he continued:

I-er-um-I think I-I need-er-if-if could-er-er-somebody er-er-er-er-er-er-er give me a little-er-give me a little help here because-er-I-er-I'm-er-er-h-h-having a-a-a real problem-er-right now and I-er-if somebody could help me out it would-it would-er-er s-s-ure be-sure be good . . . because-er-there-er-er-a cause I-er-I-uh-I've got a-a-one of the-er-sei-----er-er-things coming on and-

---

2. To test whether the order in which the subjects spoke in the first discussion round significantly affected the subjects' speed of report, the order in which the subjects spoke was varied (in the six-person group). This had no significant or noticeable effect on the speed of the subjects' reports.

and-and I could really-er-use some help so if somebody would-er-give me a little h-help-uh-er-er-er-er-er c-could somebody-er-er-help-er-uh-uh-uh (choking sounds) . . . I'm gonna die-er-er-I'm . . . gonna die-er-help-er-er-seizure-er-[chokes, then quiet].

The experimenter began timing the speed of the real subject's response at the beginning of the victim's speech. Informed judges listening to the tape have estimated that the victim's increasingly louder and more disconnected ramblings clearly represented a breakdown about 70 seconds after the signal for the victim's second speech. The victim's speech was abruptly cut off 125 seconds after this signal, which could be interpreted by the subject as indicating that the time allotted for that speaker had elapsed and the switching circuits had switched away from him. Times reported in the results are measured from the start of the fit.

Group Size Variable
The major independent variable of the study was the number of other people that the subject believed also heard the fit. By the assistant's comments before the experiment, and also by the number of voices heard to speak in the first round of the group discussion, the subject was led to believe that the discussion group was one of three sizes: either a two-person group (consisting of a person who would later have a fit and the real subject), a three-person group (consisting of the victim, the real subject, and one confederate voice), or a six-person group (consisting of the victim, the real subject, and four confederate voices). All the confederates' voices were tape-recorded.

Variations in Group Composition
Varying the kind as well as the number of bystanders present at an emergency should also vary the amount of responsibility felt by any single bystander. To test this, several variations of the three-person group were run. In one three-person condition,

the taped bystander voice was that of a female, in another a male, and in the third a male who said that he was a premedical student who occasionally worked in the emergency wards at Bellevue hospital.

In the above conditions, the subjects were female college students. In a final condition males drawn from the same introductory psychology subject pool were tested in a three-person female-bystander condition.

Time to Help
The major dependent variable was the time elapsed from the start of the victim's fit until the subject left her experimental cubicle. When the subject left her room, she saw the experimental assistant seated at the end of the hall, and invariably went to the assistant. If 6 minutes elapsed without the subject having emerged from her room, the experiment was terminated.

As soon as the subject reported the emergency, or after 6 minutes had elapsed, the experimental assistant disclosed the true nature of the experiment, and dealt with any emotions aroused in the subject. Finally the subject filled out a questionnaire concerning her thoughts and feelings during the emergency, and completed scales of Machiavellianism, anomie, and authoritarianism (Christie, 1964), a social desirability scale (Crowne & Marlowe, 1964), a social responsibility scale (Daniels & Berkowitz, 1964), and reported vital statistics and socioeconomic data.

RESULTS

Plausibility of Manipulation
Judging by the subjects' nervousness when they reported the fit to the experimenter, by their surprise when they discovered that the fit was simulated, and by comments they made during the fit (when they thought their microphones were off), one can conclude that almost all of the subjects perceived the fit as real. There were two exceptions in different experimental condi-

tions, and the data for these subjects were dropped from the analysis.

Effect of Groups Size on Helping

The number of bystanders that the subject perceived to be present had a major effect on the likelihood with which she would report the emergency (Table 1). Eighty-five percent of the subjects who thought they alone knew of the victim's plight reported the seizure before the victim was cut off, only 31% of those who thought four other bystanders were present did so.

Every one of the subjects in the two-person groups, but only 62% of the subjects in the six-person groups, ever reported the emergency. The cumulative distributions of response times for groups of different perceived size (Figure 1) indicates that, by any point in time, more subjects from the two-person groups had responded than from the three-person groups, and more from the three-person groups than from the six-person groups.

Ninety-five percent of all the subjects who ever responded did so within the first half of the time available to them. No subject who had not reported within 3 minutes after the fit ever did so. The shape of these distributions suggest that had the experiment been allowed to run for a considerably longer time, few additional subjects would have responded.

Speed of Response

To achieve a more detailed analysis of the results, each subject's time score was transformed into a "speed" score by taking the reciprocal of the response time in seconds and multiplying by 100. The effect of this transformation was to deemphasize differences between longer time scores, thus reducing the contribution to the results of the arbitrary 6-minute limit on scores. A high speed score indicates a fast response.

An analysis of variance indicates that the effect of group size is highly significant ($p < .01$). Duncan multiple-range tests indicate that all but the two- and three-person groups differ significantly from one another ($p < .05$).

Victim's Likelihood of Being Helped

An individual subject is less likely to respond if he thinks that others are present. But what of the victim? Is the inhibition of the response of each individual strong enough to counteract the fact that with five onlookers there are five times as many people available to help? From the data of this experiment, it is possible mathematically to create hypothetical groups with one, two, or five observers.[3] The calculations indicate that the victim is about equally likely to get help from one bystander as from two. The victim is considerably more likely to have gotten help from one or two observers than

Table 1. Effects of groups size on likelihood and speed of response

Group size	N	% responding by end of fit	Time in sec.	Speed score
2 (S & victim)	13	85	52	.87
3 (S, victim, & 1 other)	26	62	93	.72
6 (S, victim, & 4 others)	13	31	166	.51

Note.—p value of differences: $\chi^2 = 7.91$, $p < .02$; $F = 8.09$, $p < .01$, for speed scores.

3. The formula for the probability that at least one person will help by a given time is $1 - (1 - P)^n$ where n is the number of observers and P is the probability of a single individual (who thinks he is one of n observers) helping by that time.

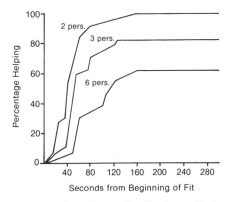

Figure 1. Cumulative distributions of helping responses.

from five during the first minute of the fit. For instance, by 45 seconds after the start of the fit, the victim's chances of having been helped by the single bystanders were about 50%, compared to none in the five observer condition. After the first minute, the likelihood of getting help from at least one person is high in all three conditions.

Effect of Group Composition on Helping the Victim

Several variations of the three-person group were run. In one pair of variations, the female subject thought the other bystander was either male or female; in another, she thought the other bystander was a premedical student who worked in an emergency ward at Bellevue hospital. As Table 2 shows, the variations in sex and medical competence of the other bystander had no important or detectable affect on speed of response. Subjects responded equally frequently and fast whether the other bystander was female, male, or medically experienced.

Sex of the Subject and Speed of Response

Coping with emergencies is often thought to be the duty of males, especially when females are present, but there was no evidence that this was the case in this study. Male subjects responded to the emergency with almost exactly the same speed as did females (Table 2).

Reasons for Intervention or Nonintervention

After the debriefing at the end of the experiment each subject was given a 15-item checklist and asked to check those thoughts which had "crossed your mind when you heard Subject 1 calling for help." Whatever the condition, each subject checked very few thoughts, and there were no significant differences in number or kind of thoughts in the different experimental groups. The only thoughts checked by more than a few subjects were "I didn't know what to do" (18 out of 65 subjects), "I thought it must be some sort of fake" (20 out of 65), and "I didn't know exactly what was happening" (26 out of 65).

It is possible that subjects were ashamed to report socially undesirable rationalizations, or, since the subjects checked the list *after* the true nature of the experiment had been explained to them, their memo-

Table 2. Effects of group composition on likelihood and speed of response [a]

Group composition	N	% responding by end of fit	Time in sec.	Speed score
Female *S*, male other	13	62	94	74
Female *S*, female other	13	62	92	71
Female *S*, male medic other	5	100	60	77
Male *S*, female other	13	69	110	68

[a] Three-person group, male victim.

ries might have been blurred. It is our impression, however, that most subjects checked few reasons because they had few coherent thoughts during the fit.

We asked all subjects whether the presence or absence of other bystanders had entered their minds during the time that they were hearing the fit. Subjects in the three- and six-person groups reported that they were aware that other people were present, but they felt that this made no difference to their own behavior.

Individual Difference Correlates of Speed of Report

The correlations between speed of report and various individual differences on the personality and background measures were obtained by normalizing the distribution of report speeds within each experimental condition and pooling these scores across all conditions ($n=62-65$). Personality measures showed no important or significant correlations with speed of reporting the emergency. In fact, only one of the 16 individual difference measures, the size of the community in which the subject grew up, correlated ($r=-.26$, $p<.05$) with the speed of helping.

DISCUSSION

Subjects, whether or not they intervened, believed the fit to be genuine and serious. "My God, he's having a fit," many subjects said to themselves (and were overheard via their microphones) at the onset of the fit. Others gasped or simply said "Oh." Several of the male subjects swore. One subject said to herself, "It's just my kind of luck, something has to happen to me!" Several subjects spoke aloud of their confusion about what course of action to take, "Oh God, what should I do?"

When those subjects who intervened stepped out of their rooms, they found the experimental assistant down the hall. With some uncertainty, but without panic, they reported the situation. "Hey, I think Number 1 is very sick. He's having a fit or something." After ostensibly checking on the situation, the experimenter returned to report that "everything is under control." The subjects accepted these assurances with obvious relief.

Subjects who failed to report the emergency showed few signs of the apathy and indifference thought to characterize "unresponsive bystanders." When the experimenter entered her room to terminate the situation, the subject often asked if the victim was "all right." "Is he being take care of?" "He's all right isn't he?" Many of these subjects showed physical signs of nervousness; they often had trembling hands and sweating palms. If anything, they seemed more emotionally aroused than did the subjects who reported the emergency.

Why, then, didn't they respond? It is our impression that nonintervening subjects had not decided *not* to respond. Rather they were still in a state of indecision and conflict concerning whether to respond or not. The emotional behavior of these nonresponding subjects was a sign of their continuing conflict, a conflict that other subjects resolved by responding.

The fit created a conflict situation of the avoidance-avoidance type. On the one hand, subjects worried about the guilt and shame they would feel if they did not help the person in distress. On the other hand, they were concerned not to make fools of themselves by overreacting, not to ruin the ongoing experiment by leaving their intercom, and not to destroy the anonymous nature of the situation which the experimenter had earlier stressed as important. For subjects in the two-person condition, the obvious distress of the victim and his need for help were so important that their conflict was easily resolved. For the subjects who knew there were other bystanders present, the cost of not helping was reduced and the conflict they were in more acute. Caught between the two negative alternatives of letting the victim continue to suffer or the costs of rushing in to help, the nonresponding bystanders vacillated between them rather than choosing not to respond. This distinction may be academic for the victim, since he got no help in either case, but it is an extremely important one for arriving at an understanding of the causes of bystanders' failures to help.

Although the subjects experienced stress and conflict during the experiment, their general reactions to it were highly positive. On a questionnaire administered after the experimenter had discussed the nature and purpose of the experiment, every single subject found the experiment either "interesting" or "very interesting" and was willing to participate in similar experiments in the future. All subjects felt they understood what the experiment was about and indicated that they thought the deceptions were necessary and justified. All but one felt they were better informed about the nature of psychological research in general.

Male subjects reported the emergency no faster than did females. These results (or lack of them) seem to conflict with the Berkowitz, Klanderman, and Harris (1964) finding that males tend to assume more responsibility and take more initiative than females in giving help to dependent others. Also, females reacted equally fast when the other bystander was another female, a male, or even a person practiced in dealing with medical emergencies. The ineffectiveness of these manipulations of group composition cannot be explained by general insensitivity of the speed measure, since the group-size variable had a marked effect on report speed.

It might be helpful in understanding this lack of difference to distinguish two general classes of intervention in emergency situations: direct and reportorial. Direct intervention (breaking up a fight, extinguishing a fire, swimming out to save a drowner) often requires skill, knowledge, or physical power. It may involve danger. American cultural norms and Berkowitz's results seem to suggest that males are more responsible than females for this kind of direct intervention.

A second way of dealing with an emergency is to report it to someone qualified to handle it, such as the police. For this kind of intervention, there seem to be no norms requiring male action. In the present study, subjects clearly intended to report the emergency rather than take direct action. For such indirect intervention, sex or medical competence does not appear to affect one's qualifications or responsibilities. Anybody, male or female, medically trained or not, can find the experimenter.

In this study, no subject was able to tell how the other subjects reacted to the fit. (Indeed, there were no other subjects actually present.) The effects of group size on speed of helping, therefore, are due simply to the perceived presence of others rather than to the influence of their actions. This means that the experimental situation is unlike emergencies, such as a fire, in which bystanders interact with each other. It is, however, similar to emergencies, such as the Genovese murder, in which spectators knew others were also watching but were prevented by walls between them from communication that might have counteracted the diffusion of responsibility.

The present results create serious difficulties for one class of commonly given explanations for the failure of bystanders to intervene in actual emergencies, those involving apathy or indifference. These explanations generally assert that people who fail to intervene are somehow different in kind from the rest of us, that they are "alienated by industrialization," "dehumanized by urbanization," "depersonalized by living in the cold society," or "psychopaths." These explanations serve a dual function for people who adopt them. First, they explain (if only in a nominal way) the puzzling and frightening problem of why people watch others die. Second, they give individuals reason to deny that they too might fail to help in a similar situation.

The results of this experiment seem to indicate that such personality variables may not be as important as these explanations suggest. Alienation, Machiavellianism, acceptance of social responsibility, need for approval, and authoritarianism are often cited in these explanations. Yet they did not predict the speed or likelihood of help. In sharp contrast, the perceived number of bystanders did. The explanation of bystander "apathy" may lie more in the bystander's response to other observers than in presumed personality deficiencies of "apathetic" individuals. Although this realization may force us to face the guilt-provoking possibility that we too might fail to intervene, it also suggests that individuals are not, of necessity, "noninterveners" because of their personalities. If people understand the situational forces that can make them hesitate to intervene, they may better overcome them.

REFERENCES

Aronfreed, J. The origin of self-criticism. *Psychological Review*, 1964, 71, 193–219.

Berkowitz, L, Klanderman, S., & Harris, R. Effects of experimenter awareness and sex of subject on reactions to dependency relationships. *Sociometry*, 1964, 27, 327–329.

Christie, R. The prevalence of machiavellian orientations. Paper presented at the meeting of the American Psychological Association, Los Angeles, 1964.

Crowne, D., & Marlowe, D. *The approval motive.* New York: Wiley, 1964.

Daniels, L., & Berkowitz, L. Liking and response to dependency relationships. *Human Relations*, 1963, 16, 141–148.

Milgram, S., & Hollander, P. Murder they heard. *Nation*, 1964, 198, 602–604.

Miller, N., & Dollard, J. *Social learning and imitation.* New Haven: Yale University Press, 1941.

Rosenthal, A. M. *Thirty-eight witnesses.* New York: McGraw-Hill, 1964.

Whiting, J. W. M., & Child, I. *Child training and personality.* New Haven: Yale University Press, 1953.

GROUP INHIBITION OF BYSTANDER INTERVENTION IN EMERGENCIES[1]

Bibb Latané[2]
COLUMBIA UNIVERSITY

John M. Darley[3]
NEW YORK UNIVERSITY

Male undergraduates found themselves in a smoke-filling room either alone, with 2 nonreacting others, or in groups of 3. As predicted, Ss were less likely to report the smoke when in the presence of passive others (10%) or in groups of 3 (38% of groups) than when alone (75%). This result seemed to have been mediated by the way Ss interpreted the ambiguous situation; seeing other people remain passive led Ss to decide the smoke was not dangerous.

Reprinted from *Journal of Personality and Social Psychology*, 1968, *10*, 215–221. Copyright 1968 by the American Psychological Association. Reprinted by permission.
1. We thank Lee Ross and Keith Gerritz for their thoughtful efforts. This research was supported by

Emergencies, fortunately, are uncommon events. Although the average person may read about them in newspapers or watch fictionalized versions on television, he probably will encounter fewer than half a dozen in his lifetime. Unfortunately, when he does encounter one, he will have had little direct personal experience in dealing with it. And he must deal with it under conditions of urgency, uncertainty, stress, and fear. About all the individual has to guide him is the secondhand wisdom of the late movie, which is often as useful as "Be brave" or as applicable as "Quick, get lots of hot water and towels!"

Under the circumstances, it may seem surprising that anybody ever intervenes in an emergency in which he is not directly involved. Yet there is a strongly held cultural norm that individuals should act to relieve the distress of others. As the Old Parson puts it, "In this life of froth and bubble, two things stand like stone—kindness in another's trouble, courage in your own." Given the conflict between the norm to act and an individual's fears and uncertainties about getting involved, what factors will determine whether a bystander to an emergency will intervene?

We have found (Darley & Latané, 1968) that the mere perception that other people are also witnessing the event will markedly decrease the likelihood that an individual will intervene in an emergency. Individuals heard a person undergoing a severe epileptic-like fit in another room. In one experimental condition, the subject thought that he was the only person who heard the emergency; in another condition, he thought four other persons were also aware of the seizure. Subjects alone with the victim were much more likely to intervene on his behalf, and, on the average, reacted in less than one-third the time required by

subjects who thought there were other bystanders present.

"Diffusion of responsibility" seems the most likely explanation for this result. If an individual is alone when he notices an emergency, he is solely responsible for coping with it. If he believes others are also present, he may feel that his own responsibility for taking action is lessened, making him less likely to help.

To demonstrate that responsibility diffusion rather than any of a variety of social influence processes caused this result, the experiment was designed so that the onlookers to the seizure were isolated from one another and could not discuss how to deal with the emergency effectively. They knew the others could not see what they did, nor could they see whether somebody else had already started to help. Although this state of affairs is characteristic of many actual emergencies (such as the Kitty Genovese murder in which 38 people witnessed a killing from their individual apartments without acting), in many other emergencies several bystanders are in contact with and can influence each other. In these situations, processes other than responsibility diffusion will also operate.

Given the opportunity to interact, a group can talk over the situation and divide up the helping action in an efficient way. Also, since responding to emergencies is a socially prescribed norm, individuals might be expected to adhere to it more when in the presence of other people. These reasons suggest that interacting groups should be better at coping with emergencies than single individuals. We suspect, however, that the opposite is true. Even when allowed to communicate, groups may still be worse than individuals.

Most emergencies are, or at least begin as, ambiguous events. A quarrel in the

—————

National Science Foundation Grants GS 1238 and GS 1239. The experiment was conducted at Columbia University.
2. Now at the Ohio State University.
3. Now at Princeton University.

street may erupt into violence, but it may be simply a family argument. A man staggering about may be suffering a coronary or an onset of diabetes; he may be simply drunk. Smoke pouring from a building may signal a fire; on the other hand, it may be simply steam or air-conditioning vapor. Before a bystander is likely to take action is such ambiguous situations, he must first define the event as an emergency and decide that intervention is the proper course of action.

In the course of making these decisions, it is likely that an individual bystander will be considerably influenced by the decisions he perceives other bystanders to be taking. If everyone else in a group of onlookers seems to regard an event as nonserious and the proper course of action as nonintervention, this consensus may strongly affect the perceptions of any single individual and inhibit his potential intervention.

The definitions that other people hold may be discovered by discussing the situation with them, but they may also be inferred from their facial expressions or their behavior. A whistling man with his hands in his pockets obviously does not believe he is in the midst of a crisis. A bystander who does not respond to smoke obviously does not attribute it to fire. An individual, seeing the inaction of others, will judge the situation as less serious than he would if he were alone.

In the present experiment, this line of thought will be tested by presenting an emergency situation to individuals either alone or in the presence of two passive others, confederates of the experimenter who have been instructed to notice the emergency but remain indifferent to it. It is our expectation that this passive behavior will signal the individual that the other bystanders do not consider the situation to be dangerous. We predict that an individual faced with the passive reactions of other people will be influenced by them, and will thus be less likely to take action than if he were alone.

This, however, is a prediction about individuals; it says nothing about the original question of the behavior of freely interacting groups. Most groups do not have preinstructed confederates among their members, and the kind of social influence process described above would, by itself, only lead to a convergence of attitudes within a group. Even if each member of the group is entirely guided by the reactions of others, then the group should still respond with a likelihood equal to the average of the individuals.

An additional factor is involved, however. Each member of a group may watch the others, but he is also aware that the others are watching him. They are an audience to his own reactions. Among American males it is considered desirable to appear poised and collected in times of stress. Being exposed to public view may constrain an individual's actions as he attempts to avoid possible ridicule and embarrassment.

The constraints involved with being in public might in themselves tend to inhibit action by individuals in a group, but in conjunction with the social influence process described above, they may be expected to have even more powerful effects. If each member of a group is, at the same time, trying to appear calm and also looking around at the other members to gauge their reactions, all members may be led (or misled) by each other to define the situation as less critical than they would if alone. Until someone acts, each person only sees other nonresponding bystanders, and, as with the passive confederates, is likely to be influenced not to act himself.

This leads to a second prediction. Compared to the performance of individuals, if we expose groups of naive subjects to an emergency, the constraints on behavior in public coupled with the social influence process will lessen the likelihood that the members of the group will act to cope with the emergency.

It has often been recognized (Brown,

1954, 1965) that a crowd can cause contagion of panic, leading each person in the crowd to overreact to an emergency to the detriment of everyone's welfare. What is implied here is that a crowd can also force inaction on its members. It can suggest, implicitly but strongly, by its passive behavior, that an event is not to be reacted to as an emergency, and it can make any individual uncomfortably aware of what a fool he will look for behaving as if it is.

METHOD

The subject, seated in a small waiting room, faced an ambiguous but potentially dangerous situation as a stream of smoke began to puff into the room through a wall vent. His response to this situation was observed through a one-way glass. The length of time the subject remained in the room before leaving to report the smoke was the main dependent variable of the study.

Recruitment of Subjects

Male Columbia students living in campus residences were invited to an interview to discuss "some of the problems involved in life at an urban university." The subject sample included graduate and professional students as well as undergraduates. Individuals were contacted by telephone and most willingly volunteered and actually showed up for the interview. At this point, they were directed either by signs or by the secretary to a "waiting room" where a sign asked them to fill out a preliminary questionnaire.

Experimental Manipulation

Some subjects filled out the questionnaire and were exposed to the potentially critical situation while alone. Others were part of three-person groups consisting of one subject and two confederates acting the part of naive subjects. The confederates attempted to avoid conversation as much as possible.

Once the smoke had been introduced, they started at it briefly, made no comment, but simply shrugged their shoulders, returned to the questionnaires and continued to fill them out, occasionally waving away the smoke to do so. If addressed, they attempted to be as uncommunicative as possible, and to show apparent indifference to the smoke. "I dunno," they said, and no subject persisted in talking.

In a final condition, three naive subjects were tested together. In general, these subjects did not know each other, although in two groups, subjects reported a nodding acquaintanceship with another subject. Since subjects arrived at slightly different times and since they each had individual questionnaires to work on, they did not introduce themselves to each other, or attempt anything but the most rudimentary conversation.

Critical Situation

As soon as the subjects had completed two pages of their questionnaires, the experimenter began to introduce the smoke through a small vent in the wall. The "smoke" was finely divided titanium dioxide produced in a stoppered bottle and delivered under slight air pressure through the vent.[2] It formed a moderately fine-textured but clearly visible stream of whitish smoke. For the entire experimental period, the smoke continued to jet into the room in irregular puffs. By the end of the experimental period, vision was obscured by the amount of smoke present.

All behavior and conversation was observed and coded from behind a one-way window (largely disguised on the subject's side by a large sign giving preliminary instructions). If the subject left the experimental room and reported the smoke, he was told that the situation "would be taken care of." If the subject had not reported the presence of smoke by 6 minutes from the

---

[2] Smoke was produced by passing moisturized air, under pressure, through a container of titanium tetrachloride, which, in reaction with the water vapor, creates a suspension of titanium dioxide in air.

time he first noticed it, the experiment was terminated.

RESULTS

Alone Condition

The typical subject, when tested alone, behaved very reasonably. Usually, shortly after the smoke appeared, he would glance up from his questionnaire, notice the smoke, show a slight but distinct startle reaction, and then undergo a brief period of indecision, perhaps returning briefly to his questionnaire before again staring at the smoke. Soon, most subjects would get up from their chairs, walk over to the vent, and investigate it closely, sniffing the smoke, waving their hands in it, feeling its temperature, etc. The usual alone subject would hesitate again, but finally walk out of the room, look around outside, and, finding somebody there, calmly report the presence of the smoke. No subject showed any sign of panic; most simply said, "There's something strange going on in there, there seems to be some sort of smoke coming through the wall. . . ."

The median subject in the alone condition had reported the smoke within 2 minutes of first noticing it. Three-quarters of the 24 people who were run in this condition reported the smoke before the experimental period was terminated.

Two Passive Confederates Condition

The behavior of subjects run with two passive confederates was dramatically different; of 10 people run in this condition, only 1 reported the smoke. The other 9 stayed in the waiting room as it filled up with smoke, doggedly working on their questionnaire and waving the fumes away from their faces. They coughed, rubbed their eyes, and opened the window—but they did not report the smoke. The difference between the response rate of 75% in the alone condition and 10% in the two passive confederates condition is highly significant ($p < .002$ by Fisher's exact test, two-tailed).

Three Naive Bystanders

Because there are three subjects present and available to report the smoke in the three naive bystander condition as compared to only one subject at a time in the alone condition, a simple comparison between the two conditions is not appropriate. On the one hand, we cannot compare speeds in the alone condition with the average speed of the three subjects in a group, since, once one subject in a group had reported the smoke, the pressures on the other two disappeared. They legitimately could (and did) feel that the emergency had been handled, and any action on their part would be redundant and potentially confusing. Therefore the speed of the *first* subject in a group to report the smoke was used as the dependent variable. However, since there were three times as many people available to respond in this condition as in the alone condition, we would expect an increased likelihood that *at least* one person would report the smoke even if the subjects had no influence whatsoever on each other. Therefore we mathematically created "groups" of three scores from the alone condition to serve as a base line.[3]

In contrast to the complexity of this procedure, the results were quite simple. Subjects in the three naive bystander condition were markedly inhibited from reporting the smoke. Since 75% of the alone subjects reported the smoke, we would expect over 98% of the three-person groups to contain at least one reporter. In fact, in only 38% of the eight groups in this condition did even 1 subject report ($p < .01$). Of the 24 people

[3] The formula for calculating the expected proportion of groups in which at least one person will have acted by a given time is $1 - (1 - p)^n$ where p is the proportion of single individuals who act by that time and n is the number of persons in the group.

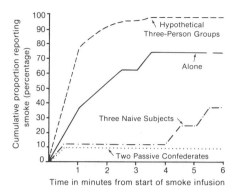

Figure 1. Cumulative proportion of subjects reporting smoke over time.

run in these eight groups, only 1 person reported the smoke within the first 4 minutes before the room got noticeably unpleasant. Only 3 people reported the smoke within the entire experimental period.

Cumulative Distribution of Report Times
Figure 1 presents the cumulative frequency distributions of report times for all three conditions. The figure shows the proportion of subjects in each condition who had reported the smoke by any point in the time following the introduction of the smoke. For example, 55% of the subjects in the alone condition had reported the smoke within 2 minutes, but the smoke had been reported in only 12% of the three-person groups by that time. After 4 minutes, 75% of the subjects in the alone condition had reported the smoke; no additional subjects in the group condition had done so. The curve in Figure 1 labeled "Hypothetical Three-Person Groups" is based upon the mathematical combination of scores obtained from subjects in the alone condition. It is the expected report times for groups in the three-person condition if the members of the groups had no influence upon each other.

It can be seen in Figure 1 that for every point in time following the introduction of the smoke, a considerably higher proportion of subjects in the alone condition had reported the smoke than had subjects in either the two passive confederates condition or in the three naive subjects condition. The curve for the latter condition, although considerably below the alone curve, is even more substantially inhibited with respect to its proper comparison, the curve of hypothetical three-person sets. Social inhibition of response was so great that the time elapsing before the smoke was reported was greater when there were more people available to report it (alone versus group $p < .05$ by Mann-Whitney U test).

Superficially, it appears that there is a somewhat higher likelihood of response from groups of three naive subjects than from subjects in the passive confederates condition. Again this comparison is not justified; there are three people free to act in one condition instead of just one. If we mathematically combine scores for subjects in the two passive confederates condition in a similar manner to that described above for the above condition we would obtain an expected likelihood of response of .27 as the hypothetical base line. This is not significantly different from the .37 obtained in the actual three-subject groups.

Noticing the Smoke
In observing the subject's reaction to the introduction of smoke, careful note was taken of the exact moment when he first saw the smoke (all report latencies were computed from this time). This was a relatively easy observation to make, for the subjects invariably showed a distinct, if slight, startle reaction. Unexpectedly, the presence of other persons delayed, slightly but very significantly, noticing the smoke. Sixty-three percent of subjects in the alone condition and only 26% of subjects in the combined together conditions noticed the smoke within the first 5 seconds after its introduction ($p < .01$ by chi-square). The median latency of noticing the smoke was under 5 seconds in the alone condition; the

median time at which the first (or only) subject in each of the combined together conditions noticed the smoke was 20 seconds (this difference does not account for group-induced inhibition of reporting since the report latencies were computed from the time the smoke was first noticed).

This interesting finding can probably be explained in terms of the constraints which people feel in public places (Goffman, 1963). Unlike solitary subjects, who often glanced idly about the room while filling out their questionnaires, subjects in groups usually kept their eyes closely on their work, probably to avoid appearing rudely inquisitive.

Postexperimental Interview
After 6 minutes, whether or not the subjects had reported the smoke, the interviewer stuck his head in the waiting room and asked the subject to come with him to the interview. After seating the subject in his office, the interviewer made some general apologies about keeping the subject waiting for so long, hoped the subject hadn't become too bored and asked if he "had experienced any difficulty while filling out the questionnaire." By this point most subjects mentioned the smoke. The interviewer expressed mild surprise and asked the subject to tell him what had happened. Thus each subject gave an account of what had gone through his mind during the smoke infusion.

Subjects who had reported the smoke were relatively consistent in later describing their reactions to it. They thought the smoke looked somewhat "strange," they were not sure exactly what it was or whether it was dangerous, but they felt it was unusual enough to justify some examination. "I wasn't sure whether it was a fire but it looked like something was wrong." "I thought it might be steam, but it seemed like a good idea to check it out."

Subjects who had not reported the smoke also were unsure about exactly what it was,

but they uniformly said that they had rejected the idea that it was a fire. Instead, they hit upon an astonishing variety of alternative explanations, all sharing the common characteristic of interpreting the smoke as a nondangerous event. Many thought the smoke was either steam or air-conditioning vapors, several thought it was smog, purposely introduced to simulate an urban environment, and two (from different groups) actually suggested that the smoke was a "truth gas" filtered into the room to induce them to answer the questionnaire accurately. (Surprisingly, they were not disturbed by this conviction.) Predictably, some decided that "it must be some sort of experiment" and stoicly endured the discomfort of the room rather than overreact.

Despite the obvious and powerful report-inhibiting effect of other bystanders, subjects almost invariably claimed that they had paid little or no attention to the reactions of the other people in the room. Although the presence of other people actually had a strong and pervasive effect on the subjects' reactions, they were either unaware of this or unwilling to admit it.

DISCUSSION

Before an individual can decide to intervene in an emergency, he must, implicitly or explicitly, take several preliminary steps. If he is to intervene, he must first *notice* the event, he must then *interpret* it as an emergency, and he must decide that it is his personal *responsibility* to act. At each of these preliminary steps, the bystander to an emergency can remove himself from the decision process and thus fail to help. He can fail to notice the event, he can fail to interpret it as an emergency, or he can fail to assume the responsibility to take action.

In the present experiment we are primarily interested in the second step of this decision process, interpreting an ambiguous event. When faced with such an event, we suggest, the individual bystander is likely to look at the reactions of people around him and be powerfully influenced by them. It was predicted that the sight of other, nonresponsive bystanders would lead the individual to interpret the emergency as not serious, and consequently lead him not to act. Further, it was predicted that the dynamics of the interaction process would lead each of a group of naive onlookers to be misled by the apparent inaction of the others into adopting a nonemergency interpretation of the event and a passive role.

The results of this study clearly support our predictions. Individuals exposed to a room filling with smoke in the presence of passive others themselves remained passive, and groups of three naive subjects were less likely to report the smoke than solitary bystanders. Our predictions were confirmed—but this does not necessarily mean that our explanation for these results is the correct one. As a matter of fact, several alternatives are available.

Two of these alternative explanations stem from the fact that the smoke represented a possible danger to the subject himself as well as to others in the building. Subjects' behavior might have reflected their fear of fire, with subjects in groups feeling less threatened by the fire than single subjects and thus being less concerned to act. It has been demonstrated in studies with humans (Schachter, 1959) and with rats (Latané, 1968; Latané & Glass, 1968) that togetherness reduces fear, even in situations where it does not reduce danger. In addition, subjects may have felt that the presence of others increased their ability to cope with fire. For both of these reasons, subjects in groups may have been less afraid of fire and thus less likely to report the smoke than solitary subjects.

A similar explanation might emphasize not fearfulness, but the desire to hide fear. To the extent that bravery or stoicism in the face of danger or discomfort is a socially desirable trait (as it appears to be for American male undergraduates), one might expect individuals to attempt to appear more brave or more stoic when others are watching then when they are alone. It is possible that subjects in the group condition saw themselves as engaged in a game of "Chicken," and thus did not react.

Although both of these explanations are plausible, we do not think that they provide an accurate account of subjects' thinking. In the postexperimental interviews, subjects claimed, *not* that they were unworried by the fire or that they were unwilling to endure the danger; but rather that they decided that there was no fire at all and the smoke was caused by something else. They failed to act because they thought there was no reason to act. Their "apathetic" behavior was reasonable—given their interpretation of the circumstances.

The fact that smoke signals potential danger to the subject himself weakens another alternative explanation, "diffusion of responsibility." Regardless of social influence processes, an individual may feel less personal responsibility for helping if he shares the responsibility with others (Darley & Latané, 1968). But this diffusion explanation does not fit the present situation. It is hard to see how an individual's responsibility for saving himself is diffused by the presence of other people. The diffusion explanation does not account for the pattern of interpretations reported by the subjects or for their variety of nonemergency explanations.

On the other hand, the social influence processes which we believe account for the results of our present study obviously do not explain our previous experiment in which subjects could not see or be seen by each other. Taken together, these two studies suggest that the presence of bystanders may affect an individual in several ways; including both "social influence" and "diffusion of responsibility."

Both studies, however, find, for two

quite different kinds of emergencies and under two quite different conditions of social contact, that individuals are less likely to engage in socially responsible action if they think other bystanders are present. This presents us with the paradoxical conclusion that a victim may be more likely to get help, or an emergency may be more likely to be reported, the fewer people there are available to take action. It also may help us begin to understand a number of frightening incidents where crowds have listened to but not answered a call for help. Newspapers have tagged these incidents with the label "apathy." We have become indifferent, they say, callous to the fate of suffering others. The results of our studies lead to a different conclusion. The failure to intervene may be better understood by knowing the relationship among bystanders rather than that between a bystander and the victim.

REFERENCES

Brown, R. W. Mass phenomena. In G. Lindzey (Ed.), *Handbook of social psychology.* Vol. 2. Cambridge: Addison-Wesley, 1954.

Brown, R. *Social psychology.* New York: Free Press of Glencoe, 1965.

Darley, J. M., & Latané, B. Bystander intervention in emergencies: Diffusion of responsibility. *Journal of Personality and Social Psychology,* 1968, 8, 377–383.

Goffman, E. *Behavior in public places.* New York: Free Press of Glencoe, 1963.

Latané, B. Gregariousness and fear in laboratory rats. *Journal of Experimental Social Psychology,* 1968, in press.

Latané, B., & Glass, D. C. Social and nonsocial attraction in rats. *Journal of Personality and Social Psychology,* 1968, 9, 142–146.

Schachter, S. *The psychology of affiliation.* Stanford: Stanford University Press, 1959.

GOOD SAMARITANISM: AN UNDERGROUND PHENOMENON?[1]

Irving M. Piliavin
UNIVERSITY OF PENNSYLVANIA

Judith Rodin
COLUMBIA UNIVERSITY

Jane Allyn Piliavin[2]
UNIVERSITY OF PENNSYLVANIA

A field experiment was performed to investigate the effect of several variables on helping behavior, using the express trains of the New York 8th Avenue Independent Subway as a laboratory on wheels. Four teams of students, each one made up of a victim, model, and two observers, staged standard collapses in which type of victim (drunk or ill), race of victim (black or white) and presence or absence of a model were varied. Data recorded by observers

Reprinted from *Journal of Personality and Social Psychology,* 1969, *13,* 289–299. Copyright 1969 by the American Psychological Association. Reprinted by permission.

[1] This research was conducted while the first author was at Columbia University as a Special National Institute of Mental Health Research Fellow under Grant 1-F3-MH-36, 328-01. The study was par-

included number and race of observers, latency of the helping response and race of helper, number of helpers, movement out of the "critical area," and spontaneous comments. Major findings of the study were that (a) an apparently ill person is more likely to receive aid than is one who appears to be drunk, (b) race of victim has little effect on race of helper except when the victim is drunk, (c) the longer the emergency continues without help being offered, the more likely it is that someone will leave the area of the emergency, and (d) the expected decrease in speed of responding as group size increases—the "diffusion of responsibility effect" found by Darley and Latané—does not occur in this situation. Implications of this difference between laboratory and field results are discussed, and a brief model for the prediction of behavior in emergency situations is presented.

Since the murder of Kitty Genovese in Queens, a rapidly increasing number of social scientists have turned their attentions to the study of the good Samaritan's act and an associated phenomenon, the evaluation of victims by bystanders and agents. Some of the findings of this research have been provocative and nonobvious. For example, there is evidence that agents, and even bystanders, will sometimes derogate the character of the victims of misfortune, instead of feeling compassion (Berscheid & Walster, 1967; Lerner & Simmons, 1966). Furthermore, recent findings indicate that under certain circumstances there is not "safety in numbers," but rather "diffusion of responsibility." Darley and Latané (1968) have reported that among bystanders hearing an epileptic seizure over earphones, those who believed other witnesses were present were less likely to seek assistance for the victim than were bystanders who believed they were alone. Subsequent research by Latané and Rodin (1969) on response to the victim of a fall confirmed this finding and suggested further that assistance from a group of bystanders was less likely to come if the group members were strangers than if they were prior acquaintances. The field experiments of Bryan and Test (1967), on the other hand, provide interesting findings that fit common sense expectations; namely, one is more likely to be a good Samaritan if one has just observed another individual performing a helpful act.

Much of the work on victimization to date has been performed in the laboratory. It is commonly argued that the ideal research strategy over the long haul is to move back and forth between the laboratory, with its advantage of greater control, and the field, with its advantage of greater reality. The present study was designed to provide more information from the latter setting.

The primary focus of the study was on the effect of type of victim (drunk or ill) and race of victim (black or white) on speed of responding, frequency of responding, and the race of the helper. On the basis of the large body of research on similarity and liking as well as that on race and social distance, it was assumed that an individual would be more inclined to help someone of his race than a person of another race. The expectation regarding type of victim was that help would be accorded more frequently and rapidly to the apparently ill victim. This expectation was derived from two considerations. First, it was assumed that people who are regarded as partly responsible for their plight would receive less sympathy and consequently less help than

tially supported by funds supplied by this grant and partially by funds from National Science Foundation Grant GS-1901 to the third author. The authors thank Virginia Joy for allowing the experimental teams to be recruited from her class, and Percy Tannenbaum for his reading of the manuscript and his helpful comments.
[2] Requests for reprints should be sent to Jane Allyn Piliavin, Department of Psychology, University of Pennsylvania, 3813–15 Walnut Street, Philadelphia, Pennsylvania 19104.

people seen as not responsible for their circumstances (Schopler & Matthews, 1965).

Secondly, it was assumed that whatever sympathy individuals may experience when they observe a drunk collapse, their inclination to help him will be dampened by the realization that the victim may become disgusting, embarrassing, and/or violent. This realization may, in fact, not only constrain helping but also lead observers to turn away from the victim—that is, to leave the scene of the emergency.

Aside from examining the effects of race and type of victim, the present research sought to investigate the impact of modeling in emergency situations. Several investigators have found that an individual's actions in a given situation lead others in that situation to engage in similar actions. This modeling phenomenon has been observed in a variety of contexts including those involving good Samaritanism (Bryan & Test, 1967). It was expected that the phenomenon would be observed as well in the present study. A final concern of the study was to examine the relationship between size of group and frequency and latency of the helping response, with a victim who was both seen and heard. In previous laboratory studies (Darley & Latané, 1968; Latané & Rodin, 1969) increases in group size led to decreases in frequency and increases in latency of responding. In these studies, however, the emergency was only heard, not seen. Since visual cues are likely to make an emergency much more arousing for the observer, it is not clear that, given these cues, such considerations as crowd size will be relevant determinants of the observer's response to the emergency. Visual cues also provide clear information as to whether anyone has yet helped the victim or if he has been able to help himself. Thus, in the laboratory studies, observers lacking visual cues could rationalize not helping by assuming assistance was no longer needed when the victim ceased calling for help. Staging emergencies in full view of observers eliminates the possibility of such rationalization.

To conduct a field investigation of the above questions under the desired conditions required a setting which would allow the repeated staging of emergencies in the midst of reasonably large groups which remained fairly similar in composition from incident to incident. It was also desirable that each group retain the same composition over the course of the incident and that a reasonable amount of time be available after the emergency occurred for good Samaritans to act. To meet these requirements, the emergencies were staged during the approximately 7½-minute express run between the 59th Street and 125th Street stations of the Eighth Avenue Independent (IND) branch of the New York subways.

METHOD

Subjects

About 4,450 men and women who traveled on the 8th Avenue IND in New York City, weekdays between the hours of 11:00 A.M. and 3:00 P.M. during the period from April 15 to June 26, 1968, were the unsolicited participants in this study. The racial composition of a typical train, which travels through Harlem to the Bronx, was about 45% black and 55% white. The mean number of people per car during these hours was 43; the mean number of people in the "critical area," in which the staged incident took place, was 8.5.

Field situation. The A and D trains of the 8th Avenue IND were selected because they make no stops between 59th Street and 125th Street. Thus, for about 7½ minutes there was a captive audience who, after the first 70 seconds of their ride, became bystanders to an emergency situation. A single trial was a nonstop ride between 59th and 125th Streets, going in either direction. All trials were run only on the old New York subway cars which serviced the 8th Avenue line since they had two-person

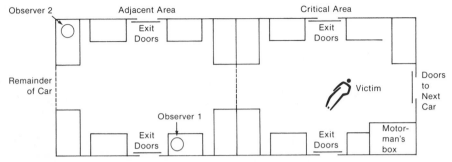

Figure 1. Layout of adjacent and critical areas of subway car.

seats in group arrangement rather than extended seats. The designated experimental or critical area was that end section of any car whose doors led to the next car. There are 13 seats and some standing room in this area on all trains (see Figure 1).

Procedure

On each trial a team of four Columbia General Studies students, two males and two females, boarded the train using different doors. Four different teams, whose members always worked together, were used to collect data for 103 trials. Each team varied the location of the experimental car from trial to trial. The female confederates took seats outside the critical area and recorded data as unobtrusively as possible for the duration of the ride, while the male model and victim remained standing. The victim always stood next to a pole in the center of the critical area (see Figure 1). As the train passed the first station (approximately 70 seconds after departing) the victim staggered forward and collapsed. Until

receiving help, the victim remained supine on the floor looking at the ceiling. If the victim received no assistance by the time the train slowed to a stop, the model helped him to his feet. At the stop, the team disembarked and waited separately until other riders had left the station. They then proceeded to another platform to board a train going in the opposite direction for the next trial. From 6 to 8 trials were run on a given day. All trials on a given day were in the same "victim condition."

Victim. The four victims (one from each team) were males between the ages of 26 and 35. Three were white and one was black. All were identically dressed in Eisenhower jackets, old slacks, and no tie. On 38 trials the victims smelled of liquor and carried a liquor bottle wrapped tightly in a brown bag (drunk condition), while on the remaining 65 trials they appeared sober and carried a black cane (cane condition). In all other aspects, victims dressed and behaved identically in the two conditions. Each victim participated in drunk and cane trials.[3]

3. It will be noted later that not only were there more cane trials than drunk trials, they were also distributed unevenly across black and white victims. The reason for this is easier to explain than to correct. Teams 1 and 2 (both white victims) started the first day in the cane condition. Teams 3 (black) and 4 (white) began in the drunk condition. Teams were told to alternate the conditions across days. They arranged their running days to fit their schedules. On their fourth day, Team 2 violated the instruction and ran cane trials when they should have run drunk trials; the victim "didn't like" playing the drunk! Then the Columbia student strike occurred, the teams disbanded, and the study of necessity was over. At this point, Teams 1 and 3 had run on only 3 days each, while 2 and 4 had run on 4 days each.

Model. Four white males between the ages of 24 and 29 assumed the roles of model in each team. All models wore informal clothes, although they were not identically attired. There were four different model conditions used across both victim conditions (drunk or cane).

1. *Critical area—early.* Model stood in critical area and waited until passing fourth station to assist victim (approximately 70 seconds after collapse).

2. *Critical area—late.* Model stood in critical area and waited until passing sixth station to assist victim (approximately 150 seconds after collapse).

3. *Adjacent area—early.* Model stood in middle of car in area adjacent to critical area and waited until passing fourth station.

4. *Adjacent area—late.* Model stood in adjacent area and waited until passing sixth station.

When the model provided assistance, he raised the victim to a sitting position and stayed with him for the remainder of the trial. An equal number of trials in the no-model condition and in each of the four model conditions were preprogrammed by a random number table and assigned to each team.

Measures. On each trial one observer noted the race, sex, and location of every rider seated or standing in the critical area.

In addition, she counted the total number of individuals in the car and the total number of individuals who came to the victim's assistance. She also recorded the race, sex, and location of every helper. A second observer coded the race, sex, and location of all persons in the adjacent area. She also recorded the latency of the first helper's arrival after the victim had fallen and on appropriate trials, the latency of the first helper's arrival after the programmed model had arrived. Both observers recorded comments spontaneously made by nearby passengers and attempted to elicit comments from a rider sitting next to them.

RESULTS AND DISCUSSION

As can be seen in Table 1, the frequency of help received by the victims was impressive, at least as compared to earlier laboratory results. The victim with the cane received spontaneous help, that is, before the model acted, on 62 of the 65 trials. Even the drunk received spontaneous help on 19 of 38 trials. The difference is not explicable on the basis of gross differences in the numbers of potential helpers in the cars. (Mean number of passengers in the car on cane trials was 45; on drunk trials, 40. Total range was 15–120.)

On the basis of past research, relatively long latencies of spontaneous helping were

Table 1. Percentage of trials on which help was given, by race and condition of victim, and total number of trials run in each condition

Trials	White victims		Black victim	
	CANE	DRUNK	CANE	DRUNK
No model	100%	100%	100%	73%
Number of trials run	54	11	8	11
Model trials	100%	77	—	67%
Number of trials run	3	13	0	3
Total number of trials	57	24	8	14

Note.—Distribution of model trials for the drunk was as follows: critical area: early, 4; late, 4; adjacent area: early, 5; late, 3. The three model trials completed for the cane victim were all early, with 2 from the critical area and 1 from the adjacent area.

Table 2. Time and responses to the incident

Trials on which help was offered	Total number of trials		% of trials on which 1 + persons left critical area [b]		% of trials on which 1 + comments were recorded [b]		Mean number of comments	
	WHITE VICTIMS	BLACK VICTIM	WHITE VICTIMS	BLACK VICTIM	WHITE VICTIMS	BLACK VICTIM	WHITE VICTIMS	BLACK VICTIM
Before 70 sec.								
Cane	52	7	4%	14%	21%	0%	.27	.00
Drunk	5	4	20%	0%	80%	50%	1.00	.50
Total	57	11	5%	9%	26%	18%	.33	.18
After 70 sec.								
Cane	5	1	40%	—	60%	—	.80	—
Drunk	19	10	42%	60%	100%	70%	2.00	.90
Total	24	11	42%	64%	96%	64%	1.75	.82
χ^2	36.83	[a]	$\chi^2_{time} = 23.19$		$\chi^2_{time} = 31.45$			
p	<.001	<.03	$p < .001$		$p < .001$			
			$\chi^2_{cane-drunk} = 11.71$		$\chi^2_{cane-drunk} = 37.95$			
			$p < .001$		$p < .001$			

Note.—Percentage and means not calculated for *n*'s less than 4.
[a]Fisher's exact test, estimate of two-tailed probability.
[b]Black and white victims are combined for the analyses of these data.

expected; thus, it was assumed that models would have time to help, and their effects could be assessed. However, in all but three of the cane trials planned to be model trials, the victim received help before the model was scheduled to offer assistance. This was less likely to happen with the drunk victim. In many cases, the early model was able to intervene, and in a few, even the delayed model could act (see Table 1 for frequencies).

A direct comparison between the latency of response in the drunk and cane conditions might be misleading, since on model trials one does not know how long it might have taken for a helper to arrive without the stimulus of the model. Omitting the model trials, however, would reduce the number of drunk trials drastically. In order to get around these problems the trials have been dichotomized into a group in which someone helped *before* 70 seconds (the time at which the early model was programmed to help) and a group in which no one had helped by this time. The second group includes some trials in which people helped the model and a very few in which no one helped at all.[4] It is quite clear from the first section of Table 2 that there was more immediate, spontaneous helping of the victim with the cane than of the drunk. The effect seems to be essentially the same for the black victim and for the white victims.[5]

What of the total number of people who

4. If a comparison of latencies is made between cane and drunk nonmodel trials only, the median latency for cane trials is 5 seconds and the median for drunk trials is 109 seconds (assigning 400 seconds as the latency for nonrespondents). The Mann-Whitney *U* for this comparison is significant at $p < .0001$.
5. Among the white victim teams, the data from Team 2 differ to some extent from those for Teams 1 and 4. All of the cane-after 70 seconds trials are accounted for by Team 2, as are 4 of the 5 drunk-before 70 trials. Median latency for cane trials is longer for Team 2 than for the other teams; for drunk trials, shorter. This is the same team that violated the "alternate days" instruction. It would appear that this team is being rather less careful—that the victim may be getting out of his role. The

helped? On 60% of the 81 trials on which the victim received help, he received it not from one good Samaritan but from two, three, or even more.[6] There are no significant differences between black and white victims, or between cane and drunk victims, in the number of helpers subsequent to the first who came to his aid. Seemingly, then, the presence of the first helper has important implications which override whatever cognitive and emotional differences were initially engendered among observers by the characteristics of the victim. It may be that the victim's uniformly passive response to the individual trying to assist him reduced observers' fear about possible unpleasantness in the drunk conditions. Another possibility is that the key factor in the decisions of second and third helpers to offer assistance was the first helper. That is, perhaps assistance was being offered primarily to him rather than to the victim. Unfortunately the data do not permit adequate assessment of these or other possible explanations.

*Characteristics of Spontaneous
First Helpers*

Having discovered that people do, in fact, help with rather high frequency, the next question is, "Who helps?" The effect of two variables, sex and race, can be examined. On the average, 60% of the people in the critical area were males. Yet, of the 81 spontaneous first helpers, 90% were males. In this situation, then, men are consider-

ably more likely to help than are women ($\chi^2 = 30.63$; $p < .001$).

Turning now to the race variable, of the 81 first helpers, 64% were white. This percentage does not differ significantly from the expected percentage of 55% based on racial distribution in the cars. Since both black and white victims were used, it is also possible to see whether blacks and whites are more likely to help a member of their own race. On the 65 trials on which spontaneous help was offered to the white victims, 68% of the helpers were white. This proportion differs from the expected 55% at the .05 level ($\chi^2 = 4.23$). On the 16 trials on which spontaneous help was offered to the black victim, half of the first helpers were white. While this proportion does not differ from chance expectation, we again see a slight tendency toward "same-race" helping.

When race of helper is examined separately for cane and drunk victims, an interesting although nonsignificant trend emerges (see Table 3). With both the black and white cane victims, the proportion of helpers of each race was in accord with the expected 55%–45% split. With the drunk, on the other hand, it was mainly members of his own race who came to his aid.[7]

This interesting tendency toward same-race helping only in the case of the drunk victim may reflect more empathy, sympathy, and trust toward victims of one's own racial group. In the case of an innocent victim (e.g., the cane victim), when sympa-

---

data from this team have been included in the analysis although they tend to reduce the relationships that were found.

6. The data from the model trials are not included in this analysis because the model was programmed to behave rather differently from the way in which most real helpers behaved. That is, his role was to raise the victim to a sitting position and then appear to need assistance. Most real helpers managed to drag the victim to a seat or to a standing position on their own. Thus the programmed model received somewhat more help than did real first helpers.

7. It is unfortunate from a design standpoint that there was only one black victim. He was the only black student in the class from which our crews were recruited. While it is tenuous to generalize from a sample of one, the problems attendant upon attributing results to his race rather than to his individual personality characteristics are vitiated somewhat by the fact that response latencies and frequencies of help to him in the cane condition fall between responses to Teams 1 and 4 on the one hand and Team 2 on the other.

Table 3. Spontaneous helping of cane and drunk by race of helper and race victim

Race of helper	White victims			Black victim			All victims		
	CANE	DRUNK	TOTAL	CANE	DRUNK	TOTAL	CANE	DRUNK	TOTAL
Same as victim	34	10	44	2	6	8	36	16	52
Different from victim	20	1	21	6	2	8	26	3	29
Total	54	11	65	8	8	16	62	19	81

Note.—Chi-squares are corrected for continuity. White victims, $\chi^2 = 2.11, p. = 16$; black victim, $p = .16$ (two-tailed estimate from Fisher's exact probabilities test); all victims, $\chi^2 = 3.26, p = .08$.

thy, though differentially experienced, is relatively uncomplicated by other emotions, assistance can readily cut across group lines. In the case of the drunk (and potentially dangerous) victim, complications are present, probably blame, fear, and disgust. When the victim is a member of one's own group—when the conditions for empathy and trust are more favorable—assistance is more likely to be offered. As we have seen, however, this does not happen without the passing of time to think things over.

Recent findings of Black and Reiss (1967) in a study of the behavior of white police officers towards apprehended persons offer an interesting parallel. Observers in this study recorded very little evidence of prejudice toward sober individuals, whether white or black. There was a large increase in prejudice expressed towards drunks of both races, but the increase in prejudice towards blacks was more than twice that towards whites.

Modeling Effects
No extensive analysis of the response to the programmed model could be made, since there were too few cases for analysis. Two analyses were, however, performed on the effects of adjacent area versus critical area models and of early versus late models within the drunk condition. The data are presented in Table 4. While the area variable has no effect, the early model elicited help significantly more than did the late model.

Other Responses to the Incident
What other responses do observers make to the incident? Do the passengers leave the car, move out of the area, make comments about the incident? No one left the car on any of the trials. However, on 21 of the 103 trials, a total of 34 people did leave the criti-

Table 4. Frequency of help as a function of early (70 seconds) versus late (150 seconds) and adjacent versus critical area programmed models

Help	Critical area			Adjacent area			Both areas		
	EARLY	LATE	BOTH	EARLY	LATE	BOTH	EARLY	LATE	TOTAL
Received	4	2	6	5	1	6	9	3	12
Not received	0	2	2	0	2	2	0	4	4
Total	4	4	8	5	3	8	9	7	16

Note.—Early versus late: $p < .04$ (two-tailed estimate from Fisher's exact test). All three cane-model trials were early model trials; two critical area, one adjacent. Help was received on all. Table includes drunk trials only.

cal area. The second section of Table 2 presents the percentage of trials on which someone left the critical area as a function of three variables: type of victim, race of victim, and time to receipt of help (before or after 70 seconds). People left the area on a higher proportion of trials with the drunk than with the cane victim. They also were far more likely to leave on trials on which help was not offered by 70 seconds, as compared to trials on which help was received before that time.[8] The frequencies are too small to make comparisons with each of the variables held constant.

Each observer spoke to the person seated next to her after the incident took place. She also noted spontaneous comments and actions by those around her. A content analysis of these data was performed, with little in the way of interesting findings. The distribution of number of comments over different sorts of trials, however, did prove interesting (see Section 3 of Table 2). Far more comments were obtained on drunk trials than on cane trials. Similarly, most of the comments were obtained on trials in which no one helped until after 70 seconds. The discomfort observers felt in sitting inactive in the presence of the victim may have led them to talk about the incident, perhaps hoping others would confirm the fact that inaction was appropriate. Many women, for example, made comments such as, "It's for men to help him," or "I wish I could help him—I'm not strong enough," "I never saw this kind of thing before—I don't know where to look," "You feel so bad that you don't know what to do."

A Test of the Diffusion
of Responsibility Hypothesis
In the Darley and Latané experiment it was predicted and found that as the number of

bystanders increased, the likelihood that any individual would help decreased and the latency of response increased. Their study involved bystanders who could not see each other or the victim. In the Latané and Rodin study, the effect was again found, with bystanders who were face to face, but with the victim still only heard. In the present study, bystanders saw both the victim and each other. Will the diffusion of responsibility finding still occur in this situation?

In order to check this hypothesis, two analyses were performed. First, all non-model trials were separated into three groups according to the number of males in the critical area (the assumed reference group for spontaneous first helpers). Mean and median latencies of response were then calculated for each group, separately by type and race of victim. The results are presented in Table 5. There is no evidence in these data for diffusion of responsibility; in fact, response times, using either measure, are consistently faster for the 7 or more groups compared to the 1 to 3 groups.[9]

As Darley and Latané pointed out, however, different-size real groups cannot be meaningfully compared to one another, since as group size increases the likelihood that one or more persons will help also increases. A second analysis as similar as possible to that used by those authors was therefore performed, comparing latencies actually obtained for each size group with a base line of hypothetical groups of the same size made up by combining smaller groups. In order to have as much control as possible the analysis was confined to cane trials with white victims and male first helpers coming from the critical area. Within this set of trials, the most frequently occurring natural groups (of males in the critical area)

8. Individuals are also somewhat more likely to leave the area with the black victim than with the white victims ($\chi^2 = 3.24, p < .08$). This race effect is most probably an artifact, since the black victim ran more drunk trials than cane trials, the white victims, vice versa.
9. The total number of people in the car was strongly related to the number of males in the critical area. Similar results are obtained if latencies are examined as a function of the total number of people in the car.

Table 5. Mean and median latencies as a function of number of males in the critical area

No. males in critical area	Cane WHITE VICTIMS	Cane BLACK VICTIM	Cane TOTAL	Drunk WHITE VICTIMS	Drunk BLACK VICTIM	Drunk TOTAL
1–3						
M	16	12	15	—	309	309
Mdn.	7	12	7	—	312	312
N	17	2	19		4	4
4–6						
M	20	6	18	155	143	149
Mdn.	5	4	5	105	70	73
N	23	4	27	4	4	8
7 and up						
M	3	52	9	107	74	97
Mdn.	1	52	1.5	102	65	84
N	14	2	16	7	3	10
Kruskal-Wallis Test (H)			5.08			6.01
p			.08			.05

Note.—Means and medians in seconds. Model trials omitted; no response assigned 400 seconds.

were those of sizes 3 ($n = 6$) and 7 ($n = 5$). Hypothetical groups of 3 ($n = 4$) and 7 ($n = 25$) were composed of all combinations of smaller sized groups. For example, to obtain the hypothetical latencies for groups of 7, combinations were made of (*a*) all real size 6 groups with all real size 1 groups, plus (*b*) all real size 5 groups with all real size 2 groups, etc. The latency assigned to each of these hypothetical groups was that recorded for the faster of the two real groups of which it was composed. Cumulative response curves for real and hypothetical groups of 3 and 7 are presented in Figure 2.

As can be seen in the figure, the cumulative helping response curves for the hypothetical groups of both sizes are lower than those for the corresponding real groups. That is, members of real groups responded more rapidly than would be expected on the basis of the faster of the two scores obtained from the combined smaller groups. While these results together with those summarized in Table 5 do not necessarily contradict the diffusion of responsibility hypothesis, they do not follow the pattern of findings obtained by Darley and Latané

and are clearly at variance with the tentative conclusion of those investigators that "a victim may be more likely to receive help . . . the fewer people there are to take action [Latané & Darley, 1968, p. 221]."

Two explanations can be suggested to account for the disparity between the findings of Table 5 and Figure 2 and those of Darley and Latané and Latané and Rodin. As indicated earlier in this paper, the conditions of the present study were quite different from those in previous investigations. First, the fact that observers in the present study could see the victim may not only have constrained observers' abilities to conclude there was no emergency, but may also have overwhelmed with other considerations any tendency to diffuse responsibility. Second, the present findings may indicate that even if diffusion of responsibility *is* experienced by people who can actually see an emergency, when groups are larger than two the increment in deterrence to action resulting from increasing the number of observers may be less than the increase in probability that within a given time interval at least one of the observers will take action to assist the victim.

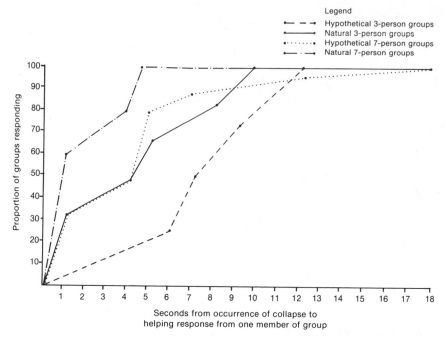

Figure 2. Cumulative proportion of groups producing a helper over time (cane trials, white victims, male helpers from inside critical area).

Clearly, more work is needed in both natural and laboratory settings before an understanding is reached of the conditions under which diffusion of responsibility will or will not occur.

CONCLUSIONS

In this field study, a personal emergency occurred in which escape for the bystander was virtually impossible. It was a public, face-to-face situation, and in this respect differed from previous lab studies. Moreover, since generalizations from field studies to lab research must be made with caution, few comparisons will be drawn. However, several conclusions may be put forth:

1. An individual who appears to be ill is more likely to receive aid than is one who appears to be drunk, even when the immediate help needed is of the same kind.

2. Given mixed groups of men and women, and a male victim, men are more likely to help than are women.

3. Given mixed racial groups, there is some tendency for same-race helping to be more frequent. This tendency is increased when the victim is drunk as compared to apparently ill.

4. There is no strong relationship between number of bystanders and speed of helping; the expected increased "diffusion of responsibility" with a greater number of bystanders was not obtained for groups of these sizes. That is, help is not less frequent or slower in coming from larger as compared to smaller groups of bystanders; what effect there is, is in the opposite direction.

5. The longer the emergency continues without help being offered (*a*) the less impact a model has on the helping behavior of observers; (*b*) the more likely it is that individuals will leave the immediate area; that

is, they appear to move purposively to another area in order to avoid the situation; (c) the more likely it is that observers will discuss the incident and its implications for their behavior.

A model of response to emergency situations consistent with the previous findings is currently being developed by the authors. It is briefly presented here as a possible heuristic device. The model includes the following assumptions: Observation of an emergency creates an emotional arousal state in the bystander. This state will be differently interpreted in different situations (Schachter, 1964) as fear, disgust, sympathy, etc., and possibly a combination of these. This state of arousal is higher (a) the more one can empathize with the victim (i.e., the more one can see oneself in his situation—Stotland, 1966), (b) the closer one is to the emergency, and (c) the longer the state of emergency continues without the intervention of a helper. It can be reduced by one of a number of possible responses: (a) helping directly, (b) going to get help, (c) leaving the scene of the emergency, and (d) rejecting the victim as undeserving of help (Lerner & Simmons, 1966). The response that will be chosen is a function of a cost-reward matrix that includes costs associated with helping (e.g., effort, embarrassment, possible disgusting or distasteful experiences, possible physical harm, etc.), costs associated with not helping (mainly self-blame and perceived censure from others), rewards associated with helping (mainly praise from self, victim, and others), and rewards associated with not helping (mainly those stemming from continuation of other activities). Note that the major motivation implied in the model is not a positive "altruistic" one, but rather a selfish desire to rid oneself of an unpleasant emotional state.

In terms of this model, the following after-the-fact interpretations can be made of the findings obtained:

1. The drunk is helped less because costs for helping are higher (greater disgust) and costs for not helping are lower (less self-blame and censure because he is in part responsible for his own victimization).

2. Women help less because costs for helping are higher in this situation (effort, mainly) and costs for not helping are lower (less censure from others; it is not her role).

3. Same-race helping, particularly of the drunk, can be explained by differential costs for not helping (less censure if one is of opposite race) and, with the drunk, differential costs for helping (more fear if of different race).

4. Diffusion of responsibility is not found on cane trials because costs for helping in general are low and costs for not helping are high (more self-blame because of possible severity of problem). That is, the suggestion is made that the diffusion of responsibility effect will increase as costs for helping increase and costs for not helping decrease. This interpretation is consistent with the well-known public incidents, in which possible bodily harm to a helper is almost always involved, and thus costs for helping are very high, and also with previous research done with nonvisible victims in which either (a) it was easy to assume someone had already helped and thus costs for not helping were reduced (Darley & Latané) or (b) it was possible to think that the emergency was minor, which also reduces the costs for not helping (Latané & Rodin).

5. All of the effects of time are also consistent with the model. The longer the emergency continues, the more likely it is that observers will be aroused and therefore will have chosen among the possible responses. Thus, (a) a late model will elicit less helping, since people have already reduced their arousal by one of the other methods; (b) unless arousal is reduced by other methods, people will leave more as time goes on, because arousal is still increasing; and (c) observers will discuss the incident in an attempt to reduce self-blame and arrive at the fourth resolution, namely a justification for not helping based on rejection of the victim.

Quite obviously, the model was derived from these data, along with data of other studies in the area. Needless to say, further work is being planned by the authors to test the implications of the model systematically.

REFERENCES

Berscheid, E., & Walster, E. When does a harm-doer compensate a victim? *Journal of Personality and Social Psychology*, 1967, 6, 435–441.

Black, D. J., & Reiss, A. J. *Studies in crime and law enforcement in major metropolitan areas.* (Report submitted to the President's Commission on Law Enforcement and Administration of Justice) Washington, D.C.: United States Government Printing Office, 1967.

Bryan, J. H., & Test, M. A. Models and helping: Naturalistic studies in aiding behavior. *Journal of Personality and Social Psychology*, 1967, 6, 400–407.

Darley, J., & Latané, B. Bystander intervention in emergencies: Diffusion of responsibility. *Journal of Personality and Social Psychology*, 1968, 8, 377–383.

Latané, B., & Darley, J. Group inhibition of bystander intervention in emergencies. *Journal of Personality and Social Psychology*, 1968, 10, 215–221.

Latané, B., & Rodin, J. A lady in distress: Inhibiting effects of friends and strangers on bystander intervention. *Journal of Experimental Social Psychology*, 1969, 5, 189–202.

Lerner, M. J., & Simmons, C. H. Observer's reaction to the "innocent victim": Compassion or rejection? *Journal of Personality and Social Psychology*, 1966, 4, 203–210.

Schachter, S. The interaction of cognitive and physiological determinants of emotional state. In L. Berkowitz (Ed.), *Advances in experimental social psychology.* Vol. 1. New York: Academic Press, 1964.

Schopler, J., & Matthews, M. W. The influence of the perceived causal locus of partner's dependence on the use of interpersonal power. *Journal of Personality and Social Psychology*, 1965, 4, 609–612.

Stotland, E. A theory and experiments in empathy. Paper presented at the meeting of the American Psychological Association, New York, September 1966.

Summary of Darley, J. M. & Latané, B., Bystander intervention in emergencies: Diffusion of responsibility, *Journal of Personality and Social Psychology*, 1968, *8*, 377–382.

Method: Between-subjects experiment

Hypothesis: "The more bystanders to an emergency, the less likely, or the more slowly, any one bystander will intervene to provide aid."

Independent variables/operational definitions: All subjects participated in "groups" that included a person identifying himself as an epileptic. This person, actually a recorded voice, went into an apparent seizure.

(1) The main independent variable was the number of recorded voices in the "group." Subjects heard only the future victim (two-person group), the victim and one other (three-person group), or the victim and four others (six-person group).

(2) Sex of subject self-explanatory; this was a variable only in three-person groups.

(3) Sex of bystander (manipulated only with female subject in three-person groups). Sex of recorded voice other than the victim's.

(4) Medical experience of bystander. In some of the three-person groups with female subjects and male bystanders, the bystander said, during the period before the seizure, that he had worked in the emergency ward at Bellevue Hospital.

(5) Individual difference measures (e.g., Alienation, Machiavellianism, need for approval, etc.). No clear operational definition is given for these non-manipulated variables. We are left to assume that some standardized tests were used.

Dependent variables/operational definitions: Speed of intervention. The reciprocal of the number of seconds between the start of the seizure speech and subject's response of reporting the emergency, multiplied by 100. The longest time allowed before responding was 360 seconds, after which the experiment was ended.

Findings: Hypothesis was supported: Subjects in "groups" responded less frequently and less quickly than subjects who thought they were the only bystanders. This seemed unaffected by the sex of either subjects or bystanders, by the bystanders' medical expertise, and by personality and social variables in the subject.

Controlled extraneous variables:

Type of emergency

Some organismic variables (the fact that several "individual difference measures" were not related to the dependent variables provided an after-the-fact control for the variables measured).

Sex of subject and bystander (controlled by being specifically studied as independent variables; they have no effect on the dependent variable).

Medical experience of other bystanders (again, controlled by being manipulated; this has no effect on the dependent variable at least with female subjects in this situation).

Uncontrolled extraneous variables/alternative explanations:

(1) The size of the community in which subjects grew up was found to be related to speed of helping. The correlation (r) was reported as negative ($-.26$), which means an inverse relationship: the larger the community a person came from the lower her/his speed score. People from big cities don't help fast. If the large-group subjects were mainly city-dwellers, this fact can explain their failure to help. If subjects were randomly assigned to treatments (the authors don't say), this organismic variable is randomized.

(2) The "individual difference measures" that the authors found to be unrelated to helping behavior were in fact collected only after the experiment had been explained to subjects (see last paragraph of PROCEDURE section). If subjects who did not intervene were impeded by their apathetic or Machiavellian atti-

tudes, they would hardly admit this after finding out what the experiment was about. Thus, the authors have not clearly ruled out explanations based on causes within the nonhelping individuals.

(3) Some subjects appear to have questioned whether the seizure was real. The authors reported that 20 of 65 subjects noted that "I thought it must be some sort of a fake," when asked to identify their thoughts during the experiment. If subjects had doubts, the presence of a group of others might have tipped the balance of decision in favor of nonintervention: "Let the others take the chance of looking foolish; it may be an experiment to see if I will follow directions and stay in my room." Thus, the results may hold only when there is doubt about whether the "emergency" is real.

Sample/Population sampled: The sample consisted of 59 female and 13 male students from a population of Introductory Psychology students at New York University. The authors appear to have generalized beyond this population to all adults.

Sampling biases: None evident; subjects could not freely choose whether or not to be in the experiment. We do not know, however, what method was used to choose these 72 students from the Introductory Psychology class.

Interactions: Though the authors did not expect to find any, they looked for some. For example, the sex of subject and of the other bystander, and the bystander's medical expertise did not influence the subject's behavior in three-person groups. Any of these variables could possibly have influenced people, and the influence could have depended on the size of the group. (This was not carefully investigated: These other variables were manipulated only with one group size.)

Conclusions: In emergencies in which bystanders do not see each other, and in which indirect action is possible, group size inhibits bystander intervention. This effect does not result from the bystanders' personalities or attitudes, or the social group to which they belong. Note that the authors have generalized from one emergency situation to a large class of emergencies. Whether this generalization holds must await further evidence.

Summary of Latané, B. & Darley, J. M., Group inhibition of bystander intervention in emergencies, *Journal of Personality and Social Psychology,* 1968, *10*, 215–221.

Method: Between-subjects experiment

Hypothesis: Being in a group decreases the probability that an individual will respond to an emergency. This happens partly by group influence on the individual's interpretation of events.

Independent variables/operational definitions: All subjects filled out a questionnaire in a room that filled with smoke coming through a vent.

(1) Size of group. Subjects were alone or with two others in room.

(2) Response of others to event. In some three-person groups, two people were the experimenter's confederates, and acted indifferent to the smoke. In the other three-person groups, all people were real subjects, and their responses to the smoke were not controlled.

Dependent variables/operational definitions:

(1) Reporting the smoke in room. (a) Did subject report smoke within six minutes after noticing it? (b) Length of time after subject noticed smoke before reporting it.

(2) Other: Notes were taken on subjects' behavior, based on observation through one-way mirror. Postexperimental interviews were used to obtain subjects' perceptions of the events.

Findings: Subjects in groups responded less frequently and less quickly than people alone. This was true both when bystanders were naive and when they were the experimenter's confederates and acted passively.

Controlled extraneous variables:

Type of emergency (held constant)

Reactions of confederates (held constant) (also other variables)

Uncontrolled extraneous variables/alternative explanations:

(1) Authors mention that people may fear fire less in groups, and may therefore be less inclined to act (some evidence against this is presented).

(2) Authors mention that people may desire to hide their fears more when in groups, and thus be less inclined to act (authors argue against this interpretation too).

(3) Authors mentioned that some subjects thought "it must be some sort of experiment" when the smoke came in. These were subjects who did not report the smoke, so most came from the group conditions. This reaction should be more common in a university research setting than elsewhere. Thus, while these subjects didn't report the emergency, they might have if they hadn't seen the situation as an experiment.

Sample/Population sampled: The sample consisted of 58 volunteers from the population of male Columbia students living on campus. The authors generalize to "American males," and then, in the last paragraph, to "individuals."

Sampling biases: Volunteer subjects were used. Though "most" people contacted did volunteer, it is also true that volunteer subjects are usually more interested and willing to please than the average person. If the sample includes people who suspect that "it must be some sort of experiment," the tendency not to respond should be exaggerated by sampling bias because volunteers would not like to ruin the experiment.

Interactions: Not studied or reported.

Conclusions: "Individuals are less likely to engage in socially responsible action if they think other bystanders are present."

This is a conclusion from the present study and the one by Darley and Latané (1968). Note that the conclusion is about all "individuals."

Summary of Piliavin, I. M., Rodin, J., & Piliavin, J. A., Good Samaritanism: An underground phenomenon? *Journal of Personality and Social Psychology,* 1969, *13*, 289–299.

Method: Since the number of bystanders was not manipulated, any conclusions on the relationship of crowd size to intervention are based on *correlational* evidence. On the other hand, the study is a between-subjects experiment in that it manipulates the race and physical appearance (cane-using versus drunk) of the victim, and the presence of helping models. Thus, even though the study is experimental, it is only correlational with respect to the independent variable of greatest interest to us.

Hypothesis: There are several, though not all are related to the issue we are looking for data on:

(1) People will be more likely to help a victim of their own race.

(2) People will be more likely to help a sick person than a drunken one.

(3) People exposed to helping models will be more likely to help.

(4) Crowd size may or may not influence the likelihood of helping.

Only this last hypothesis is of major interest to us.

Independent variables/operational definitions: We can save ourselves some writing here by deciding which variables to look at. Though they are all interesting, we are only interested in crowd size as an independent variable. If the other independent variables in this study are investigated in interaction with crowd size, we might have to take notice of them, since the effect of crowd size might depend on other variables, such as the racial composition of the group, and so on. The data on crowd size (Table 5 in the study) report its effect in relationship to two variables: type of victim (cane versus drunk) and race of victim. No data are reported on the relationship of group size to race of helpers or response to models. We are only concerned with group size and the variables that might interact with it:

(1) Size of group: Operationally, this was defined in terms of the number of *male* bystanders in the "critical area" (that is, the half of the subway car in which the victim "collapsed"). Specifically, all groups were divided into those containing 1–3, 4–6, and 7 or more males.

(2) Race of victim: White or black (all victims 26–35 years old, identically dressed).

(3) Type of victim: Drunk condition victims "smelled of liquor and carried a liquor bottle tightly wrapped in a brown bag." Cane condition victims "appeared sober and carried a black cane." All victims dressed and behaved identically except for the above.

Dependent variables/operational definitions: Likelihood of a victim receiving help. This was operationalized as the length of time between the start of the "emergency" and the arrival of the first helper on the scene (in nonmodel trials).

Findings: Victims (black or white, drunk or ill) were likely to receive help quicker when there were a larger number of men in the critical area. Also, large groups responded faster than mathematically created combinations of smaller groups.

Controlled extraneous variables:
Victim's dress and behavior
Scene of emergency
Opportunity for potential helpers to escape was equal in all trials (also other variables)

Uncontrolled extraneous variables/alternative explanations: Because the group size variable was organismic, not manipulated, we should look for correlates of this variable that might influence helping behavior. Here are some possibilities:

(1) Time of day and type of passengers: The number of riders in the subway car was said to vary between 15 and 120—quite a range! Suppose the subway was always most crowded during a certain part of the 11 AM to 3 PM period during which the trials were run. Further suppose that the riders at that time (say it was lunch hour) were a different sort of people (more responsible, since they are working) from those who ride the subway just before and just after lunchtime. If these assumptions hold, it may be that what was interpreted as an effect of group size was really an effect of the type of people in the group. While there is no evidence to support these assumptions, they are at least plausible, and there is no evidence presented to refute them.

(2) Time of year and type of passengers: The study ran from April to June. Time of year may influence both the size and helpfulness of the subway crowds. You can make up several plausible explanations of the results based on this possibility.

Sample/Population sampled: The authors studied about 4450 weekday riders of the 8th Avenue Subway (between 59th and 125th Streets, on the express) between 11 AM and 3 PM from April to June 1968.

It is difficult to say what population this sample is drawn from. I'd say it is a sample of New York City subway riders, though it is a biased sample (see below). The authors appear to generalize beyond this population to the population of anyone in a similar emergency. They consider this emergency to be similar to, and to generalize to, other emergencies in which bystanders can see each other, and in which there is little chance for them to escape.

Sampling biases: The sample is biased because it excludes all those subway riders who are working on weekdays between the hours of eleven and three, as well as those who are attending school. Thus, the sample probably over-represents homemakers, retired people, and the unemployed. If the sample is considered to be a sample of the population of New Yorkers, it is further biased by excluding motorists and taxi riders, most of whom are of higher socioeconomic status than the average subway rider.

Interactions: Group size does *not* seem to interact with the race of the victim, or with whether he appeared drunk or ill. The data exist in Table 5 to look for these interactions, but they do not seem to be present.

Conclusions: In this situation, group size does not inhibit helping behavior. The authors also speculate on the possible reasons why these results do not agree with those of other studies (including Darley and Latané, 1968). They suggest that the difference may have been due to subjects' ability to see (as well as hear) the victim, or to the fact that escape was "virtually impossible" in this study. Another explanation is also offered (see last paragraph of RESULTS AND DISCUSSION).

You now have some detailed notes on a group of articles. Your next job, before writing a review, is to try and make sense out of the results of all the studies. Although there is no foolproof procedure that will guide you through a tangle of research to a clear view, there is a procedure that can be of some help. Try to proceed in this way:

(1) Look at your notes on the FINDINGS of the studies.

If the relationship between the variables you are interested in is always the same, you are almost home free. Go to step 5.

This rarely happens. Usually some results will point in one direction and others will either point the other way, or find no relationship, or conclude that the relationship depends on other variables (interaction effects). You could decide the point by "majority vote" (the most common result "wins"), but that isn't a very satisfactory way to proceed because it doesn't explain why some results don't fit. Besides, the unusual result often points the way to deeper knowledge. So, if the results do not agree, go to step 2.

(2) Look at your notes on INTERACTIONS.

See if any of the studies you read discovers a third variable that influences the relationship between the ones you have chosen to study. If you do find an interaction, look back at the other studies to see if they measured the third variable. If they did, was the same interaction present? (If there was no interaction effect, you have another problem to solve: Why isn't the interaction universal?) If other studies did find the interaction, or if no other studies measured the third variable, look at the other research in terms of the third variable.

An example is the research on sex differences in conformity, mentioned on page 171. Sistrunk and McDavid (1971) suspected that the sex differences most researchers found may have resulted from the type of tasks (male-or-female-interest) studied. Their research demonstrated that an interaction between sex and type of task did influence conformity. Knowing this, it becomes possible to look back at the earlier research on sex and conformity to see if the studies that found women to conform more did, in fact, use tasks like those Sistrunk and McDavid called male-interest tasks. If so, the apparent conflict between the results of Sistrunk and McDavid and those of the earlier researchers begins to be resolved.

If you are able to find a third variable that makes sense out of some of the discrepancies in the research, you have one possible way to make sense of all the literature you have found. But whether you have found such an explanation or not, go on to step 3.

(3) Look at each of the ALTERNATIVE EXPLANATIONS you have suggested for each study reviewed.

Can any of these explain the results of more than one study? If so, you have something worth noting, especially if you are able to use an alternative explanation to explain the results of studies that seem, on the surface, to contradict each other.

Are there studies that provide evidence against an alternative explanation you have suggested for a different study? If so, you can think about ruling out that explanation. (If you find this, you might briefly mention it in your review.)

We can look at the articles on bystander intervention for an example of this process. The first alternative explanation mentioned for Darley and Latané's results (1968) concerned the size of the community from which the subjects came. People from larger home towns were more likely to stand by and do nothing in emergencies. Checking this explanation against the other studies, we find that Latané and Darley (1968) used a sample of Columbia University students living on campus. It is not clear whether these students were small-towners or city people, though a university like Columbia probably attracts mainly urban and suburban people. The study by Piliavin et al. (1969) clearly used predominantly city-dwellers. Relatively few out-of-towners ride the subways, especially on the run to Harlem. Yet in this study the bystanders *did* intervene when in groups. This was a case of big city people who didn't just stand by. It seems likely that the difference between Latané's and Darley's results and those of the Piliavin group are not due to the size city the subjects came from, but probably result from some other variable.

This is the general line of thinking. Until you have a sense of which alternative explanations look the most promising, it might pay to look through them all, methodically, trying to see if any of them helps you make sense out of several different studies. After you have done this, you will have some idea of which studies seem to make sense together (on the basis of the same assumptions), and which ones you still feel are unexplained. Then go on to step 4.

(4) Compare the studies in terms of

OPERATIONAL DEFINITIONS OF INDEPENDENT VARIABLES

OPERATIONAL DEFINITIONS OF DEPENDENT VARIABLES

POPULATIONS SAMPLED

SETTINGS USED IN GATHERING DATA

The task is to try to find some consistency between one of these four things and the results reported. Sometimes the results you get depend on the way you measure the variables, or the subjects you use, or the place and time you choose to gather data. When two studies get different results, the difference might be explained by a difference in any of these areas. When two studies get the same results, one is tempted to conclude that differences between them in these four areas are unimportant in terms of the variables being studied. A good way to begin is to *take two studies that seem most inconsistent with each other* and look for differences between them in terms of operational definitions, populations sampled, and/or settings. Use any difference you find as a hypothesis, and test it using the evidence of the other studies.

Here is an example from the bystander intervention studies. The Piliavin study stands out because large groups were more helpful than small ones, while the reverse was found in the two other studies. One difference between Piliavin and the other studies was in the subjects used (subway riders in Piliavin, college students in the other studies). Once you find this difference between the Piliavin study and *one* of the others, you can suggest a tentative explanation: There is a difference between college students and the run-of-the-mill New Yorker that makes students more averse to taking action and looking foolish. You predict that with students there will be less helping as the group gets larger, while the reverse will be true of other New Yorkers. And indeed the third study, which uses students, finds that they help less in groups. This is support for your explanation, and it has made sense of the three articles. (Of course, it has not made sense of the fact that the Kitty Genovese murder, which prompted the research, was witnessed by 38 run-of-the-mill New Yorkers who did nothing.) There are other differences between Piliavin and the other studies, and some of these may yield more convincing explanations of the bystander intervention phenomenon (see the sample review that begins on page 211).

The goal of this step in your thinking is to find one or more consistent relationships between some detail of the studies and the results they report. If you can find a detail that is consistently correlated with a particular result, you have something worth mentioning, because it may help explain why different researchers get different results. This is the way reviews of empirical literature can be useful in extending knowledge. Armed with a hypothesis about what makes the results turn out different, a reviewer like you can suggest further research to test the new hypothesis. It would not be difficult, for example, to expose college students and other New York dwellers to the same carefully controlled emergency, and compare their reactions. This would provide direct evidence on the hypothesis that college students behave differently from other people in emergencies.

With this ground work done, you can proceed closer to writing.

(5) Decide on a logical order in which to present your articles (or other scientific evidence).

You might present articles in the chronological order in which they were written. This organization makes good sense when the authors were aware of each other's work, as is the case with these articles on bystander intervention (Latané and Darley cite Darley and Latané, and Piliavin et al. cite Latané and Darley). When each article reviews the older ones, chronological order makes good sense because the studies follow *logically* as well.

Another form of organization is topical. You might group laboratory studies together and field research together, or you might divide the research according to the population sampled or according to the ways the variables were operationalized, and so on. With topical organization, you should use a category system that will make sense in terms of your ultimate conclusion. If, for example; you decide that Piliavin's results differed from those of the other studies because Piliavin's was a field study, it makes sense to separate field studies from lab studies. You could then summarize the lab studies, summarize the field studies, and compare the two summaries. Your point would be strongly made.

You could also organize your review like a detective story. You would start with a problem (Why wasn't Kitty Genovese's murderer stopped, with so many people watching?), and present articles to piece together an answer. Begin with a general or preliminary piece of research that still leaves open several possibilities, and then present other pieces of research that slowly eliminate alternative explanations, or else suggest new ones. Again, the order of presentation depends on the final point you want to make. In social science, many of the mysteries are unsolved, and it is often interesting to see how what everybody thought was true turned out to be false.

With a logical organization, you are ready to write.

(6) WRITE.

In preparing a review for a professional journal, space is at a premium and you are writing for an audience of experts in the field. Thus, in such reviews it is unnecessary or undesirable to include a great deal of detail about each study you review. For a beginner, however, some detail is desirable. If you are not used to writing reviews of research articles, or if your audience is nonexpert, you should write with a fair amount of detail about each study you are evaluating. You can learn a lot about how to do this concisely by reading the abstracts that appear at the head of many articles in the professional journals. Here is an outline of what you should probably tell your reader about each article:

> What was the general question?
> What was the hypothesis?
> What method was used to collect the data?
> What population was sampled?
> What were the variables important to your review?
> How were these operationalized (briefly)?
> What results were found?
> What was the author's conclusion?

This is a good approximate order in which to present the information, and it is the order most frequently used in abstracts. Once you have said all this, the reader is "with you"—he or she knows what the study was all about. You may then go on with your critique (alternative explanations due to uncontrolled extraneous variables, sampling bias, etc.) and discuss other articles, in the order you have planned.

Unfortunately, there is no rule concerning how much criticism of an article is appropriate while you are first summarizing it. It is a matter of judgment whether to put your commentary after each article or to save it for the end. The most crucial point is not to lose the reader in details.

These suggestions should help you organize your thinking and writing about a group of scientific articles. The following student review of the three articles on bystander intervention may also help.

THE EFFECT OF GROUP SIZE ON BYSTANDER INTERVENTION IN EMERGENCIES

Robert Dietrich
ELMIRA COLLEGE

The murder of Kitty Genovese which 38 people watched for half an hour without extending aid of any kind has prompted considerable research into a phenomenon termed "bystander apathy." The researchers who did the studies contained within the current review disclaim that apathy is a factor in nonintervention by bystanders in an emergency. The first two studies cited in this review by Darley and Latané (1968) and Latané and Darley (1968) claim that dynamics peculiar to group size are responsible for this inaction by groups of bystanders in an emergency; the third and final study of this review, by Piliavin, Rodin, and Piliavin (1969), hypothesized that action or inaction by bystanders is due to situational factors exclusive of group size.

What effect does group size have on the helping behavior of individuals witnessing an emergency? It has been hypothesized that as the number of witnesses to an emergency increases, the likelihood that one or more of these witnesses will intervene, decreases.

The first study of this review (Darley & Latané, 1968) advances this hypothesis. The researchers claim that diffusion of responsibility is the cause of inaction by witnesses to an emergency. Since the responsibility to act in an emergency is diffused throughout the number of people present, then the more people present the more diffusion there will be, and consequently motivation to act by any single individual will be weaker. To test their hypothesis the researchers constructed a between-subjects experiment in the laboratory.

The subjects used in this experiment were 13 males and 59 females enrolled in an introductory psychology course at New York University. Their participation was mandatory as a class requirement and they had no knowledge that they were participating in an experiment.

To manipulate group size, a subject was placed in a room by himself in which a communication system monitored the voices of supposedly other people in the subject's group. The voices were actually recordings and group size as perceived by the subject was the number of different voices that he heard. There were three group sizes: (1) a two-person group consisting of the subject and the voice of a future emergency victim; (2) a three-person group consisting of an added voice merely serving as another bystander to the planned emergency; and (3) a six-person group consisting of three added voices serving as bystanders.

The emergency situation was defined as the hearing of one of the supposed group members having an epileptic seizure. The dependent variable of reaction to the emergency by the subject was measured by the amount of time it took the subject to initiate a helping behavior (notifying the experimenter who was sitting outside the room). Time was measured from the onset of the seizure until the subject reported the seizure; if no report was made within six minutes it was considered as no response to the emergency and the particular session was terminated. To deemphasize the six minute time limit for a response to be issued, a "speed" score was derived from the time taken for a particular response by taking the reciprocal of the response time in seconds and multiplying it by 100.

The subjects in their respective groups listened to each person in their group talk in turn for 125 seconds under the guise that they were to discuss personal problems facing them due to urban pressures. The future victim always talked first and the subject always talked last. Upon the victim's second turn to talk the seizure condition was initiated. The subject was led to believe that the only time he could be heard by the other members of the group was when it was his turn to talk; and likewise, the only time he could hear the other members was on their turn to talk. Informed judges estimated that the emergency should be undeniably perceived by the subject by 70 seconds after the beginning of the victim's second turn to talk (onset of the seizure). If a subject did not respond within six minutes after the onset of the seizure that particular experimental session was terminated.

The results showed that subjects in the two-person groups reported the emergency significantly faster than subjects in the three-person groups; and subjects in the three-person groups reported the emergency faster than those in the six-person groups.

The researchers concluded that these results confirmed their hypothesis and that diffusion of responsibility was a cause of less responding as the size of the group became larger. To further support their conclusion and to discredit the apathy theory, the researchers made note of emotional response of the subjects who didn't act in the emergency. Diffusion of responsibility, and thus inaction, caused an inner conflict demonstrated by such emotional responses as sweating hands, general nervousness, etc.

In their results the researchers didn't take into consideration that nearly one third of the subjects commented that they believed the emergency situation was a "fake."

Thus, it is reasonable to speculate that subjects who thought themselves to be in groups would be less apt to act than lone subjects, for why should they respond to a faked emergency and look foolish in the eyes of the other "bystanders." Perhaps failure to respond in this situation was a function of the number of bystanders present, but instead of diffusion of responsibility, the larger the group of people to witness a subject's reaction to a faked emergency, the more foolish the subject would feel. Whether or not the subjects guessed that the emergency was merely contrived, just such statements alone from so many subjects demonstrates a weakness in the experimenters' conclusions. Such sources of confounding are especially a problem in laboratory experiments and the conclusions drawn from this study should be regarded with reserve.

What about the emotional response of the subjects that did not give aid? It is difficult to take the emotional responses reported into consideration since the researchers didn't quantify them. How many subjects actually emitted such responses; what was the degree of emotional response per subject; is it possible that an emotional response was, at least in some cases, misperceived, and maybe such a report was even a product of experimenter bias? In addition, wouldn't concerned bystanders show emotion even if they believed help to be on its way?

In the between-subjects experiment by Latané and Darley (1968) the subjects were put with other real people in composing the groups for this study. In this study the hypothesis was basically the same as in the former study, except this time it was speculated that the more people witnessing an emergency the less apt anyone will be to respond because interaction between the bystanders will tend to minimize the immediacy of the situation. The subjects for this study were 58 male Columbia professional, graduate, and undergraduate students.

They were asked to participate in the study under the guise that they would be discussing problems involved in life at an urban university. Group size for this study was manipulated by the use of a single-subject situation, a subject placed with two confederates of the experimenter, and three subjects together in a group.

The subjects were guided to a room in which they were to fill out a questionnaire consistent with the supposed purpose of the study. The emergency situation in this study was induced by the injection of bursts of white "smoke" into a room in which the subjects were contained. The smoke was injected into the room until a subject reported it or until the room was filled with smoke and interfered with visibility. If the (a) subject did not report the smoke by six minutes after its onset, that particular experimental session was terminated.

The dependent variable was measured by the amount of time it took a subject to report the smoke (emergency) after he had noticed it. If the smoke was unreported after six minutes, the experimental session was terminated.

The subject-alone condition resulted in the highest incidence of reporting the smoke. Although more subjects from the three-subject group reported smoke than from the group containing one subject and two confederates, the differences between these two groups were not significant.

According to a post interview, none of the subjects was overly alarmed by the smoke. The subjects who reported the smoke were not sure what it was from, but thought that it might hold some potential danger. Those that did not report the smoke claimed that they thought that it was harmless. Some even perceived the situation as being a possible experiment.

From the response measures and the self-reports of the subject, Latané and Darley concluded that people in groups do not see a situation as being as dangerous as persons who are alone and witnessing a potentially hazardous situation. The researchers ruled out diffusion of responsibility as a major factor in this study because the danger of the situation was aimed at the subject rather than someone else; thus, and in support of their hypothesis, in order for inaction to prevail it was reasoned that being in a group lessened the perception of danger by a subject.

Latané and Darley offer an alternative explanation in that American culture stresses composure in an emergency situation. Thus, subjects in groups did not react due to not wanting to lose their composure in the eyes of others present. Fear could be a component of lost composure which the subject did not want to show by "overreacting" and reporting the smoke. Also, according to the researchers, people tend to feel safe in groups and therefore able to better cope with fear and endure a threatening situation.

The evidence seems somewhat weak in support of a major difference between the perception of danger by subjects alone and the perception (lack of perception) by subjects in groups. No subject really displayed alarm due to the smoke. This puts in doubt, as in the previously cited study, how real the emergency was to any of the subjects. Contrary to what the researchers claim, another alternate explanation could be diffusion of responsibility. If the smoke really was perceived as not immediately dangerous it is reasonable to assume that individuals alone would report it before someone from a group. If the smoke was more of a nuisance than a threat to the subjects, those in groups tended to wait it out with the idea that someone else would report it. Whatever the precise explanation for the results of this study, it appears as though the number of bystanders present (one or three bystanders) makes a difference in responding to an emergency.

In a field study by Piliavin et al. (1969) factors besides the size of the group witnessing an emergency were examined. Contradicting the former two studies Piliavin hypothesized that group size was not the determiner of aid in an emergency.

The subjects for this study were approximately 4,450 men and women who traveled the 8th Avenue Ind. subway in New York City weekdays between 11:00 A.M. and 3:00 P.M. April 15 to June 26, 1968. The subway used traveled between Harlem and the Bronx and contained about 45% black and 55% white people. The mean number of people per car was 43 and the mean number of people in the critical area of the staged emergency was 8.5.

Group size for this study was taken as the number of males within a critical area at the onset of the "emergency" situation. The most frequently occurring group sizes were 3-person and 7-person groups.

The emergency situation was either a confederate acting as though he was intoxicated and falling on the floor of a subway car, or a confederate using a cane and falling on the floor of a subway car.

Response to the emergency was measured by the amount of time it took from the onset of the emergency to the extending of aid by a bystander.

The subway trains selected for staging the emergencies were ones which made no stops for 7½ minutes; thus, the confederates had a captive audience for this amount of time. 70 seconds after the train would leave its station the confederate would collapse on the floor of the car.

The results showed that some of the variables being studied did make a difference in the helping behavior of the bystanders, but group size did not make a significant difference in whether or not the victim was helped. Although it was not a significant effect, the researchers found that a larger group size was more apt to offer help than a smaller group size.

This is a marked deviance from the former two studies cited. The researchers

explain this difference due to the particular situation at hand: The bystanders could not help but see the incident and were very close to it; and they could not ignore the emergency because they were exposed to it whether or not they wanted to be. Although the researchers do not elaborate on such effects, perhaps proximity to an emergency and the impossibility of escape from it promotes an attitude in a bystander such that he is compelled to act. In the case of Piliavin's study this disposition to help might be enhanced by the fact that a bystander could give direct assistance in the emergency; whereas, in the former two studies cited the subject could only give aid indirectly through the experimenter. This "hands on" capability of the current study may be the critical element causing the discrepancy in results between it and the previously cited studies.

Another factor that may have influenced the results of this study could be the type of subjects used. The experiments previously cited used college students as opposed to the different but particular population sample used in the current study. Perhaps college students are more apt to perceive particulars of an experiment and therefore introduce a source of confounding; whereas a different population sample might be more naive. To further illustrate possible differences due to different population samples, it might be noted that the murder of Kitty Genovese occurred in a middle class neighborhood. Possibly the majority of people riding on the subway in the Piliavin et al. study were lower class people, and maybe lower class people are more inclined to help someone in distress than would middle class people.

The Piliavin study has some good features. It is especially impressive because it was done in the field. Undoubtedly the subjects were less prone to discover the study's deceptive purpose than were the subjects in the laboratory studies. Although Piliavin's subjects were not a true representation of the general population, they were a better representation than the subjects used in the two former studies cited. These features may have had important influence on the results obtained.

All the studies cited attempted to generalize to the general population, a generalization that has no merit since none of the samples were truly representative of the general population.

The accumulated evidence is not impressive enough to support any hypothesis concerning intervention by bystanders to an emergency, as being a function of the number of bystanders present. The study by Piliavin et al. impressively contradicts the conclusions of the first two studies reviewed in that no relationship was found between number of bystanders and helping behavior of the bystanders. Impressive as the Piliavin et al. study is, it must be remembered that only Piliavin et al. found this effect, and, as the others, their study has its noted weaknesses.

In a final comparison of all the studies and the Genovese incident, major differences are evident. Along with the sample and setting differences, the defined emergency situation was different in each case. The Darley and Latané experiment had a victim that couldn't be seen by the subjects; the Latané and Darley study placed the subject in the position of being a possible victim; the Piliavin et al. study's victim was in full view of and close proximity to the subjects; and in the Genovese case the victim was in full view of the bystanders, but the bystanders were removed from the actual scene of the emergency; plus, direct intervention by a bystander in the Genovese case presented a possible danger to that bystander. These differences suggest a strong possibility that the bystanders in each case had different potentials to react.

The differences between the cases seem to be great enough to suggest that other factors are involved in bystander intervention in an emergency in addition to the number of bystanders present. Perhaps it is a combination of factors peculiar to each situation which determines whether bystanders respond to an emergency. Walster and Piliavin (1972) present an interesting discussion of the issue. They claim that an ordered progression of factors determine whether or not help is forthcoming from bystanders, and that each factor in itself is influenced by a number of variables. For instance, recognition of an emergency situation is the initial factor in the chain. Did this recognition occur in the first two studies cited? Arousal is a factor following recognition. Arousal is effected by how great the emergency is, affective reaction toward a victim, etc. Was arousal present in the Genovese case? Response cost is considered after arousal. If arousal was sufficiently present in the Genovese case, was the response cost structure such that it inhibited help to the victim (i.e., the cost of helping was greater than the reward for helping)? Based on these factors it could be assumed that the proper combination of variables influencing these factors was present in the Piliavin study, thus resulting in a helping behavior on the part of the bystanders in that study. Although the previous is but a partial explanation, it suggests direction for further research on the current issue. Thus a feasible direction of further research would be studying the interaction of several variables in emergency situations as relating to intervention by bystanders.

REFERENCES

Darley, J. M. & Latané, B. Bystander intervention in emergencies: Diffusion of responsibility. *Journal of Personality and Social Psychology*, 1968, *8*, 377–383.

Latané, B. & Darley, J. Group inhibition of bystander intervention in emergencies. *Journal* of *Personality and Social Psychology*, 1968, *10*, (3), 215–221.

Piliavin, I. M., Rodin, J., & Piliavin, J. A. Good Samaritanism: An underground phenomenon? *Journal of Personality and Social Psychology*, 1969, *13*, (4), 289–299.

Walster, E. & Piliavin, J. A. Equity and the innocent bystander. *Journal of Social Issues*, 1972, *28*, 165–189.

The preceding paper is by a student who has learned how to write a critical review. While it is imperfectly written—and takes only one of the possible approaches to its task—it is a very good example of how to review a set of articles bearing on a general question and you may safely use it as a model.

Certain features of the paper are discussed below.

Style: This paper is written in the standard style of professional work in psychology. The references are cited in psychological style (American Psychological Association, 1974), and are listed, using that style, at the end of the paper. Students in psychology may use the paper as a stylistic model.

Organization: The paper can be divided into four major sections.

(1) Introduction—the first two paragraphs tell us the general question, the hypotheses that have been made, and something about how the articles will be organized: two that suggest the same conclusion, and then one that disagreed.

(2) Description of the studies—the studies are described one at a time, and all the crucial information is given, in about the order suggested (see page 210). You will note that the longest part of these descriptions is devoted to telling how variables were operationalized. This usually takes longest to describe, especially with experimental research. The writer has ended his discussion of each article by suggesting some possible alternative explanations. He could have saved these for the end of the paper, but they are highly appropriate where he put them.

(3) Comparison of the studies—here we see some of the writer's thinking. He has shown us where he has looked for possible explanations of the findings of all three studies together and points out the differences between studies, in terms of the subject populations sampled, procedures used, and so forth. This is a good way to proceed since it makes your thinking clear to the reader. It is possible, however, to combine this section with the one to follow.

(4) Conclusions and suggestions for research—the last three paragraphs of the paper give the writer's conclusions. You can see that he is very doubtful about concluding anything from these three studies. You may

reach this conclusion yourself and it is not an uncommon one. He perhaps could have come up with a formulation that at least *might* make sense of these three studies and the Genovese murder, but he has stopped short of doing this. Instead, he has done some extra research (admirable, but not always necessary), and found a formulation, by Walster and Piliavin, that points out the complexity of the problem and allows him to duck out by suggesting directions for research, without solving anything. It is regrettable that he has had to do this, but it is a fairly well-respected ending for a critical review.

Content: Let's look at selected parts of the paper.

(1) *Method of gathering data:* Once, the writer explicitly identifies the method used to collect data in a study (he identified the first study as a between-subjects experiment). This is all right to do, but not necessary. What is necessary is to give the reader enough information to tell what method was used. Thus, in describing the Latané and Darley study (page 213) he tells the reader that the independent variable (group size) was manipulated, and that this was done by using three situations. It is clear that this is a comparison group design; a between-subjects experiment.

(2) *Alternative explanations:* The writer seems to have given only those alternative explanations he feels may truly explain the results. The size of the community from which subjects came, for example, is not mentioned. This may be either because he didn't think of it or because he noticed that Piliavin's results didn't fit the explanation. As a rule, don't burden yourself and the reader by discussing alternative explanations that you will later identify as useless.

(3) *Conclusions:* The writer has suggested a few. First, he hints that the college students may have been more sophisticated about the possibility they were being experimented on, and this may have led them to behave in an atypical manner. This conclusion is plausible, and it fits the data of all three studies, though not of the Genovese murder, where people knew it wasn't an experiment yet did nothing. Second, he suggests social class as a possible explanation: The subjects who did nothing in two experiments and the real murder were all presumably middle-class or higher, while the subway riders who helped were probably lower-class. This suggestion handles *all* the data, and is therefore worth a second look. Finally, several differences among studies are noted in the situations used, and it is suggested that these differences may hold the key to the bystander intervention question. This a plausible conclusion. Obviously, there are other possible explanations that aren't mentioned, yet this does not detract from the paper. The writer has successfully described the literature, pointed to the contradictions and inconsistencies, and suggested some possible meanings of the whole body of information. This is all one can ask of a reviewer.

If you have followed and understood what you have read and practiced to this point, you should be ready to try to do what Bob Dietrich did, with other material. No examples are provided because it is time for you to go out on your own. If you must find research on your own before writing your review, use the Appendix as a reference, and be sure that all the evidence you have is really about the same general question. Be sure the studies you choose deal with the same variables, or closely related ones. If they do, the procedures suggested in this chapter, together with what you know, should guide you to a competent critical review.

This is the payoff from all your work so far. By now, you should be able to draw your own conclusions and be fairly certain of your opinions in an area you care about—even if you must decide that you aren't sure. I hope that you continue to use your skills to evaluate evidence, and that you use them responsibly.

Asking Answerable Questions and Finding Scientific Evidence

This Appendix is to help you transform an interest of yours into a question that is answerable by appeal to scientific evidence. This is a necessary process before you can evaluate the available facts pertaining to your question.

If you have completed Chapter 2, there should be little new vocabulary to learn here because you will mainly be applying what you have learned as well as practicing some library skills. However, the term *answerable question* should be defined before we go further. According to Doherty and Shemberg, "in order for a question to be answered scientifically, it must be asked so that *repeatable, controlled observations of all significant items* in the question can be made" (1970, p. 6, emphasis added).

The crucial point is that whether a question is answerable by appeal to evidence *depends on how it is asked*. This seems obvious. However, the implication is that whether a question can have a scientific answer does *not* depend on how important it is, or whether you feel you have a good idea of what you want to know; you can get an answer *only* if you frame the question properly. Let's look back at the definition.

"*So that repeatable . . . observations can be made*." This means that abstractions must be concretized well enough for independent observers to agree on what is what.

"*So that . . . controlled observations . . . can be made*." Essentially, this means you must be able to rule out alternative explanations for what you observe. I'm not sure whether you can always tell before you ask the question if fully controlled observations are possible. We may not have the technology needed to measure what you want to observe, or it may be unethical to control the conditions of observation, or, if you are studying real life events, such as the functioning of governments, control is impossible. The goal of ruling out alternatives is still desirable, no matter how hard it may be to attain in practice.

"*So that . . . observations of all significant items . . . can be made.*" The "significant items" are *variables*. This means that you must identify the relevant variables, concretize them, and observe them.

Thus, to have an answerable question, you must identify variables and concretize them, so that they may be observed under conditions that rule out possible effects of other events ("extraneous variables"). An example may make this clearer. To use the one given by Doherty and Shemberg (1970), you may begin with a general question: "Why does one's personality change when under stress?" The significant items here are personality, change, and stress. Personality and stress are variables, and the fact that they change is what makes them variables. Since the variables are unconcretized, the question is unanswerable. "Personality" can be concretized in many ways. If we use, for example, scores on the CPI (California Personality Inventory, a standard personality test), we can now look, concretely, for different scores depending on whether the person is under "stress." "Stress" can also be concretized in many ways (e.g., deprivation of sleep for 96 hours, or incarceration in a concentration camp, or immersion in ice water, etc.). Once the variables are concretized (in any way you choose), the question becomes answerable. You need only to make the necessary observations.

You probably cannot help noticing the difference between measuring the effect of sleep deprivation on CPI scores (for example) and understanding why personality changes with stress. When you concretize the variables, you only know about a certain kind of stress and its effects on those aspects of personality the CPI measures. In short, you have evidence on only part of the original question. Worse yet, even if you find out that changes occur, and even if you know *which* changes occur, you still don't know *why*, which was the question.

(You will usually find that in the process of making questions answerable, "why" questions tend to be transformed into "under what conditions," because, given evidence, independent observers can rarely agree about "why" something happened. It is much easier to agree on what conditions surrounded the event. One way is to get clear evidence of how CPI scores change under conditions of 96 hours' sleep deprivation. If we find that similar changes occur under other conditions, we can conclude that these conditions have something in common, and identifying the common element gets us closer to a satisfying answer to "why?")

Let's try to relate this to your own interests. If your background in your field is limited, you may well not be able to ask a question even as specific as "Why does one's personality change when under stress?" This is a fairly common position for students to be in since many don't yet know their subjects well enough to ask a question that is phrased in variables, let alone concretized ones. Thus, the purposes of this Appendix are:

> To assist you in using library resources to focus your interests
> To help you to ask a question in answerable terms
> To aid you in finding a bibliography of the evidence relevant to your question.

There is a more or less logical progression that people take in accomplishing these goals:

> (1) Identify an area you are interested in.
> (2) Gather general information, noting whether scientific evidence exists.
> (3) Identify a variable you are interested in, and about which evidence exists.
> (4) Get information about the variable. What other variables are related to it?
> (5) If you can, choose a second variable that has been related to the first by some scientific evidence.
> (6) Make a bibliography of evidence about the relationship of the variables.
> (7) Assess the amount of evidence available, and redefine the variables so that it is possible to evaluate all evidence within your time limits.

Let us slowly go through these steps, with an example, and comment on some problems you may run into along the way. You may use the following as a guide when you have to assemble a bibliography of scientific evidence on a question that interests you.

Step 1. Identify an Area You Are Interested in.

You should be able to do this without help. It's all right to start with something very general. For example, we'll start with the topic of "body language," sometimes also called "nonverbal communication."

Step 2. Gather General Information, Noting Whether Scientific Evidence Exists.

Use as resources textbooks in your area of interest, the library card catalog, and handbooks.

Textbooks

These can be very useful for beginning a search. If you look through several recent ones in your area of interest, you will quickly get an idea of whether there is much research on the question you are interested in. There may be no way to predict (without knowledge of the field) whether there are hundreds of good studies on a topic, or a few, or nothing but a lot of unsupported conjecture. A look at several books will give you a feel for this. Textbooks will also help you identify the key terms used in connection with your topic. Knowing these, you can look them up when you are ready to use sources of more detailed information.

We're interested in "body language." Not being sure, we might seek textbooks on introductory psychology, language, communication, sociology, and social psychology. Look in the index under anything that might be relevant (e.g., body language, nonverbal, language, communication). See how much coverage is given to what you are interested in. Keep in mind that some topics will get coverage in one textbook but not in another, even though both texts are on the same subject. Look in several similar books before you give up. This won't take too long: textbooks on the same subject are usually on the same library shelf.

In our search for material on "body language," let's suppose we don't get much from textbooks (this could easily happen). The linguistics books use a lot of fancy language, but don't seem to provide scientific observations, and most of the psychology and sociology books have little coverage. This may be what you would find in a search on this topic; if so, go to another source.

Card Catalog

This is an easy source to consult, and you are probably familiar with it. For most topics it will not be fruitful, because few questions in the social sciences have had whole books written about them. Still, if you *do* find a recent book on your subject, you may save yourself a lot of searching.

The topic of "body language" is one that you will find in the card catalog. (Don't forget to use both title and subject headings.) Some of the books are popularized, and contain mostly unsupported assertions. Others seem more scholarly, and contain a mixture of scientific evidence, casual observation, and speculation. By looking through these books, you find that there seem to be many kinds of body language or nonverbal communication: posture, gestures, tone of voice, eye contact, facial expression, and proxemics (the use of interpersonal space), to name the most prominent ones. You also find that there is a fair amount of scientific evidence that seems to be available about at least some of these. If your topic is "body language," you are ready to go on to the next step. You know that there is enough evidence available to continue.

If you still haven't found out whether there is scientific evidence on your topic, you might look for some useful *handbooks*.

Handbooks

Handbooks are reference works in specialized fields. They often contain reviews of research and theory on particular subjects related to the topic of the handbook (e.g., *Handbook of organizations, Handbook of psychotherapy and behavior change*). Articles are written by experts, and are usually valuable for some years after the publication date. If you can find a relevant article, it will be useful at all steps of the process of preparing your question. The articles may, however, presume more technical knowledge than you have at the beginning of your search. Handbooks may be found either in the reference section or with ordinary books and you may locate them through the card catalog or by asking an instructor or reference librarian.

At this stage, you are mainly interested in finding out whether there is a body of scientific evidence on your topic. If you can find a handbook article that seems to cover your subject, look at the references cited in the article that are in your area of interest. If there are several, and if they seem to involve scientific observation, you are safe to go on to the next step. If you don't think you can understand the article, make a note of it and return to it when you have read a bit more.

Step 3. Identify a Variable You Are Interested in, About Which Evidence Exists.

This step involves thinking. When you found that "body language" includes posture, gesture, tone of voice, eye contact, and so on, you found a list of variables that might be of interest. You may realize that some of them are more complex than others. For example, there are many ways that facial expressions can differ, but few ways that eye contact can vary (mainly, contact is made or it isn't). At this stage, this difference will not matter much. You can feel free to pursue any of the types of body language you are interested in, as long as you are sure there is scientific evidence about it. Your main task is to narrow your focus from the broad topic (body language) to a variable (say, interpersonal space).

Step 4. Get Information About the Variable. What Other Variables Are Related to it?

Ideally, what you want to find now is a "review article" about your variable. Review articles are articles summarizing what has been written (both theory and factual evidence) on a subject.

Resources for review articles include: textbooks, card catalog, handbooks, and serials.

Textbooks

Look back at the useful texts you may have found to see if there is a chapter or a subchapter section on your variable. If there is, make a list of the variables that are supposedly related to it, noting whether this relationship is merely speculative or is based on casual or scientific observation.

Card Catalog

Treat any useful books you may have found in the card catalog as textbooks, and look for sections on your variable. You may also want to look again at the card catalog, under the name of your variable. If it is a variable such as personal space, you may find a book on the subject.

Handbooks

If you found a handbook article covering your topic, look now for a subsection on the variable you are interested in. Get the same information you would get from a book.

Serials

A serial is a periodical, published usually once a year or so (regularly or irregularly), that contains articles of current interest in a particular field. Like handbooks, serials often contain articles reviewing research and theory on specific topics. A particularly useful serial is the *Annual Reviews* series, which is published for psychology, sociology, anthropology, and other disciplines. These contain *only* reviews of recent work in areas in which progress is being made. If you can find a recent review of this type, which covers your variable, much of your work is done. The author will have carefully searched for all the latest published work in the field, and you will have not only a good overview, but a valuable source of bibliography.

If you can find a review article in any of the above sources, or even a discussion of several pages' length about your variable, you can begin to identify other variables related to it. Compile a list of other variables, and note the kind of evidence that seems to link each to the variable you are interested in. If there appears to be scientific evidence, about how much is there?

Judging from the books you find, personal space seems to be related to the individual's personality, to attraction between people, to stress, to whether people are same-sex or opposite-sex, to eye contact, and to the setting in which the people meet. These relationships are in some cases supported by casual observation, and in other cases, there seem to be scientific studies (one or more) that relate the variable to interpersonal space. Do not attempt to judge whether personal space is, in fact, related to personal attraction for example. All you want to do is note that there is some evidence bearing on the question of whether the variables are related. You can decide whether there is a relationship only after you have evaluated the evidence.

Step 5. If You Can, Choose a Second Variable That Has Been Related to the First by Some Scientific Evidence.

After you have finished Step 4, you can perform Step 5 from your notes.

It's possible that you can find nothing but unsupported assertions and casual observations about your variable. If this seems to be happening, it's a good time to look for help from an instructor or an advanced student who might have more experience with the area your question deals with. Such a person may be able to direct you to a source that mentions scientific evidence, or may confirm your suspicion that there just *isn't* much scientific evidence in the field. If the latter occurs, you would be wasting your time trying to review the scientific literature on the subject. (This does not mean your interest was not a good one. Many important questions lack evidence because nobody has shown the interest or because no one has figured out how to collect scientific evidence on them that would be relevant.)

You may find that there is scientific evidence relating your variable to each of several other variables. This is what would probably happen in researching interpersonal space. Suppose you have found only one or two scientific studies relating interpersonal space to each of the other variables mentioned. Since two studies are not enough to review, you might try to define a variable yourself; for example, you might relate interpersonal space to *social comfort*. You could assume that both stress and lack of interpersonal attraction make people socially uncomfortable and should have the same effects. In this way, it would make sense to look at studies on stress and personal space together with studies on attraction and personal space. (If both stress and lack of attraction make people stand further apart, the evidence would support your assumption that there is such a thing as "social comfort" that involves both stress and attraction.) You should understand that inventing a variable of your own is a little risky, but if several of the "other variables" seem to you to form a cluster, you can study them all, as long as you make your assumptions explicit when you review the research. You are in better shape if one of the "second variables" is related to the first variable in several scientific articles. In this case, you do not have to go out on a limb by inventing variables.

For interpersonal space, let's say we have found several scientific studies relating it to interpersonal attraction, and also several relating it to eye contact. We have a choice of which relationship to explore. Before going on to the next step, we should look carefully at the kind of relationship between the two variables. For example, are we conceiving of one as the independent variable and the other as the dependent variable? With personal space and attraction, the relationship might go either way. Attraction may determine the amount of space people keep between each other, or—at least with people meeting for the first time—the space they keep between them may determine attraction. There are at least two different questions concerning the relatinship between attraction and personal space, and *evidence relevant to one question may be irrelevant to the other.*

Before you go on, frame a tentative question about the relationship between the two variables you plan to study. Be sure you understand whether you are assuming a causal relationship between the variables and, if so, be clear about the direction of causality. Your choice may be dictated by the practical consideration of available evidence. You may be more interested in how personal space influences attraction, but most of the evidence may be on how attraction influences personal space. If this happens, you may choose to look at the less interesting question, to examine both questions but discuss them separately, or you may decide to select a different variable.

When you have a second variable, and a tentative question relating your variables, go to the next step. Let's decide to ask "How does attraction influence people's use of interpersonal space?"

Step 6. Make a Bibliography of Evidence About the Relationship of the Variables.

Use as resources review articles in books, handbooks, or serials; recent journals, abstracts, indexes.

Review Articles in Books, Handbooks, or Serials

If you have found one of these, look through it for the sources it cites relating your two variables. Put these in your bibliography. Also, be alert for review articles on your *second* variable in the same way you looked for articles on the first. An article on interpersonal attraction may include some useful references. What you find in review articles should be current to within a year or so of the publication date. Check the dates of the references. For newer work, you will have to look elsewhere.

Recent Journals

This might be a good place to begin your search, especially if textbooks or other information suggest that research is currently going on. Journals are the most up-to-date source of evidence you can find, and a *single* recent article will lead you, through its bibliography, to other related research. You also may discover that in tracing the bibliographies of journal articles, you come upon a fairly recent review article, which will give you more bibliography.

If you don't know which recent journals to look at, you might start with current issues of the journals that published the older articles in your bibliography.

Abstracts and Indexes

Indexes are reference works that give author, title, and source for articles of theory and research. They are most useful if you know what terms to look up (look for the names of your variables), or if you know the name(s) of author(s) who have done work in the field. One way to get more recent information is to look up the names of the authors of older articles you have found to see if they are still doing work. The most recent work will probably cite what has been done in the interim.

Abstracts resemble indexes, but also include brief summaries of all works indexed. These are highly useful in making bibliographies because the summaries can save you the effort of tracking down articles that have interesting titles but which turn out, on inspection, to be irrelevant.

Abstracts and indexes usually exist for whole disciplines: *Psychological Abstracts, Social Science and Humanities Index, Crime and Delinquency Abstracts,* and *Sociological Abstracts* are some examples. The larger ones run to thousands of pages annually. It is therefore useful to have a fairly specific idea of what you are looking for so that you are not bogged down in masses of irrelevant material. A good method is to look up the variable that has *fewer* scientific articles on it. Since abstracts and indexes are generally cross-referenced by subject, this will give you the articles that relate your two variables with the least time spent attending to irrelevant articles on only one variable. You will quickly find that there are many more studies done on attraction than on personal space and consequently you will save time by looking up personal space.

Other Resources

There may be *specialized bibliographies* in some area that includes your question. Your instructor may know if there is such a source, and a reference librarian may also be helpful. Specialized bibliographies are coming out all the time, and even professors may not be aware of the newest ones unless they are working in the particular specialized field.

Ask for help. This is a good general rule if you are having trouble finding material. Instructors, librarians, and sometimes advanced students may be able to suggest a source that you can use.

Computerized literature search services are valuable (and expensive) for someone doing very serious research. These services are most useful if your research project is highly technical, or if you can expect useful information to come from obscure sources. For a student with relatively little background in a field, the use of such a service would probably be superfluous.

The following are some general notes on preparing a bibliography:

(1) It will save time to begin by looking for very recent work in the field. The bibliography of a recent study will cite older sources, but the reverse never occurs. In using abstracts, indexes, serials, and recent journals, always begin with the most recent and work backwards.

(2) Your bibliographic sources will often give you only the title of an article. You should try to determine whether the article is a report of scientific evidence, a review article, a theoretical article, or a statement of opinion. Without prior experience, it will often be impossible to do this from the title alone. But reviews often leave the word "review" in the title, and titles that include mention of your variables by name and are very specific and technical-sounding are generally articles containing scientific evidence. Very general titles for very short articles (e.g., a five-page article called "personal space") will usually contain speculation or an oversimplified review of the literature, often without bibliography. In your notes, keep the reports of scientific evidence separate from review and theoretical articles.

(3) If you are working with a deadline, check to see if the articles you need are available in your library. When you are working in a carefully defined research area, you may find some references that cannot be instantly located. Ask about inter-library loan services in your library, and request material early so you will have it when you are ready to read it.

(4) In gathering your bibliography, make a note of all the standard information (title and author, place of publication, date, and volume number and pages, if applicable). It is usually helpful to also make a note summarizing the nature of the reference, if the title does not make it obvious. This can save you many trips back to a journal because you couldn't remember exactly what an article was about.

Step 7. Assess the Amount of Evidence Available, and Redefine the Variables so That It Is Possible To Evaluate All the Evidence Within Your Time Limits.

After doing Step 6, you can do this step by careful thinking.

To know how much evidence is available, you must first have some idea whether you have found it all. The easiest way to determine this is to look at the references listed in each new source you find. When all the interesting references you find are already in your own bibliography, you can get ready to stop. If other people working in the same subject area can't find more references than you can, you have probably found almost all of them.

At this point, you have a practical decision to make. You want to do a complete job yet you don't have unlimited time to do it. The skills involved in reviewing and evaluating a body of scientific literature are difficult and take quite a bit of practice. Assuming that you haven't done this sort of review before, and assuming that you have not read many scientific papers before, you can count on a lot of rereading and a good investment of time for each article you try to review carefully. For a typical term paper, a careful review of, say, five to ten scientific articles should be quite a bit. (You may decide that you can handle more, but don't commit yourself to doing so until you have tried writing a review, as in Chapter 5.)

With your bibliography fairly well complete, you should have an idea if the number of scientifically acceptable sources is only a few, or a few dozen, or a few hundred. If your bibliography is about the size you want, after you have completed a fairly exhaustive search for the evidence, you are lucky, and are ready to go ahead. If not, one of two things has happened:

(a) You *do not have enough references* to satisfy your needs. The following are some possible solutions:

> Seek help. There may be sources of evidence you haven't found yet.
>
> Redefine one of your variables to make it broader (including stress and attraction in a common category of "social comfort" is an example of this strategy).
>
> Loosen the criteria of evidence to include some casual observations. This is a risky option, since you are including poor evidence that may lead to weakly supported conclusions, or otherwise cause confusion. Casual observations are hard to interpret, and are very open to bias. It is best to avoid casual observations entirely, unless you feel that the question is of such importance that it must be discussed even in the absence of a good body of acceptable evidence. If you decide to include casual observations in your review, justify this decision early in the paper, and carefully note the limitations of the evidence.
>
> Eliminate one of your variables, and switch to another one (that is, go back to step 5).
>
> Give up the whole thing (go back to step 3 or step 1). Of course, this is not recommended if you are genuinely interested in your question. It *is* done, unfortunately, by students who are mainly concerned with getting a paper in on time.

(b) You have *too many references* to do an adequate job on them all. Here are some possible solutions:

Redefine one of your variables to make it narrower. We might narrow "personal space" by considering only studies measuring the face-to-face distance between people, and ignoring studies of how close they sit on benches or how much they touch each other.

Narrow the range of evidence you will consider while keeping the same variables. For example, you might choose to consider only evidence about use of personal space by children or same-sex pairs of people.

Restrict yourself to certain research methods. You might, for example, consider only research based on observation of the actual behavior of people, and reject studies measuring personal space by the placement of cardboard models or other symbols of people. With some questions, you might choose to evaluate only experimental evidence, and not to consider correlational studies.

The general rule is to narrow your topic in some way that makes conceptual sense and keeps the focus on what you think is most interesting or important. It is always good to make your decisions to narrow explicit at the start of your written review. This shows your reader that you have done your homework, and that your choice of a subject and of which research to discuss was rational, rather than arbitrary. It is much better to do a complete job of reviewing carefully selected research than to do a superficial review of a large number of loosely related studies.

By the time you have completed these steps, you will have used the library to help you define a question and to compile a bibliography of the relevant scientific evidence. These are two of the three objectives of this chapter. The other is to ask a question in answerable terms. We have said that an answerable question is one asked in terms of variables, in such a way that reliable observations of the variables can be made. If you were gathering your own data, you would be responsible for concretizing the variables. To review research, you need only be sure that different studies are in fact dealing with the same variable. (This sounds easy enough, but as you begin to read research, you will see that a major reason why similar studies get different results is that they do not concretize the same variable in the same way. In effect, they are studying different variables without knowing it beforehand.)

If your question is asked in terms of variables that can be concretized, you will have an answerable question for the purpose of reviewing the literature. You could try to concretize your variables as an exercise, but you may find that no published research has concretized them in the way you would choose.

No formal exercises or problems are offered to test your ability to reach the objectives of this Appendix. The obvious exercise is to pursue an interest of yours as far as you can in the direction of preparing a complete bibliography on a carefully asked question. You can evaluate your success by your ability to proceed through the steps. If you aren't sure whether you are proceeding in the most efficient way, or if you would like comments on what you have done, you can have your work (reformulated questions, bibliography, etc.) evaluated by an instructor or other well-informed person. If you are not making good progress, don't get discouraged; it takes experience to know where to look for material. Ask someone with the experience—this is one purpose of a teacher.

References

Agnew, N., & Pyke, S. *The science game*. Englewood Cliffs, N.J.: Prentice-Hall, 1969.

American Psychological Association, Committee on Ethical Standards in Psychological Research. *Ethical principles in the conduct of research with human participants*. Washington, D.C.: Author, 1973.

American Psychological Association. *Publication manual of the American Psychological Association*. (2nd ed.) Washington, D.C.: Author, 1974.

Antunes, G., & Gaitz, M. Ethnicity and participation: A study of Mexican-Americans, blacks, and whites. *American Journal of Sociology*, 1975, *80*, 1192–1211.

Bardwick, J. Psychological factors in the acceptance and use of oral contraceptives. In J. T. Fawcett (Ed.), *Psychological perspectives on population*. New York: Basic Books, 1973.

Bell, J. E. *Critical evaluation in psychology*. Columbia, Md.: Howard Community College, 1974.

Brady, J. V. Ulcers in executive monkeys. *Scientific American*, 1958, *199*(3), 95–104.

Braginsky & Braginsky. *Mainstream psychology: A critique*. New York: Holt, Rinehart, and Winston, 1974.

Cameron, J., Livson, N., & Bayley, N. Infant vocalizations and their relationship to mature intelligence. *Science*, 1967, *157*, 331–333.

Campbell, D. T., & Stanley, J. C. *Experimental and quasi-experimental designs for research*. Chicago: Rand-McNally, 1963.

Carrigan, W. C., & Julian, J. W. Sex and birth-order differences in conformity as a function of need affiliation arousal. *Journal of Personality and Social Psychology*, 1966, *3*, 479–483.

Cox, D. E., & Supprelle, C. N. Coercion in participation as a research subject. *American Psychologist*, 1971, *26*, 726–728.

Darley, J. M., & Latané, B. Bystander intervention in emergencies: Diffusion of responsibility. *Journal of Personality and Social Psychology*, 1968, *8*, 377–383.

Doherty, M. E., & Shemberg, K. M. *Asking questions about behavior*. Glenview, Ill.: Scott, Foresman, 1970.

Doob, A. N., & Gross, A. E. Status of frustrator as an inhibitor of horn-honking responses. *Journal of Social Psychology*, 1968, *76*, 213–218.

Duncan, S., Rosenberg, M. J., & Finkelstein, J. The paralanguage of experimenter bias. *Sociometry*, 1969, *32*, 207–219.

Duncan, S., & Rosenthal, R. Vocal emphasis in experimenters' instruction reading as unintended determinant of subjects' responses. *Language and Speech*, 1968, *11*, 20–26.

Fanon, F. *The wretched of the earth*. New York: Grove Press, 1966.

Freedman, J. L. The effects of population density on humans. In J. T. Fawcett (Ed.), *Psychological perspectives on population.* New York: Basic Books, 1973.

Freedman, J. L. *Crowding and behavior.* San Francisco: Freeman, 1975.

Freedman, J. L., Levy, A., Buchanan, R. W., & Price, J. Crowding and human aggressiveness. *Journal of Experimental Social Psychology,* 1972, *8,* 528–548.

Friedman, H. *Introduction to statistics.* New York: Random House, 1972.

Gaertner, S., & Bickman, L. A non-reactive indicator of racial discrimination: The wrong number technique. In L. Bickman & T. Henchy (Eds.), *Beyond the laboratory: Field research in social psychology.* New York: McGraw-Hill, 1972.

Gamsky, N. Team teaching, student achievement, and attitudes. *Journal of Experimental Education,* 1970, *39*(1), 42–45.

Glaser, D. *The effectiveness of a prison and parole system.* Indianapolis: Bobbs-Merrill, 1964.

Glock, C. Y., Ringer, B. B., & Babbie, E. R. *To comfort and to challenge.* Berkeley: University of California Press, 1967.

Goodman, N., & Ofshe, R. Empathy, communication efficiency, and marital status. *Journal of Marriage and the Family,* 1968, *30,* 597–603.

Gottman, J. M., McFall, R. M., & Barnett, J. T. Design and analysis of research using time series. *Psychological Bulletin,* 1969, *72,* 299–306.

Hays, W. L. *Statistics for psychologists.* New York: Holt, Rinehart, and Winston, 1963.

Heise, D. R. Problems in path analysis and causal inference. In E. F. Borgatta & G. W. Bohrnstedt (Eds.), *Sociological methodology.* San Francisco: Jossey-Bass, 1969.

Hersen, M., & Barlow, D. H. *Single-case experimental designs: Strategies for studying behavior change.* New York: Pergamon, 1976.

Janis, I. L., & Field, P. B. Sex differences and personality factors related to persuasibility. In C. I. Hovland & I. L. Janis (Eds.), *Personality and persuasibility.* New Haven, Conn.: Yale University Press, 1959.

Janis, I. L., & Mann, L. Effectiveness of emotional role-playing in modifying smoking habits and attitudes. *Journal of Experimental Research in Personality,* 1965, *1,* 84–90.

Johnson, D. W. (Ed.) *Contemporary social psychology.* Philadelphia: Lippincott, 1973.

Jourard, S. *Self-disclosure: Experimental investigations of the transparent self.* New York: Van Nostrand Reinhold, 1971.

Kerlinger, F. N. *Foundations of behavioral research.* (2nd ed.) New York: Holt, Rinehart, and Winston, 1973.

Kytle, R. *Clear thinking for composition.* New York: Random House, 1969.

Land, K. C. Principles of path analysis. In E. F. Borgatta & G. W. Bohrnstedt (Eds.), *Sociological methodology.* San Francisco: Jossey-Bass, 1969.

Landauer, T., & Whiting, J. Infantile stimulation and adult stature of human males. *American Anthropologist,* 1964, *66,* 1007–1028.

Latané, B., & Darley, J. Group inhibition of bystander intervention in emergencies. *Journal of Personality and Social Psychology,* 1968, *10,* 215–221.

Lawick-Goodall, J. van. *In the shadow of man.* Boston: Houghton-Mifflin, 1971.

Lieberman, L. R. Untitled letter, *Science,* 1973, *180,* 369.

Loo, C. M (Ed.) *Crowding and behavior.* New York: MSS Information Corp., 1972.

Lorenz, K. *On aggression.* New York: Harcourt Brace Jovanovich, 1966.

McCroskey, J. C., Larson, C. E., & Knapp, M. L. *Introduction to interpersonal communication.* Englewood Cliffs, N.J.: Prentice-Hall, 1971.

Mitchell, R. E. Some social implications of high-density housing. *American Sociological Review,* 1971, *36,* 18–29.

National Advisory Commission on Civil Disorders. *Report of the National Advisory Commission on Civil Disorders.* New York: Bantam Books, 1968.

Orne, M. T. On the social psychology of the psychological experiment: With particular reference to demand characteristics and their implications. *American Psychologist,* 1962, *17,* 776–783.

Piliavin, I. M., Rodin, J., & Piliavin, J. A. Good Samaritanism: An underground phenomenon? *Journal of Personality and Social Psychology,* 1969, *13,* 289–299.

Rabin, A. I. Motivation for parenthood. *Journal of Projective Techniques and Personality Assessment,* 1965, *29,* 405–411.

Ransford, H. E. Isolation, powerlessness, and violence: A study of attitudes and participation in the Watts riot. *American Journal of Sociology*, 1968, *73*, 581–591.

Roethlisberger, F. J., & Dickson, W. J. *Management and the worker*. Cambridge, Mass.: Harvard University Press, 1939.

Rogers, Carl R. *Carl Rogers on encounter groups*. New York: Harper and Row, 1970.

Rosenberg, M. J. When dissonance fails: On eliminating evaluation apprehension from attitude measurement. *Journal of Personality and Social Psychology*, 1965, *1*, 18–42.

Rosenberg, M. J. The conditions and consequences of evaluation apprehension. In R. Rosenthal & R. L. Rosnow (Eds.), *Artifact in behavioral research*. New York: Academic Press, 1969.

Rosenhan, D. L. On being sane in insane places. *Science*, 1973, *179*, 250–258.

Rosenthal, R. *Experimenter effects in behavioral research*. New York: Appleton-Century-Crofts, 1966.

Schachter, S. *The psychology of affiliation*. Stanford: Stanford University Press, 1959.

Schaefer, V. H. Teaching the concept of interaction and sensitizing students to its implications. *Teaching of Psychology*, 1976, *3*, 103–114.

Schein, E. H. Interpersonal communication, group solidarity, and social influence. *Sociometry*, 1960, *23*, 148–161.

Scott, J. P. Social behavior, organization, and leadership in a small flock of domestic sheep. *Comparative Psychology Monographs*, 1945, *18* (Whole No. 4).

Sistrunk, F., & McDavid, J. W. Sex variable in conforming behavior. *Journal of Personality and Social Psychology*, 1971, *17*, 200–207.

Small families are smarter, IQ boom ahead, Zajonc birth order study predicts. *Intercom*, June, 1976, pp. 2–3.

Strodtbeck, F. L., & Hook, L. H. The social dimensions of a twelve man jury table. *Sociometry*, 1961, *24*, 397–415.

Tryon, R. C. Genetic differences in maze learning in rats. In *National Society for the Study of Education, the thirty-ninth yearbook*. Bloomington, Ill.: Public School Publishing, 1940.

Watson, G., & Johnson, D. W. *Social psychology: Issues and insights*. (2nd ed.) Philadelphia: Lippincott, 1972.

Webb, E. J., Campbell, D. T., Schwartz, R., & Sechrest, L. *Unobtrusive measures: Nonreactive research in the social sciences*. Chicago: Rand McNally, 1966.

Winer, B. J. *Statistical principles in experimental design*. New York: McGraw-Hill, 1962.

Wolfenstein, M. Fun morality: An analysis of recent American child-training literature. *Journal of Social Issues*, 1951, *7*(4), 15–25.

Wrightsman, L. S. Wallace supporters and adherence to "law and order." *Journal of Personality and Social Psychology*, 1969, *13*, 17–22.

Zimbardo, P. G., Haney, C., Banks, W. C., & Jaffe, D. The psychology of imprisonment: Privation, power, and pathology. Unpublished manuscript, Stanford University, 1973.

Zucker, R., Manosevitz, M., & Lanyon, R. Birth order, anxiety, and affiliation during a crisis. *Journal of Personality and Social Psychology*, 1968, *8*, 354–359.

Index

Page references in *italics* indicate definitions of indexed terms.

ABA design, 93–94, 95(table)
Abstract, in scientific report, 137–38, 140
Abstraction, 10–12, 29
  concretized, *11–14*, 64
  unconcretized, 11n
Abstracts, as bibliographic resources, 227
Aggression, and crowding, 26–30, 38, 40–41, 168
Agnew, N., 65, 91
Algeria, 10–14
Alternative explanation, *63–64*, 71(table), 76(table), 83, 94–95, 96(table), 144
  comparisons of, 169, 207–8, 217
  examples of, 101–5, 112–13, 144–45, 164–65, 201–5
Annual Reviews, 224
Answerable question, *219–20*
Appeal to authority, *9–10*
Archival records, 75, 76(table)
Articles, scientific, format, 136–37
  procedure for reading, 138–46
Artifacts, 65–66, 69

Babbie, E. R., 61–63
Behavior modification, 93
Bell, J. F., 8n
Between-subjects design, 40–42, 95(table)
  distinguished from between-subjects experiment, 83
Between-subjects experiment, *40–42*, 83, 92
  controls in, 94, 96(table)

distinguished from between-subjects design, 83
  examples of, 40–41, 46, 51
  extraneous variables in, 96(table)
Biases. *See* Distortion; Sampling bias
Bibliographic resources, 221–28
Birth control, 77–80
Blind measurement, 69, 71(table), 74, 76(table)
Body language, 221–23
Brady, J. V., 86
Bystander intervention in emergencies, 172–218

Campbell, D. T., 62, 66, 92, 94
"Canned" researcher, 70, 71(table)
Card catalog, as bibliographic resource, 222–24
Casual observation, *13–14*, 15
Churches, 61–63
Comparison group, as control, 67, 83, 92, 95(table)
Comparison group design. *See* Between-subjects design
Complete recording, 25
Computerized literature searches, 227–28
Conclusions, of scientific reports, 171
  examples of, 202, 204, 206
Concrete language, 25, 64
Conformity, sex differences in, 169–71, 207
Confounding, *77*, 83, 95(table)
Control, *63–64.* *See also specific research methods; specific methods of control*

Correlational study, 33, *34–37*, 82–91
  advantages of, 37
  and causation, 37, 39, 112(example)
  controls in, 83–91, 94, 96(table)
  distinguished from experiment, 36
  distinguished from retrospective case study, 53
  distinguished from sample study, 35
  examples of, 33–36, 46–47, 49
  extraneous variables in, 82–91, 96(table)
  limitations of, 37, 82–83, 90–91
Counterbalancing, 92–94, 95(table)
Covariance, analysis of, 87
Cross-lagged panel design, 92
Crowding, 25–35, 38–43, 168. *See also* Aggression

Darley, J. M., 172, 180–81, 187–90, 196–97, 200–216
Deception, 66–67, 71(table)
  ethics of, 67
Demand characteristics, 65
  controls for, 67, 71(table)
Dependent variable, *38–39*
Dickson, W. J., 68
Discussion section, in scientific report, 137, 144
Distortion, by researcher, 73–74, 96(table)
  controls for, 74, 76(table)
Doherty, M. E., 219–20
Double-blind technique, 69, 71(table)

Emergencies, bystander intervention in, 172–218
Error
  random, 78
  systematic, 79
Evaluation apprehension, 65
  control for, 67, 71(table)
Evidence, 8–10. *See also* Scientific evidence
Executive monkeys, 86
Expectancy, researcher's, 68
  controls for, 69–70, 71(table)
Experiment, 36–*38*
  advantages of, 42. *See also* Between-subjects experiment; Within-subjects experiment
Extraneous variable, *63–64*
  controlled, *143–44*, 164
  examples of controlled, 102–5, 111–12, 201–5
  examples of uncontrolled, 101–5, 112–13, 201–5
  uncontrolled, *144–45*, 164–65

Fact, questions of, 3–4
Fact, statements of, 7–9, 14–16
  decision-making procedure for, 16(figure)
Faking bad, 65
  controls for, 71(table)
Fanon, F., 10–15
Findings, 110, 137, 140, 206
  comparisons of, 169, 206
  examples of, 101–5, 111, 142–43, 164, 201–5
Freedman, J. L., 40–43
Freud, S., 4

Glock, C. Y., 61–63

Handbooks, as bibliographic resource, 223–24, 226
Hawthorne effect, 68
  controls for, 70, 71(table)
  example of, 104
Holding procedures constant, 80–81, 95(table)
  examples. *See* Extraneous variable, controlled
Hong Kong, 34–35
Hospitalization, psychiatric, 146–66
Human Relations Area Files, 120, 139–40, 145–46
Hypothesis, *29*
  causal and noncausal, *38–39*
  in correlational studies, 39
  in experiments, 38–39

Independent variable, *38–39*
Indexes, as bibliographic resource, 227
Infantile stress, 117–28, 138–46
Insane places, 146–66
Interaction of variables, *88–90*, 146, 169–71, 206–7
  examples of, 146, 169–71, 202, 206, 207
Introduction, in scientific report, 137
Invalid operational definitions, 77, 94, 95(table), 96(table)
  examples of, 101–2, 105, 112

Journals, as bibliographic resource, 226–27

Kerner Commission (National Advisory Commission on Civil Disorders), 27–30, 75

Landauer, T. K., 117, 136–46
Latané, B., 172, 180–81, 187–90, 196–97, 200–216
Lawick-Goodall, J. van, 26
Loo, C., 40–42
Lorenz, K., 26, 29, 30

Males, adult stature of human, 117–28, 138–46
Manhattan, and crowding, 30–33
Manipulation of variables, 35–36, 40–41
  as a control, 81–82, 95(table)
  example, 52
Marital happiness, 36–38
Marx, K., 4
Matching, 37, 85–87, 90, 95(table)
Memoraid, 91–93
Memory, selective, 25, 29, 75–76, 96(table)
  controls for, 75–76(table)
Method section, in scientific report, 137–39, 143–44
Methods of gathering evidence, 24–45, 64. *See also* *specific methods*
  characteristics, 43(table)
  decision-making procedure, 45(figure)
Michigan, University of, 9–10

Minimal interference, 25
Mitchell, R. E., 33–35, 37
Moreland University, 46, 80
Multiple time-series design, 92

Naturalistic observation, 24, *25–27*, 64–72
 examples of, 26, 47
 extraneous variables in, 64–72, 96(table)
 limitations of, 26–27, 64, 72
 uses of, 29, 42
Nonverbal communication, 221–22
Null hypothesis, 141

"On stage" effects, 65–67, 96(table)
 controls for, 66–67, 71(table)
 examples of, 103, 105
Operational definition, *11–12*, 29–30, 73, 139–40
 comparisons of, 208–9
 examples of, 111, 139–40, 163–64, 200–205
Organismic variables, *82–91*
 controls for, 83–91, 94, 95(table), 96(table)
 examples of uncontrolled, 101–3, 105, 112
Orne, M. T., 65

Panel design, 92
Partial correlation, 87
Path analysis, 92
Personal relationship effect, 68–69
 controls for, 69–70, 71(table)
Personal space, 223–30
Piaget, J., 26
Piliavin, I. M., 188, 204–16
Piliavin, J. A., 188, 204–16
Placebo effect, 68
 controls for, 69–70, 71(table)
Populations, *31*, 145–46, 205
 comparisons of, 169, 208, 214–15
 generalizing across, 80, 113, 145–46, 165, *168–69*, 202–3
Probability values, 140–42
Programmed instruction, 87–90
Prospective research, 75
Purposes of book, 3–5
Pyke, S., 65, 91

Quasi-experimental research, 94

Randomization, 83–85, 90, 95(table), 143–44
Relationships between variables, 34–35, 37
 strength of, 142
Reliability, *12–13*
 types of, 12–13
Results section, in scientific report, 137, 140–43
Retrospective case study, *27–29*, 72-76
 advantages of, 28–29
 distinguished from correlational study, 53
 examples of, 27–29, 48, 50
 extraneous variables in, 72–76, 96(table)
 limitations of, 29, 72
 uses of, 29, 42

Review article, as bibliographic resource, 223–24, 226
Reviewing a body of literature, 167–218
 outline for writing review, 210
 outlining articles, 169–71
 steps in reviewing, 206–10
Ringer, B. B., 61–63
Riots, 28–29, 75
Rodin, J., 188, 204–16
Roethlisberger, F. J., 68
Rosenberg, M. J., 65
Rosenhan, D. L., 146, 163–67
Rosenthal, R., 68

Sample study, *32–33*, 76–82
 advantages of, 32
 distinguished from correlational study, 35
 extraneous variables in, 76–82, 96(table)
 limitations of, 32–33, 76, 82
Samples, *31*, 145–46
 generalization from, 77–80, 145–46, 165, 169
 random, 79
 representative, 32–33, 78–80, 95(table)
Sampling bias, 73, 77–*79*, 80, 94
 controls for, 79–80, 95(table), 96(table)
 examples of, 102, 113, 145, 165, 203, 205
Sampling error, 78
Scholastic Aptitude Tests, 87–88
Schwartz, R., 66
Scientific evidence, 10–14
 finding, 221–31
Sechrest, L., 66
Selectivity, of researcher, 72–73, 76(table), 96(table)
Self-fulfilling prophecy, 68
 controls for, 69–70, 71(table)
 examples of, 101, 104
Serials, as bibliographic resource, 224, 226
Settings for gathering data, 208–9, 214–15
Sex differences, 169–71, 207
Shemberg, K. M., 219–20
Skinner, B. F., 41
Social desirability, 65
 controls for, 67, 71(table)
Specialized bibliographies, 227
Stanley, J. C., 62, 92, 94
Statistical controls, 87, 90, 95(table)
Statistical inference, 140–41
Statistical significance, 141–42
Statistics, 31, 140–42
Style, American Psychological Association, 8n, 216
Subject variables. *See* Organismic variables
Subjects as own controls, 86–87, 95(table)
Summary, in scientific report, 137–38, 140, 142–43

Territoriality, 26–29, 168
Textbooks, as bibliographic resource, 222–24

Theory
   questions of, 3–4, 168
   and researcher's selectivity, 72–73
   statements of, 8, 29
Time-series design, 92
"Time-tied" extraneous variables, 91–94, 96(table)
   controls for, 92–94, 95(table)
   example, 104

Unobtrusive measures, 66, 71(table)
Unsupported assertions, 8–10

Validity, 13. See also specific research methods
   external, 63, 167
   internal, 62–64, 167
   threats to, 94
Value
   questions of, 3
   statements of, 7
Variables, 30, 64
   inclusion in hypothesis, 87–90
   interaction of, 88–90, 146, 169–71, 206–7

Vermont, 77–80
Volunteer subjects, 80, 102

Wallace, G., 85–87
War of national liberation, 8, 10–14
Warm-up period, 70, 71(table)
Webb, E. J., 66
Whiting, J.W.M., 117, 136–46
Within-subjects design, 40–42
Within-subjects experiment, 40, 41–42, 86–87, 91–94
   controls in, 92–94, 95(table)
   examples of, 40–41, 44, 48–49
   extraneous variables in, 91–94, 96(table)
   limitations of, 91–92
Wrightsman, L. S., 85–87

Yoked control, 86

Zajonc, R., 9, 15